Alice Wood
Of Wings and Wheels

Beihefte zur Zeitschrift für die alttestamentliche Wissenschaft

Herausgegeben von
John Barton · Reinhard G. Kratz
Choon-Leong Seow · Markus Witte

Band 385

W
DE
G

Walter de Gruyter · Berlin · New York

Alice Wood

Of Wings and Wheels

A Synthetic Study of the Biblical Cherubim

W
DE
G

Walter de Gruyter · Berlin · New York

G

∞ Printed on acid-free paper which falls within the guidelines of the ANSI
to ensure permanence and durability.

ISBN 978-3-11-020528-2
ISSN 0934-2575

Library of Congress Cataloging-in-Publication Data

A CIP catalogue record for this book is available from the Library of Congress.

Bibliographic information published by the Deutsche Nationalbibliothek

The Deutsche Nationalbibliothek lists this publication in the Deutsche Nationalbibliografie;
detailed bibliographic data are available in the Internet at http://dnb.d-nb.de.

Forward

This monograph was originally submitted in accordance with the regulations for the degree of PhD (Divinity) at the University of Edinburgh, Scotland.

I would like to thank my supervisor, Dr David Reimer, for his advice and guidance in preparing this thesis, and my parents for their encouragement and support. This work was funded by means of a postgraduate scholarship from New College, Edinburgh, where I spent seven very happy years.

Alice Wood
22nd April 2008

Contents

Forward V

Contents VII

Abbreviations IX

Introduction 1

Part I: The Biblical Texts 5

§ 1.1 The Cherubim Formula (יֹשֵׁב הַכְּרֻבִים) 9

§ 1.1.1 Semantic and Syntactical Problems 9

§ 1.1.2 The Cherubim Formula and "Yahweh of Hosts" 14

§ 1.1.3 The Cherubim Formula and the Ark 18

§ 1.1.4 Summary 22

§ 1.2 כְּרֻבִים as Cultic Images 22

§ 1.2.1 The Cherubim of the Tabernacle in Exodus 23

§ 1.2.1.1 The Golden Cherubim on the כַּפֹּרֶת 23

§ 1.2.1.2 The Inspiration for the Golden Cherubim 28

§ 1.2.1.3 Do the Cherubim Statues Form a Throne? 30

§ 1.2.1.4 The Cherubim on the פָּרֹכֶת veil 32

§ 1.2.1.5 Summary 33

§ 1.2.2 The Cherubim in the Solomonic Temple 33

§ 1.2.2.1 The Statues in the דְּבִיר 34

§ 1.2.2.2 Cherubim relief (1 Kgs 6:29–35) 37

§ 1.2.2.3 The Wheeled Lavers (1 Kgs 7:27–39) 38

§ 1.2.2.4 The Source of the 1 Kings Account 41

§ 1.2.2.5 The Temple Cherubim in Chronicles 42

§ 1.2.2.6 Summary 49

§ 1.2.3 The Cherubim Iconography in Ezekiel 41:18–25 50

§ 1.3 כְּרֻבִים as Heavenly Beings 51

§ 1.3.1 Genesis 3:24 51

§ 1.3.2 Ezekiel 28:11-19 61

§ 1.3.2.1 Earlier Exegesis 63

§ 1.3.2.2 The Significance of the Masoretic Text 71

§ 1.3.2.3 A Holistic Approach 73

§ 1.3.2.4 Towards a New Interpretation of the Cherub   75
§ 1.3.2.5 Summary   84
§ 1.3.3 The Song of David   84
§ 1.3.3.1 Textual Issues   85
§ 1.3.3.2 Poetic Issues   88
§ 1.3.3.3 The Cherub in a Storm Theophany   91
§ 1.3.3.4 Theophany and Divine Attendants   92
§ 1.3.3.5 Summary   94
§ 1.3.4 Ezekiel's Visions   95
§ 1.3.4.1 Earlier Exegesis   97
§ 1.3.4.2 Critique   102
§ 1.3.4.3 The Cherubim in Ezekiel 9–11   105
§ 1.3.4.4 Summary   138
§ 1.4 Conclusions Emerging from Biblical Exegesis   139
Part II: The Root k-r-b and Comparative Semitic Material   141
Part III: The Archaeological Evidence   157
§ 3.1 Delimiting the Evidence 1   161
§ 3.2 Delimiting the Evidence 2   163
§ 3.3 The Megiddo Ivories   165
§ 3.4 Archaeological Survey   173
§ 3.4.1 Larger objects, Ivories and a Cave Drawing   174
§ 3.4.2 The Glyptic   183
§ 3.5 Evaluation   200
§ 3.6 Summary   203
Conclusion   205
Bibliography   209
Pictures   231
Index of Biblical References   245
Index of Names and Subjects   251

Abbreviations

AB	Anchor Bible
ABD	*Anchor Bible Dictionary*
AJSL	*The American Journal of Semitic Languages and Literatures*
ASOR	American Schools of Oriental Research
ANEP	J. B. Pritchard, *The Ancient Near East in Pictures Relating to the Old Testament* (2ⁿᵈ Edition with Supplement; Princeton: Princeton University Press, 1969)
ANET	J. B. Pritchard, *Ancient Near Eastern Texts Relating to the Old Testament* (3ʳᵈ Edition; Princeton: Princeton University Press, 1969)
ASTI	*Annual of the Swedish Theological Institute*
AuOr	*Aula Orientalis*
BA	*Biblical Archaeologist*
BAR	*Biblical Archaeology Review*
BASOR	*Bulletin of the American Schools of Oriental Research*
BDB	F. Brown, S. R. Driver and C. A. Briggs, *Hebrew and English Lexicon of the Old Testament*
BETL	Bibliotheca Ephemeridum theologicarum Lovaniensium
BKAT	Biblischer Kommentar: Altes Testament
BN	*Biblische Notizen*
BWANT	Beiträge zur Wissenschaft vom Alten und Neuen Testament
BZAW	Beihefte zur *ZAW*
CBQ	*Catholic Biblical Quarterly*
DJD	*Discoveries in the Judaean Desert (of Jordan)* (Oxford: Clarendon Press, 1955-)
FRLANT	Forschungen zur Religion und Literatur des Alten und Neuen Testaments
GKC	*Gesenius' Hebrew Grammar*, E. Kautzsch (ed.), translated by A. E. Cowley

HAT	*Handbuch zum Alten Testament*
HSM	Harvard Semitic Monographs
HSS	Harvard Semitic Studies
HUCA	*Hebrew Union College Annual*
ICC	The International Critical Commentary
IEJ	*Israel Exploration Journal*
JAOS	*Journal of the American Oriental Society*
JBL	*Journal of Biblical Literature*
JM	*A Grammar of Biblical Hebrew*, by P. Joüon, translated and revised by T. Muraoka (Roma: Editrice Pontificio Istituto Biblico, 1993)
JNES	*Journal of Near Eastern Studies*
JSS	*Journal of Semitic Studies*
JSOT	*Journal for the Study of the Old Testament*
JSOTSup.	Journal for the Study of the Old Testament Supplement Series
JTS	*Journal of Theological Studies*
KJV	King James Version
KTU	*Die Keilalphabetischen Texte aus Ugarit* by M. Dietrich, O. Loretz and J. Sanmartín (Alter Orient und Altes Testament 24; Kevelaer: Butzon und Bercker and Neu-kirchen-Vluyn: Neukirchener, 1976)
NCB	New Century Bible
NICOT	New International Commentary on the Old Testament
NKJV	New King James Version
NIV	New International Version
NKJV	New King James Version
NRSV	New Revised Standard Version
OBO	Orbis biblicus et orientalis
OTL	Old Testament Library
OTS	Oudtestamentische studiën
PEQ	*Palestine Exploration Quarterly*
REB	Revised English Bible
REJ	*Revue des Études Juifs*
RSV	Revised Standard Version
SBL	Society of Biblical Literature
SBS	Stuttgarter Bibelstudien

SBT	Studies in Biblical Theology
SJOT	*Scandinavian Journal of the Old Testament*
SSS	Semitic Study Series
SVT	Supplements to *VT*
TynBul	*Tyndale Bulletin*
OTL	Old Testament Library
UF	*Ugarit-Forschungen*
VT	*Vetus Testamentum*
WBC	Word Biblical Commentary
WMANT	*Wissenschaftliche Monographien zum Alten und Neuen Testament*
ZA	*Zeitschrift für Assyriologie*
ZAW	*Zeitschrift für die alttestamentliche Wissenschaft*
ZThK	*Zeitschrift für Theologie und Kirche*

Introduction

Today's popular perception that cherubim are a type of angel has a long history. Texts dating as early as the 1ˢᵗ Century B.C.E. include cherubim in the divine hierarchy, for example *The Songs of the Sabbath Sacrifice* found at Qumran (see Newsom 1985) and the apocalyptic books of Enoch.[1] Rabbi Abbahu, in the 3ʳᵈ Century C.E., etymologized the Hebrew word for cherub (כְּרוּב). He viewed the lexeme as a compound of the preposition כְּ, "like", and the Aramaic noun רביא, "youth" (Sukkah 5b). Thus, in early Jewish tradition, there existed the notion that cherubim had youthful, human features.[2] A similar idea, that a cherub was a small and plump winged boy, exists in Christian tradition but has its roots in classical art and mythology. Cherubim became associated with the Putto[3] and the god Cupid/Eros, both of which originated in the Greco-Roman period and became popular in the art of the Renaissance. The notion that cherubim are a type of angel has been disseminated in Western Christianity by means of hymns such as the *Te Deum*, "Holy, Holy, Holy" by Reginald Heber and the favourite carol by Christina Rossetti, "In the Bleak Midwinter". Hence the common understanding of cherubim as angels persists in the West today.

In the Hebrew Bible, however, the physical features, the rank and role of the cherubim (כְּרֻבִים) are never so explicitly elucidated. In most of the biblical texts in which they occur, it appears that the authors

---

1   In later rabbinic literature too, long treatises were written, expatiating upon the rank and role of the cherubim among the angelic hosts. For example, Maimonides ranks the cherubim as the ninth of the ten classes of angels ("Yad," Yesode ha-Torah, ii. 7). Also see his exposition of Ezekiel's vision in *The Guide for the Perplexed* (1919: 251–261).

2   Despite this tradition, some early midrashic literature (e.g. Midrash Tehillim 18:15; Rashi, *Song of Solomon* 1:9) conceives of the cherubim as non-corporeal. In the 1st Century C.E., Josephus claimed: "No one can tell, or even conjecture, what was the shape of these Cherubim" (*Antiquities* 8:73).

3   Putti were images of naked winged boys that were popular on sarcophagi of the 2nd Century C.E. but were revived in Renaissance art.

expected their audience to be well acquainted with the exact form and function of the כְּרֻבִים. It has proved difficult, therefore, for biblical scholars to identify exactly what the Hebrew Bible is referring to when it mentions the כְּרֻבִים. To make matters worse, in some instances we are given conflicting information as to the physical appearance of the cherubim.[4] Some of the descriptions are a far cry from the traditional Christian and Jewish conceptions of cherubim and suggest that a כְּרוּב was not the charming childlike figure that it later became.

Aside from Yahweh, the cherubim are the most frequently occurring heavenly being in the Hebrew Bible: the word כְּרוּב appears ninety-one times when referring to a cherub.[5] In view of this fact, it is surprising that a comprehensive study of the biblical כְּרֻבִים is not to be found in recent academic literature. In a two-page article in the *Biblical Archaeologist* in 1938, Albright asked the question "What were the cherubim?". At the time this was published, archaeological excavations had yielded a number of items upon which winged beings were depicted that conformed, to some degree, to the biblical descriptions of the כְּרֻבִים. Albright (1938: 2) argued that the "winged lion with human head" is "much more common than any other winged creature, so much so that its identification with the cherub is certain". This creature is found flanking thrones on iconography from Phoenicia and Israel dating from the Late Bronze period. Hence Albright argued that "the primary function of the cherub" was to form the throne of Yahweh. His article seemed to have settled the problem of the form and function of the cherubim once and for all. Indeed, two of the most recent encyclopedia articles on the biblical cherubim (Meyers 1992 and Mettinger 1999) still presuppose the tenets of Albright's argument.

In the most extensive study of the כְּרֻבִים in recent times, Freedman and O'Connor's 1995 article in the *Theological Dictionary of the Old Testament*, the relevance of archaeological evidence is called into question. Freedman and O'Connor (1995: 315) argue that an examination of the

---

4   The cherubim in Ezekiel 10 have four faces and two pairs of wings. In Ezek 41:18–20, they are portrayed with two faces, although this is probably because they are depicted in profile. Elsewhere in the Bible, they seem to have one face and one pair of wings (Ex 25:18–22; 37.7–9; 1 Kgs 6:23–28). In Ezekiel, the cherubim may be biped (Ezek 1:5, 7), whereas elsewhere they appear to be quadruped (Ps 18:10 = 2 Sam 22:11).

5   This is discounting the two references to כְּרוּב as a place name (Ezr 2:59; Neh 7:61). The כְּרֻבִים are never described as deities in the Hebrew Bible (they are never worshipped) and thus never threaten Yahweh's divine supremacy.

archaeological evidence "presupposes that the monumental cherubim of the ancient Near East can be identified with the biblical cherubim". They continue: "This presupposition is actually erroneous, since the Israelite tradition fundamentally includes no graphic representations, although archaeology has uncovered some isolated exceptions." Freedman and O'Connor thus seem to suggest that because there exists a tradition of a prohibition of images in the Hebrew Bible (e.g. in Ex 20:4, 23; 34:17; Lev 19:4; 26:1; Deut 4:16, 23, 25; 27:15), we should not expect to find comparative material for the biblical כְּרֻבִים in the archaeological record of the ancient Near East. Yet their argument seems to ignore the fact that fifty-six out of the ninety-one occurrences of the lexeme כְּרוּב refer to a cherub as an image in the temple or tabernacle. There may be a tradition concerning a ban on icons in the Hebrew Bible, but there is also a tradition that there were cherub images in the temple. We cannot allow either one tradition to take precedence. Indeed, it is precisely because the cherubim are described as cultic images that we may be justified in looking at relevant archaeological evidence in order to elucidate their physical form and cultic function.

Yet how far we should allow archaeological evidence to dictate our interpretation of the biblical כְּרֻבִים remains debatable. In Albright's article, as indeed in the work of several other scholars (e.g. Mettinger 1982a, 1982b, 1999 and Haran 1959, 1978), the archaeological evidence is allowed to take precedence and guide his interpretation of the כְּרֻבִים. Yet the כְּרֻבִים are, first and foremost, a biblical phenomenon. The relationship between text and artifact requires a close assessment and methodological parameters need to be set up before we can compare these two very different types of evidence.

One further type of evidence has been used to illuminate the biblical כְּרֻבִים: that of etymology and semantics. In 1926, Dhorme wrote an important article on the word כְּרוּב. He argued that cognates of the Hebrew noun could be found in the Akkadian words *kāribu* and the diminutive, *kurību*. The Akkadian terms are used to refer to intercessory divine beings (and statues of such beings) that plead with the gods on behalf of humanity. According to Dhorme (1926: 338), the Hebrew term כְּרוּב was borrowed from Akkadian and the function of the cherubim was influenced by this borrowing. He thus concludes that the cherubim had an intercessory role.

In Dhorme's article, like Albright's, the biblical evidence takes a subordinate position. The etymological evidence guides Dhorme's interpretation and he reaches conclusions that do not correspond to the biblical presentation of the cherubim. Yet, even in relatively recent commentaries and articles,[6] Dhorme's article is still drawn upon. It seems that biblical scholarship could benefit from a new treatment of the etymological evidence pertaining to the lexeme כְּרוּב in order to reassess its use for the elucidation of the cherubim.

It is the aim of this thesis to provide a new synthetic study of the biblical כְּרֻבִים. It will prioritize the evidence provided by the biblical texts and yet will not ignore etymological and archaeological data altogether. As our primary source of information, exegesis of the biblical texts will constitute the large part of the thesis (chapter 2). Etymological and archaeological evidence will only be evaluated after the biblical texts have been discussed (in chapters 3 and 4). The usefulness of these types of evidence will be reassessed. If useful, these types of evidence may allow us to corroborate what we have gleaned from the biblical texts and perhaps furnish our findings with additional nuances. Methodological issues relating to the interpretation of each type of evidence will be considered at the beginning of each respective section.

---

6   E.g. The entry for כְּרוּב in *The Hebrew and Aramaic Lexicon of the Old Testament: Volume 2* (1995: 497) and in the commentaries on Ezekiel by Block (1997: 306) and Zimmerli (1969: 231).

Part I
The Biblical Texts

Recent trends in Biblical Studies have emphasised the literary over the historical. The influence of modern literary criticism has occasioned a shift in scholarly interests from the historical referents to the poetic function of biblical literature (see Powell 1992: 5–6). Text and reader-oriented studies abound compared to a general decline in the number of studies that engage with the historical world, authors and audience of the biblical texts (see Barr 2000: 21). Nevertheless, it is the assumption of the present study that the lexeme כְּרוּב, and the concept signified by it, are historical phenomena and that their historical meanings remain an interesting and relevant subject of discussion.[7] As we have inherited these historical phenomena in a literary medium,[8] both historical and literary considerations will be pertinent to our investigation.

Traditional historical and literary approaches to the biblical texts have been much maligned in recent times for privileging the Western academic elite and for feigning objectivity (see Collins 2005: 1–25).[9] Yet, owing to our assumption that the כְּרֻבִים are a historical as well as a lit-

---

7   The historical meaning of the כְּרֻבִים is not monolithic. We are better to speak of historical meanings (in the plural). The meaning can shift from text to text as well as from implied author to implied audience. Historical meanings are considered irrelevant by many postmodern theorists. For the postmodern critique of historical criticism, see Barr (2000: 16–31) and Collins (2005: 1–25).

8   The lexeme כְּרוּב only occurs in the biblical texts and not in epigraphy. There is no labelled ancient representation of a כְּרוּב.

9   For descriptions of traditional historical and literary approaches see Steck (1998) and Barton (1996). It must be admitted from the outset that this study is the product of Western academic instruction. As regards the pursuit of objectivity, we will follow a traditional critical approach by attempting to allow the text to "speak for itself" as far as is possible. No researched subject can ever wholly speak for itself, but our arguments will be based on evidence, which is "public" and can be tested. This means that, although this study may be the product of Western academic instruction, its discussion is not intended to be "personal" or subjective but can be criticized according to its use of the evidence.

erary phenomenon, we are somewhat bound to these types of approach in this investigation. It is presumed from the outset that any overarching method, which approaches the texts in a systematic and similar way, will not do justice to the variety of texts under discussion. This is in line with Barton's observation that there is not one historical-critical method but, rather, biblical criticism has produced a number of theories that formalize "intelligent intuitions" (1996: 244).[10] The lexeme כְּרוּב occurs in twelve different biblical books.[11] Methodological considerations will need, therefore, to reflect differences in genre. Poetic texts, for example, will raise different questions to narrative texts. Moreover, each text presents its own unique hermeneutical problems. Sometimes (for example in our discussion of Ezekiel 9–11), the editorial history of the text will become important for our interpretation of the cherubim. However, in other texts (for example Genesis 3), the redaction of the text is irrelevant for our purposes.[12] Thus, to a certain extent, our methods for engaging with the texts reside in the texts themselves.

An important preliminary consideration, however, concerns how far the biblical texts describe the historical reality of ancient Israel. Many references to the cherubim occur in texts which appear to record historical events (e.g. the books of Samuel, Kings and Chronicles). Thus many scholars have argued that these passages witness to the historical reality of the cherubim in the cult of Israel. Mettinger (1982b) and Haran (1976), for example, use the biblical texts to reconstruct the historical form and function of the cherubim in the cults of Jerusalem and Shiloh. Yet how far the texts reflect a historical reality is difficult to ascertain. The account of the cherubim ornamentation of the wilderness tabernacle in Exodus 25–26; 36–37 may well be largely imaginary. On

---

10   Barton's remarks are taken up and developed by Barr (2000: 46–47). Steck's delineation of the major approaches to biblical exegesis (1998) illustrates the plurality of these theories.

11   The Masoretic Text is the primary text for this discussion. Since the non-Hebrew versions of the biblical texts transliterate the word כְּרוּב and do not offer a suitable translation, the Hebrew version must be prioritised. For a summary of the versional renderings of כְּרוּב see Wood (2006: 6–7, § 4). Textual differences between the Hebrew and non-Hebrew versions will be addressed where relevant.

12   Some scholars argue that the cherubim did not occur in the original version of the Eden narrative. Yet, if these scholars are correct, this does not affect how we interpret the cherubim in Gen 3:24 precisely because they would only occur in the final form and not in earlier strata.

the other hand, the description of the cherubim decoration in the temple building account of 1 Kings 6–8 may be based on administrative records and thus accurately reflect the architecture of the Solomonic temple. For the most part, we will not attempt to use the texts to postulate the historical reality of the cherubim in the temple or cult. The biblical texts can only tell us how the implied[13] authors or editors understood the sanctuaries. The accounts of the construction of the temple (1 Kings 6–8) and tabernacle (Exodus 25–31; 35–40) will be viewed as witnesses to traditions that arose concerning these sanctuaries and not to their historical reality.[14]

Additionally, it is important to emphasize that we should not expect the biblical conception of the כְּרֻבִים to be monolithic. We may observe how ideas concerning the cherubim differ from text to text. If we attempt to read the texts diachronically, we may be able to trace the historical development of beliefs concerning the cherubim. As noted at the beginning of the introduction to this thesis, post-biblical texts (even very early ones, such as *The Songs of the Sabbath Sacrifice* from Qumran) portray the cherubim in a very different light to the biblical passages. Thus we may be able to detect the first signs of a conceptual shift concerning the cherubim that inspired the authors of post-biblical texts to describe the cherubim in the way that they do.

Dating the biblical texts is an extremely difficult task. Many of the cherubim passages have a long history and have been subjected to extensive editorial work. Nevertheless, ignoring the possible chronological distinctions between the texts means that we may miss some important insights into how ideas concerning the cherubim changed over time. We will not focus on absolute dating but on relative chronology, i.e. not when exactly each text was written but rather which may have preceded, or inspired, another.[15]

---

13   We do not know who wrote any of the biblical cherubim texts. However, we can posit "implied authors" based on the information provided by the text.

14   This is not to suggest that there is no historical information contained in the biblical texts, but rather that it is very difficult to discern between history and ideology.

15   Decisions about which texts precede others and which may be dependent on others are very difficult to make. On the whole, we will favour the scholarly consensus where possible.

The lexeme כְּרוּב occurs ninety-three times in the Hebrew Bible.[16] In two of these instances it appears as a place name (Ezr 2:59; Neh 7:61), referring to a location in Babylonia from which exiles returned to Judah. The remaining ninety-one occurrences can be divided into three general uses. First, there are those that occur in the divine epithet יֹשֵׁב הַכְּרֻבִים. There are seven instances of this usage (1 Sam 4:4; 2 Sam 6:2; 2 Kgs 19:15; 1 Chr 13:6; Ps 80:1, 99:1; Isa 37:16), mainly in liturgical texts.[17] Second, the lexeme is used to denote a cherub as an image in the furnishings of the tabernacle and temple. This is the most common use and occurs fifty-six times (in Ex 25:18–22; 26:1, 31; 36:8, 35; 37:7–9; Num 7:89; 1 Kgs 6:23–29, 32, 35; 7:29, 36; 8:6, 7; 41:18, 20, 25), mostly in histo-riographical accounts describing the design of sanctuaries. Third, כְּרוּב is used twenty-eight times to denote animate heavenly beings (in Gen 3:24; 2 Sam 22:11 = Ps 18:11; Ezek 9:3; 10:1–9, 14–16, 18–20; 11:22; 28:14, 16). These texts tend to be more poetic (2 Sam 22:11 = Ps 18:11; Ezek 28:14, 16) and mythological (Genesis 2–3; Ezekiel 8–11). We will group the biblical texts under discussion according to these three general uses of the lexeme. In our discussion, we will begin with the verses in which the lexeme כְּרוּב appears and work outwards to discuss the wider liter-ary units where appropriate. It is hoped that this approach will mini-mize the chances of discussing irrelevant material.

---

16   Gen 3:24; Ex 25:18, 19 (3x), 20 (2x), 22; 26:1, 31; 36:8, 35; 37:7, 8 (3x), 9 (2x); Num 7:89;
     1 Sam 4:4; 2 Sam 6:2; 22:11; 1 Kgs 6:23, 24 (2x), 25 (2x), 26 (2x), 27 (3x), 28, 29, 32 (2x),
     35; 7:29, 36; 8:6, 7 (2x); 2 Kgs 19:15; 1 Chr 13:6; 28:18; 2 Chr 3:7, 10, 11 (2x), 12 (2x), 13,
     14; 5:7, 8 (2x); Ezr 2:59; Neh 7:61; Ps 18:11; 80:2; 99:1; Isa 37:16; Ezek 9:3; 10:1, 2 (2x), 3,
     4, 5, 6, 7 (3x), 8, 9 (3x), 14, 15, 16 (2x), 18, 19, 20; 11:22; 28:14, 16; 41:18 (4x), 20, 25.

17   It occurs in the Psalms and in hymns embedded in narratives (2 Kgs 19:15; Isa 37:16).
     The formula does occur in plain narrative in 1 Sam 4:4; 2 Sam 6:2 and the parallel
     text, 1 Chr 13:6, but again in cultic contexts.

§ 1.1 The Cherubim Formula: יֹשֵׁב הַכְּרֻבִים

The phrase יֹ׳ שֵׁב הַכְּרֻבִים, sometimes known as the "cherubim formula" (Mettinger 1982a: 112), occurs several times as a divine epithet of Yahweh (1 Sam 4:4; 2 Sam 6:2; 2 Kgs 19:15; 1 Chr 13:6; Ps 80:1, 99:1; Isa 37:16).[18] There are some semantic and syntactical issues pertaining to the phrase that will need to be investigated before any more detailed discussion can proceed. Once these problems have been considered, the relationship between the cherubim formula and the other more common epithet, יהוה צְבָאוֹת, with which it occurs four times, will be examined. Finally, the significance of the two occurrences of the cherubim formula in the Samuel "ark narrative" will be investigated.

§ 1.1.1 Semantic and Syntactical Problems

There has been some debate concerning the exact meaning and syntax of the divine title, יֹשֵׁב הַכְּרֻבִים (see Görg 1990: 434–437 for a summary). There are several reasons for this. First, the verb יֹשֵׁב has a broad semantic range, from "dwell" or "sojourn" to "sit" and, by abstraction, "rule". Second, the syntactical relationship between the two words is unclear. Grammatically, the cherubim formula seems to be a construct phrase (Görg 1990: 434), and thus denotes "sitter/sojourner/dweller of the cherubim". Yet the syntax depends on whether the phrase is *subjective* or *objective* (see Gibson 1994: 30). If the former, then the second noun (B) "possesses" the first (A), whereas if the latter, then B is "the recipient of or otherwise affected by the action implied by A" (Gibson 1994: 31). Therefore, if הַכְּרֻבִים is used *objectively*, then it would act like a direct object and יֹשֵׁב would have a transitive impetus. Finally, a third problem concerning the syntax of the phrase arises from the absence of a preposition between the two words where one might be expected.[19]

---

18 It also occurs in LXX Dan 3:55, in the prayer of Azariah.

19 Prepositions in Hebrew are left out in certain circumstances and the omission may thus be consistent with Hebrew linguistic convention (see JM §121*n*). With the exception of 1 Sam 4:4, the LXX reads ὁ καθήμενος ἐπὶ τῶν χερουβιν or καθημένου ἐπὶ χερουβιν, supplying the preposition ἐπὶ, "upon". Therefore, one might expect עַל. One might also expect בֵּין, following Ex 25:22//Num 7:89.

Owing to these three main difficulties, the epithet has been paraphrased in a number of ways, e.g. "enthroned between the cherubim"
(NIV), "enthroned upon the cherubim" (REB), "the one who dwells
between the cherubim" (NKJV). It is necessary to clarify what the epithet could mean and to determine whether it holds any clues for our
investigation into the biblical cherubim. We will survey previous arguments before proceeding to examine the title afresh.

Some earlier scholars have read the cherubim formula through the
lens of the description of the cherubim on the tabernacle in Exodus (e.g.
Schmitt 1972: 128–129). Here, in Ex 25:18–22 (//Ex 37:7–9), two golden
cherubim are fashioned and joined to either side of the כַּפֹּרֶת, facing
each other. They look down towards the כַּפֹּרֶת and shadow it with their
wings. This description of the tabernacle has inspired such paraphrases
of the cherubim formula as "He who dwells with the cherubim" or "He
who dwells between the cherubim". These interpretations suggest that
the cherubim shield or house the divine presence between their wings.
They connect יָשֵׁב to the verb שׁכן, which has the root meaning "abide"
and is used in connection with the "tabernacle". The idea is that the
divine presence dwells (יֹשֵׁב/שׁכן) in the tabernacle, between the two
cherubim.

However, there are two key problems with this interpretation of the
formula. First, the idea that the divine presence is "housed" within or
between the wings of the cherubim relies on the translation of יָשֵׁב as
"dwell" (being thus a synonym of שׁכן). Yet "dwell" is only one sense
ascribed to the root and, as we shall see, another of its meanings may
also be suitable in this context. Second, שׁכן and יָשֵׁב have different semantic values (שׁכן perhaps reflecting a less permanent state of affairs,
see Görg 1990: 428) and thus the idea that both terms are used equally
with reference to the tabernacle of Yahweh is flawed (see the difference
connoted by the juxtaposition of the two terms in 1 Kgs 8:12–13).

Other scholars, such as Mettinger (1982a: 112) and Haran (1978:
247–249), offer a different interpretation of the cherubim formula.[20]
They argue that the meaning intended by יָשֵׁב in this context is not
"dwell". Instead it is the figurative sense of the root that is meant here,
"ascend the throne" or "reign" (Görg 1990: 430; see Ex 15:14; 2 Sam 5:6;
Zech 9:5–6), which is derived from the more common, basic sense, "sit"
(Görg 1990: 424–426). They render the phrase, "enthroned upon the

---

20   A similar understanding of the cherubim formula is held by Albright (1938: 2), who
translates "He who sitteth (on) the cherubim". Albright gives no reasons for translating the formula in the way that he does.

cherubim", providing the preposition "upon", following the LXX translation (see n. 13 above). Instead of claiming that the divine presence
resides beneath the wings of the cherubim, as the description of the
Exodus tabernacle may suggest, they interpret the epithet as referring
to the deity enthroned upon, above or between the wings of the cherubim.[21]

Yet this interpretation relies heavily upon archaeological evidence.
Mettinger refers to thrones flanked by winged sphinxes[22], from Israel
and Phoenicia,[23] which he believes lend support to the idea that Yahweh is enthroned upon the cherubim. The earliest representations of
this type of throne are unique to the Syro-Palestinian area, suggesting
that it may have had its inception among Phoenician artisans (see
Bloch-Smith 1994: 25). The thrones are flanked by Phoenician-style[24]
sphinxes, whose wings are outstretched in order to form the seat. According to Mettinger, the similarities between the biblical descriptions
of cherubim and the sphinxes flanking thrones in Syro-Palestinian iconography support his idea that the cherubim formula means "enthroned upon the cherubim."[25]

Yet, aside from the archaeological evidence, there is very little textual and linguistic evidence which would support this interpretation of
the epithet. The only biblical text which links the cherubim to the throne of Yahweh is Ezekiel 10, which (as we shall see in § 1.3.4) is an extremely difficult passage. Given its obscurity, it would be ill-advised to
base any claims for the interpretation of the cherubim formula upon it.

---

21 According to Haran, it is not necessary to view this interpretation as contradicting
    the description of the tabernacle in Exodus. He argues that the two golden cherubim
    of the כַּפֹּרֶת may also form a seat (1978:257). He cites Ex 25:22 (// Num 7:89) as evi-
    dence for this. He maintains that, although the Exodus tabernacle never actually ex-
    isted, it did reflect real elements of Jerusalem cultic furniture and thus contains, to
    some degree, "a nucleus of historical truth" (Haran, 1978:203).

22 The term 'sphinx' in relation to the cherubim will be avoided in this study (espe-
    cially in Chapter 4 in our discussion of the archaeology). This is because 'sphinx' is a
    somewhat loaded term, carrying with it connotations of Greek and Egyptian my-
    thology. It is used here because this is the term employed by Mettinger.

23 A throne flanked by winged sphinxes occurs on Ahiram's sarcophagus from Byblos,
    dating to the 10th century B.C.E. A similar depiction of such a throne appears on a
    Late Bronze II ivory plaque from Megiddo. This panel depicts a victory scene with
    bound prisoners being exhibited before the king. Also discovered at Megiddo was
    an ivory model of a comparable throne (see Mettinger 1982a: 114–115) for illustra-
    tions.

24 For the characteristics of the Phoenician style, see Winter (1976).

25 See also Albright (1938), De Vaux (1967) and Mettinger (1982a).

Furthermore, the syntax of the Hebrew does not really support Mettinger's rendering "enthroned upon the cherubim". For this, we need a
preposition עַל (as occurs with כִּסֵּא) or even בֵּין as in Num 7:89. The LXX
rendering, which provides the preposition "upon" in all but one case,
may have been influenced by emerging *merkābāh* traditions at the time
of the Greek translation and is thus not strong evidence in support of
Mettinger's interpretation.[26] The fact that the LXX in 1 Sam 4:4 has
καθημένου χερουβιμ instead of ἐπὶ τῶν χερουβιν may show that the syntax
of the Hebrew epithet was not uniformly understood by the Greek
translators.

Owing to the inadequacies of the two traditional lines of interpretation of the cherubim formula, we will now take a fresh look at the semantics and syntax of the epithet, placing primary importance on the
words themselves, rather than archaeological data and the LXX translation of the phrase. The first word of the cherubim formula, יֹשֵׁב, is the
masculine singular active participle of the verb יָשַׁב, "to sit, remain,
dwell". This must refer to Yahweh as the "sitter," "sojourner" or
"dweller". The second component of the phrase is the definite noun
הַכְּרֻבִים, the meaning of which is unambiguous: "the cherubim". Our
first task when determining the overall sense of the formula, therefore,
is to decide on the relationship between the two words. As stated previously, the cherubim formula seems to be a construct phrase (see Görg
1990: 434), and thus denotes "sitter/sojourner/dweller of the cherubim".
Yet the phrase may be either *subjective* or *objective* (see Gibson 1994: 30).
If the former, then the second noun, הַכְּרֻבִים, 'possesses' (in the grammatical sense) the first noun, יֹשֵׁב, whereas if the latter, then the cherubim are, to some extent, affected by Yahweh in his role as the יֹשֵׁב. In the
latter case, יֹשֵׁב would have a transitive force and הַכְּרֻבִים may act as the
direct object.

Predominantly, the verb יָשַׁב is used intransitively. Yet, when it takes on the more figurative sense of "sit upon a throne", the verb can
adopt a transitive force. For example, in Num 21:1, the king of Arad is
referred to as יֹשֵׁב הַנֶּגֶב. This could mean "dweller of the Negev" and
thus יֹשֵׁב would be intransitive (as in Josh 24:18; Judg 1:9, 11:21) and the
construct phrase would be *subjective* ("the Negev dweller"). In this case,
B ("the Negev") "possesses" A ("the dweller"). Yet the declaration that
the king of Arad dwelt in the Negev seems almost superfluous in the

---

26 Halperin (1988: 55–60) notes the influence of *merkābāh* traditions on the LXX transla-
    tion of Ezekiel. That these traditions could also have affected the translation of the
    cherubim formula is possible.

context of the narrative and it may be that we have here an instance of יָשַׁב with the more figurative sense of "sit enthroned" (see Görg 1990: 430). If this is the case, then the verb would take on a somewhat transitive impetus. Although the literal meaning must be something like "the throne-sitter of the Negev", we would render this: "he who rules the Negev" or "ruler of the Negev".

If it is this more figurative sense of יָשַׁב that is contained in the phrase יֹשֵׁב הַכְּרֻבִים, then יֹשֵׁב may also have a transitive force here. Thus Mettinger may be wrong to paraphrase the epithet as "he who is enthroned upon the cherubim". In Num 21:1, the Negev is not *the* throne that the king of Arad sits on. Rather, the Negev is the environs of his rule. This is confirmed by Num 34:40, where the same king is described as יֹשֵׁב בַּנֶּגֶב, "ruler in the Negev". By analogy, the syntax of יֹשֵׁב הַכְּרֻבִים does not imply that the cherubim physically constitute the throne of Yahweh but rather may imply that Yahweh is the "throne-sitter of the cherubim", i.e. "ruler of the cherubim". Thus, if we have here the figurative sense of יָשַׁב, it does not follow that we should supply a preposition "upon" when we are paraphrasing the epithet and, moreover, it is certainly not the case that the epithet can be used as evidence of a cherubim throne concept in the Hebrew Bible (as Mettinger and Haran would have us believe).

On the other hand, יֹשֵׁב, in יֹשֵׁב הַכְּרֻבִים, may not have the sense of "rule" but rather the plainer sense of "dwell". When in construct relationship with a definite noun, the meaning of יֹשֵׁב is usually "dweller" or "inhabitant", e.g. in Gen 4:20; Ex 34:15;[27] Josh 24:18; Judg 1:9; 11:21. If this is what we have in the cherubim formula, then the phrase should be rendered "dweller of the cherubim". Just as in Josh 24:18, where יֹשֵׁב הָאָרֶץ refers to "the dweller of the land", יֹשֵׁב הַכְּרֻבִים, would refer to "dweller of the cherubim" or "cherubim dweller".[28] Thus the verb would have its usual intransitive sense and the construct phrase would be *subjective* in character, B ("the cherubim") "possessing" A ("the dweller").

---

27 The singular participle can be used as a collective as is evinced here. The plural verb forms which follow in this verse support this.

28 In the same way, יֹשֵׁב הָהָר, in Judg 1:9, refers to "mountain dweller" and יֹשֵׁב בָּעֵמֶק, in Num 14:25 denotes "valley dweller". In both these instances, יֹשֵׁב is used collectively, modifying a gentilic.

Both "ruler of the cherubim" and "dweller of the cherubim" are semantically appropriate paraphrases of יֹשֵׁב הַכְּרֻבִים. The epithet always appears in cultic contexts and thus seems to reflect the temple setting (Yahweh's abode, where cherubim decoration abounds – 1 Kings 6–8). In 1 Kgs 8:12–13, Solomon observes that Yahweh had said he would tabernacle (שׁכן) in a cloud but now he has built Yahweh an exalted house in which he can dwell (ישׁב) forever. Thus perhaps the idea that Yahweh is "the dweller of the cherubim" is the most likely underlying sense of the cherubim formula, as his sanctuary is covered in images of these heavenly beings. Yet, as we shall see, the cherubim are sometimes viewed as the agents of Yahweh (Gen 3:24; Ps 18:11 = 2 Sam 22:11). Thus "ruler of the cherubim" is also possible. The occurrence of the cherubim formula with the more common epithet, יהוה צְבָאוֹת, "Yahweh of Hosts", may support this.

§ 1.1.2 The Cherubim Formula and "Yahweh of Hosts"

In the Samuel passages, as well as Isa 37:16, the cherubim formula follows the title יהוה צְבָאוֹת. Likewise, it occurs at the beginning of Psalm 80 and יהוה צְבָאוֹת appears in vv 5, 8, 15 and 20. The fact that the cherubim formula occurs with this more common epithet four times out of seven occurrences has prompted scholars to argue for a connection between the two titles.

The link between the two divine titles is explored most fully by Mettinger in his article, "Yhwh Sabaoth – The Heavenly King on the Cherubim Throne" (1982a). He cites Eissfeldt (1966: 116–121), who argues that the phrase יֹשֵׁב הַכְּרֻבִים never originally existed independently but was connected with the epithet יהוה צְבָאוֹת from its inception. Mettinger (1982a: 112) agrees, arguing that the passages in which the cherubim formula occurs on its own (without יהוה צְבָאוֹת) do not imply that the formula originally existed independently. According to Mettinger, 1 Chr 13:6 is no more than a parallel to 2 Sam 6:2 (the whole of chapter 13 being a somewhat muddled reworking of the Samuel "ark narrative") and cannot be used as evidence against a link between the two divine titles. Likewise, the occurrence of the cherubim formula without יהוה צְבָאוֹת in 2 Kgs 19:15 is not reliable evidence that the epithet existed independently because it is parallel to Isa 37:16, which contains both titles. The only remaining passages that contain the formula on its own are Ps 99:1 and LXX Dan 3:55. Mettinger (1982a: 113) argues that these two occurrences are not enough to counterbalance the passages which suggest a link between the cherubim formula and צְבָאוֹת יהוה.

Schley (1989: 161), in his historical study on Shiloh, follows Mettinger, arguing that the title יהוה צְבָאוֹת was originally the name of the Shilonite deity, which was transferred to the Jerusalem cult by David in order to endorse his usurpation of the throne from Saul (2 Samuel 6). In a similar vein, Preuss (1991: 166) proposes that the fact that the Samuel references link the epithet to the cult at Shiloh may indicate that the cherubim formula originated there. Yet Mettinger goes further, arguing that not only did the full epithet, יְהוָה צְבָאוֹת יֹשֵׁב הַכְּרֻבִים, exist at Shiloh, but also a physical representation of a cherubim throne.[29] He finds evidence for this in the "Canaanite" background of the Shiloh cult.

According to Josh 18:1, Shiloh was where the Tent of Meeting was erected after the Israelites settled in the hill country of Ephraim. 1 Samuel 1–4 indicates that, according to Israelite tradition, Shiloh became the chief sanctuary of the pre-monarchic period. It is the only cult centre labelled a הֵיכָל in the Hebrew Bible, apart from the Jerusalem temple. Schley (1989: 201) maintains that, prior to Israelite control, the sanctuary existed as a non-Israelite, or at least non-Yahwistic, shrine. Consequently, the Israelite הֵיכָל may well have appropriated some of the earlier traditions associated with the shrine.

Mettinger (1982a: 130) argues that one such tradition adopted by the Israelites from the earlier "Canaanite" cult at Shiloh is the designation יהוה צְבָאוֹת, which was adapted from an original אֵל צְבָאוֹת, El being the chief Canaanite deity according to the Ugaritic texts. He claims that there are several clues which link the epithet יהוה צְבָאוֹת to El. First, in the Ugaritic texts, El is portrayed as the progenitor god and, as such, can bestow fertility. He grants children to Danel and Keret (in *KTU* 1.16 and 1.19 respectively). Similarly, in 1 Sam 1:11, Hannah prays to Yahweh Sabaoth for a son. Second, Hannah gives her child an El, rather than a Yahwistic name, שְׁמוּאֵל, meaning 'name of El'. Third, El usually appears to people in dreams (as opposed to Baal, who appears in a storm), which is how Yahweh appears to Samuel in 1 Samuel 3. Finally, El is the head of the pantheon and this is consistent with the idea that Yahweh Sabaoth is "Yahweh of Hosts", i.e. Yahweh who presides over the other deities. Thus, according to Mettinger, the designation אֵל צְבָאוֹת

---

29 This proceeds from his connection of the formula with sphinx flanked thrones and his interpretation of the epithet as having the sense "enthroned upon the cherubim".

stemmed from the notion of El as the principal deity, the king of the
gods, who presided over his heavenly council, his צְבָאוֹת, "hosts".

Although there is no concrete evidence that a cherubim throne ever
existed in the temple of Shiloh, Mettinger argues that such a throne
would "suit admirably the El qualities of YHWH" (1982a: 131). He
points to Punic representations of El seated on a sphinx-flanked throne
with his right hand raised as a sign of benediction.[30] He compares these
depictions to the Ugaritic El stele (dated two thousand years earlier) in
which El appears in a similar pose. Although sphinxes are absent on
the El stele, Mettinger argues that the affinities between the Punic and
Ugaritic representations show that the sphinx/cherubim throne was a
feature of El's, rather than Baal's, iconographic tradition.

Mettinger's argument is based on extremely patchy evidence. The
idea that the cherubim formula was linked to the epithet יהוה צְבָאוֹת
from its inception (as Mettinger 1982a: 112; Eissfeldt 1966: 116–121)
is unsustainable. If the two epithets were related from the begin
ning, and both were used with reference to Yahweh at an early stage in
Israelite/Judahite history (as Mettinger would have us believe),
then why is there such textual variety in the use of the epithets? In Isa
37:16, the cherubim formula occurs in the following format:
יְהוָה צְבָאוֹת אֱלֹהֵי יִשְׂרָאֵל יֹשֵׁב הַכְּרֻבִים. Yet, in the parallel text 2 Kgs 19:15,
the formula occurs again but with the omission of צְבָאוֹת:
יְהוָה אֱלֹהֵי יִשְׂרָאֵל יֹשֵׁב הַכְּרֻבִים. It is reasonable to assume that the more
ancient a divine title was, the more fixed it would become in the textual
transmission process. Such variety in the use of the formula is also
found in 2 Sam 6:2 and the parallel text 1 Chr 13:6. The fact that we
have the cherubim formula used both with and without יהוה צְבָאוֹת in
parallel texts must cast doubt on the idea that the two epithets were
linked from early times and should not be used as evidence in favour of
an early connection (as Mettinger argues). We also have varying usage
of the formula in the versions. In the LXX of 1 Sam 4:4, for example,
צְבָאוֹת is not represented.[31] Likewise, in the 4QSam version of 2 Sam 6:2,
there is not enough space for צְבָאוֹת between יהוה and יֹשֵׁב (see plate IV
in Fincke 2001: 286). Thus Mettinger and Eissfeldt are wrong to stress

---

30 These include a stele from Hadrumetum-Sousse and scarabs from Sardinia (Met-
    tinger 1982a: 131–132).
31 The LXX usually renders צְבָאוֹת by τῶν δυνάμεων (as in 2 Sam 6:2) or transliterates,
    σαβαωθ (as in Isa 37:16).

such a strong link between the two epithets when the transmission history suggests that their use together was by no means fixed.

Furthermore, Mettinger's claim that the cherubim formula was originally linked to Shiloh, a cult of El and a cherubim throne is entirely conjectural and gives too much credence to the historicity and structural unity of the Samuel text. First, the Samuel text is primarily a collection of narratives rather than an integral historical account. Therefore we must be wary of placing too great a weight on the historical accuracy of the text. Second, the collection of narratives may be the result of a long editorial process, whereby originally independent passages were brought together by an editor for ideological reasons.

Neglecting the possibility that the Samuel text is a pastiche of narratives is perhaps the fundamental weakness of Mettinger's argument. The link between the cherubim formula and the cult at Shiloh is only suggested by the use of the epithet in 1 Sam 4:4. This verse occurs at the very beginning of the narrative unit of 1 Samuel 4–6 and its main purpose is to link this material to the preceding story (1 Samuel 1–3), the setting of which is Shiloh.[32] Therefore the connection between the cherubim formula and the cult of Shiloh may be no more than a narrative structural link and not evidence of the historical provenance of the epithet (as Mettinger 1982a and Haran 1976: 247–249 believe). Moreover, it follows from this that the supposed "cult of El" at Shiloh may only be linked to the cherubim formula for literary reasons.

Whether or not Mettinger is right to stress that the origin of the cherubim formula was within an El cult at Shiloh, there is certainly no evidence in the Hebrew Bible (and, more significantly, none in the Ugaritic texts) that links a cherubim throne to the god El. Indeed, the idea of a cherubim throne is lacking in the Hebrew Bible. As we have seen, the cherubim formula cannot be used as evidence to support a cherubim throne concept in the Hebrew Bible. The only text that links the cherubim to Yahweh's throne is Ezekiel 10, which is an extremely problematic text (see § 1.3.4). Moreover, in Ezekiel 10, the cherubim do not

---

32   Ahlström argues that the story of 1 Sam 4:1–7:2 has been artificially grafted onto the stories set in Shiloh (Ahlström 1975: 142, esp. n. 5, 149). Auld (2004: 174) argues that the first chapters of 1 Samuel are designed to anticipate the story of the Jerusalem temple and the continuation of the Davidic line. He maintains that Shiloh in 1 Samuel 1–3 "is not being described historically: it is a stage set to evoke Solomonic Jerusalem."

form the throne (in the way that Mettinger envisages) but support and
transport the platform upon which the throne is situated (Ezek 10:1).
The archaeological evidence cited by Mettinger is largely Phoenician in
origin. The artifacts found in Israel date to the Late Bronze period,
which may be significantly earlier than the final form of the 1 and 2
Samuel texts. Even if Mettinger is right to connect the cherubim to the
sphinx thrones, it is interesting that the sphinxes mostly just flank the
throne and do not always form the seat. This perhaps indicates that the
deity or king depicted is not "enthroned upon the cherubim" (as Mettinger suggests) but enthroned *between* the cherubim. In which case, the
cherubim may be performing an entirely different function. Rather than
physically comprising the throne itself, the cherubim may be guarding
or transporting it.

Thus Mettinger's idea that the cherubim formula and the epithet
יהוה צְבָאוֹת were linked from early times and originated at an El sanctuary in Shiloh is entirely conjectural. There is remarkably little evidence
to support his thesis. The textual data suggests a link between the two
divine titles, but not one that was so strong as to prevent them from
being used independently. The two epithets could have been connected
because of a link between the cherubim and the צְבָאוֹת. The cherubim
may form part of the divine army, an idea perhaps suggested by 2 Sam
22:11 = Ps 18:11. In this case, the cherubim may have been thought to
participate in Yahweh's battles. Alternatively, there may be no real
significance in the connection. Divine epithets are sometimes employed
in conjunction with one another but it does not follow that their use
together was occasioned by a mutual underlying ideology.

§ 1.1.3 The Cherubim Formula and the Ark in 1 Sam 4:4 and
2 Sam 6:2

The cherubim formula occurs twice in the books of Samuel in 1 Sam 4:4
and 2 Sam 6:2. 1 Sam 4:4 occurs at the beginning of the narrative unit
1 Sam 4–7:2,[33] which describes how the ark is taken into battle, seized

---

33 Most scholars separate 1 Sam 4–7:2 from 1 Samuel 1–3, owing to the change in sub-
    ject matter and the absence of Samuel (the protagonist in 1 Sam 1–3) in 1 Sam 4–6.
    Fokkelman (1993), Van Seters (1983: 353) and Smelik (1992), however, all argue that
    1 Sam 4–7:2 cannot be read independently of 1 Samuel 1–3. Frolov (2004: 36) makes a

by the Philistines as booty and is then restored to the Israelites after inflicting plagues upon Philistine cities.[34] In 2 Samuel 6, David triumphantly conveys the ark to Jerusalem from Baal Judah.[35] Thus the appearance of the cherubim formula in two stories about the ark[36] may point to a connection between the ark and the cherubim.

Yet what is the nature of this connection? Did whoever included the epithets in these passages imagine the ark to have two adjoined cherubim statues as is outlined in the description of the tabernacle in Exodus (Exodus 25–31 and 35–40)? Or, do the epithets merely apply to Yahweh and thus have no special association with the ark? Haran (1978: 249) claims that the cherubim formula in 1 Sam 4:4 and 2 Sam 6:2 refers only to the majestic qualities of Yahweh and does not refer to the ark. Therefore, he argues, there is no link between the ark and the cherubim in the books of Samuel. Instead, he contends that the cherubim formula is used in 1 Sam 4:4 and 2 Sam 6:2 because of its historical association with a cherubim throne at Shiloh. He views this throne to have existed independently from the ark and likens this to the traditions concerning the ark and cherubim in the Solomonic temple, where the ark is placed under the wings of the cherubim but is entirely separate from it (1 Kgs 8:6–8), unlike Ex 25:18–22 (Haran 1959:33).

Haran's explanation for the use of the cherubim formula in the Samuel passages is untenable. As we have seen, there is little evidence for a cherubim throne at Shiloh or Jerusalem. Moreover, the view that the cherubim formula in 1 Sam 4:4 and 2 Sam 6:2 has no connection with the ark is tenuous. 2 Sam 6:2, in particular, states that the name

---

case for reading 1 Samuel 1–7 as an "integral, if complex, composition." See Eynikel (2000: 88–106) for a recent summary of the arguments.

34 Punishment is also inflicted on the people of Bethshemesh who look into the ark (1 Sam 6:19–21).

35 In 1 Sam 7:2, the ark is said to lodge in Kiriath Jearim. The different names may support the idea that 1 Sam 4–7:2 and 2 Samuel 6 do not make up a single narrative entity (see Miller and Roberts 1977: 23).

36 Earlier scholars (e.g. Rost 1926 and Campbell 1975) believed that 1 Sam 4–7:2 and 2 Samuel 6 constituted a single narrative unit, the so-called "ark narrative". Miller and Roberts, however, maintain that there are too many differences between the 1 Samuel and 2 Samuel narratives for them to be a single entity (Miller and Roberts 1977: 23). If the two passages do not constitute an integral account, then the two occurrences of the cherubim formula in the books of Samuel may not be the product of the same hand. Thus its use in 1 Sam 4:4 could have occasioned its use in 2 Sam 6:2, or vice versa.

יְהוָה צְבָאוֹת יֹשֵׁב הַכְּרֻבִים was "called over/upon"[37] the ark. Thus the appearance of the cherubim formula in 1 Sam 4:4 and 2 Sam 6:2 does seem to suggest that the author(s) made some connection between the ark and the cherubim.

It is only in the Exodus traditions (Exodus 25–31 and 35–40) that two golden cherubim are attached to the כַּפֹּרֶת on the ark. The description of the ark in Deuteronomy (Deut 10:1–5, 8) lacks any reference to the כַּפֹּרֶת and its cherubim statues.[38] In 1 Kgs 8:6–7, the ark is carried into the new Solomonic temple and placed under the wings of two giant cherubim statues (1 Kgs 6:23–28). As the Exodus tabernacle is most likely an idealized version of the Solomonic temple (see § 1.2.1.2), we should perhaps infer that the author of 1 Kings 8 also envisaged the ark to be without the כַּפֹּרֶת and the cherubim (see Haran 1978: 249). Although it is conceivable that whoever included the cherubim formula in 1 Sam 4:4 and 2 Sam 6:2 had the golden cherubim of the כַּפֹּרֶת in mind, the description of the ark and its movements in the books of Samuel does not accord with the portrayal of the ark in Exodus. Instead of the portable shrine that is described in the Exodus traditions, the ark in Samuel is more of a war palladium, used as a talisman against the enemy (1 Sam 4:3).[39] It thus seems unlikely that the use of the cherubim formula in 1 Sam 4:4 and 2 Sam 6:2 was inspired by the Exodus traditions of the cherubim statues above the ark.

Further evidence that the author of 1 Sam 4:4 did not have the Exodus description of the ark in mind is the inclusion of the term בְּרִית with reference to the ark. Carlson (1964: 70–71) argues that the expression אֲרוֹן בְּרִית is a catchphrase of the Deuteronomist, who wished to emphasize that the ark housed the law tablets. Moreover, he views the entire phrase אֲרוֹן בְּרִית־יְהוָה צְבָאוֹת יֹשֵׁב הַכְּרֻבִים (1 Sam 4:4) in a similar light. He contends (1964: 71–71): "The divine name connected with the Ark in 1 Sam 4:4 is an associative introduction to 2 Sam 6:2; thus the proclamation of the name in this verse can hardly be taken as referring to Shiloh: it must either be supposed to have taken place in Kiriath-Jearim… or, more generally, to point its connection with the deity… on

---

37   The Hebrew נִקְרָא has cultic overtones and perhaps has the sense of "invoke" (see 1 Kgs 8:43).

38   Mettinger (1982b: 51) argues that this is "the result of the conscious suppression of the notion of the God who sat enthroned in the Temple."

39   This is similar to the function of the ark in the book of Joshua and in Num 10:34–36.

Mt. Zion."[40] Thus the inclusion of the cherubim formula in these narratives may be for literary rather than historical reasons. The author(s) may have purposefully incorporated the epithet in order to evoke the Jerusalem temple cult.

Ahlström (1975: 142) argues that the 1 Sam 4–6 was attached to the preceding Shiloh material and that originally the ark had no connection with Shiloh (see also Janowski 1991: 235–240). He maintains that, in 1 Sam 4:4 and 2 Sam 6:2, the cherubim formula is used purposefully to evoke the Solomonic temple. The editor(s) wished to emphasize a "pan-Israelite doctrine", which underscored the unity of the Israelites in the pre-monarchic era.[41] The ark narratives in Samuel portray Yahweh as the "empire god", who, when captured by the enemy, brought pestilence and disease wherever his ark was taken (Ahlström 1975: 141). This story was artificially attached to the Shiloh traditions in order to give reason for the downfall of the Shilonite priesthood. This, in turn, justified David's transferral of the ark from Shiloh to Jerusalem and thereby helped legitimize the centralization of the cult. The application of the cherubim formula to Yahweh in the ark narratives helps to link the ark with Solomon's temple and thus amplify the voice of the Deuteronomistic editor (Ahlström 1975: 142, n. 5).

The idea that the cherubim formula in 1 Sam 4:4 and 2 Sam 6:2 links the ark to its "rightful" place in the temple is important. As we have seen in our discussion of the syntax and semantics of the cherubim formula, the title is most likely associated with Yahweh's dwelling place in the temple. Thus, for the author of 2 Sam 6:2, a narrative about the ark's new and "proper" position in Jerusalem, the use of the epithet would help to underscore the significance of the events (see Janowski 1991: 235–240). Yahweh's rightful dwelling place is with the cherubim in the Jerusalem temple (1 Kgs 8:6) in accordance with his divine title, יֹשֵׁב הַכְּרֻבִים. If the author of 1 Sam 4:4 draws upon 2 Sam 6:2 (so Carlson

---

40 Carlson's rendering of יֹשֵׁב הַכְּרֻבִים as "enthroned upon the cherubim" is inaccurate. Nevertheless, he is right in his view that the epithet connects the ark with the Jerusalem sanctuary.

41 Ahlström views 1 Samuel 4–6 and 2 Samuel 6 to form an integral narrative unit, which was reworked by a Deuteronomistic editor. This is in contrast to Frolov's thesis (2004) that the ideology in 1 Samuel 1–8 is an anti-Deuteronomistic polemic. Both view the theme of Yahweh's universality to be of utmost importance and the reason for the inclusion of the cherubim formula in both 1 Samuel 4 and 2 Samuel 6, but for very different reasons.

1964: 70–71, Auld 2004: 174, n. 72 and Frolov 2004: 173), then a further connection is made between the triumphal entry of the ark into Jerusalem and the loss of the ark on the battlefield at Ebenezer.

§ 1.1.4 Summary

We have seen, in our analysis of the syntax and semantics of the cherubim formula, that the epithet is best paraphrased as "dweller of the cherubim". The alternative is to render it "ruler of the cherubim". The title probably relates to Yahweh's dwelling-place in the Jerusalem temple, surrounded by images of cherubim. Mettinger's argument that the formula should be rendered "enthroned upon the cherubim" and linked to an early cult of El and his cherubim throne at Shiloh is unconvincing. His connection of the cherubim formula with יהוה צְבָאוֹת is tenuous. Likewise, the link between the cherubim formula and Shiloh may be entirely literary and not historical. Similarly, the association of the cherubim formula and the ark in 1 Sam 4:4 and 2 Sam 6:2 is probably a narrative device. The author of 2 Samuel 6 may be deliberately attempting to link the ark to its "rightful" future position in the temple (in accordance with 1 Kgs 8:6). Its use in 1 Sam 4:4 may have arisen out of a desire to link the story of 1 Samuel 4–6 with 2 Samuel 6 and ideas concerning the centralisation of the cult in Jerusalem.

§ 1.2 כְּרֻבִים as Cultic Images

The lexeme כְּרוּב occurs most frequently in prose descriptions of cultic furnishings in the books of Exodus, 1 Kings, 1 and 2 Chronicles and Ezekiel. In these descriptions, the cherubim adorn the architecture and cultic furniture in the temple and tabernacle. They also occur as freestanding statues in 1 Kgs 6:23–28; 8:6–7 (//2 Chr 3:10–13; 5:7–8). Although we learn something of the physical form of the cherubim and how they feature in the temple and tabernacle, the texts say very little about their religious and cultic significance. The texts are altogether silent as to why the cherubim feature in the places that they do. Nevertheless, it may be possible to make some inferences as to their ideological function by looking closely at the contexts in which they appear.

§ 1.2.1 The Cherubim of the Exodus Tabernacle
(Exodus 25–26; 36–37)

The first canonical references to images of cherubim occur in the instructions for the building of the ark (Exodus 25–26) and the report of
its assembly (Exodus 36–37). Haran has drawn attention to the order in
which the instructions are given. He has shown that the tabernacle
furniture is deliberately mentioned in a specific sequence, relating to
the perceived holiness of the object. Similarly, the materials and the
technical skill needed to create an object are in proportion to the sa-
credness ascribed to it. He notes, "Such a rule is ingrained in many
cultures… – the higher an item is on the scale of sanctity, the greater
man's efforts to embellish it" (1978: 164). According to this principle,
the cherubim decorating the tabernacle are at the highest end of the
scale. The two cherubim of the כַּפֹּרֶת are mentioned among the first architectural features of the tabernacle (Ex 25:18–22; 37:7–9) and are made
of solid gold. The cherubim which adorn the פָּרֹכֶת veil (which functions
as a screen for the ark and tr,PoK;, Ex 26:31; 36:35) are missing on the
less important outer veil of the tabernacle. Likewise, the tabernacle
curtains (Ex 26:1; 36:8) are embroidered with images of cherubim,
whereas no decoration is said to embellish the outer tent curtains (26:7;
36:14). Hence, the placement of cherubim within the tabernacle, and the
materials used to craft them, indicate that they are connected with the
most sacred space in the tabernacle.

§ 1.2.1.1 The Golden Cherubim on the כַּפֹּרֶת

The exact form and function of the two golden cherubim has been
much debated. It is helpful to examine in detail the five relevant verses
(Ex 25:18–22).36 Verse 18 reads:

וְעָשִׂיתָ שְׁנַיִם כְּרֻבִים זָהָב מִקְשָׁה תַּעֲשֶׂה אֹתָם מִשְּׁנֵי קְצוֹת
הַכַּפֹּרֶת:

The *athnak* under זָהָב shows that the Masoretes understood the
phrasing to be as follows: "You shall make two cherubim of gold – you

---

36   The instructions in Ex 25:18–20 are identical to the report of construction in Ex 37:7–
9. The LXX text of Exodus 37 is much shorter than its MT counterpart.

shall make them of hammered work – at the two ends of the כַּפֹּרֶת."
However, without the Masoretic punctuation, the phrasing can also
follow the LXX, "You shall make two cherubim beaten from gold, and
you shall put them on both sides of the כַּפֹּרֶת."[37] The term מִקְשָׁה most
likely derives from קשׁה, meaning "be hard, severe". Durham (1987: 357)
notes that it seems to imply hammered as opposed to poured metalwork.

As Haran (1978: 159) has observed, the use of pure gold is more or
less restricted to the inner furniture of the tabernacle, where the outer
furniture is made from the less precious metal, bronze (overlay or hammered work). The gradation of materials is again symbolic of the perceived proximity to the divine presence. The size of the cherubim is not
mentioned. However, as they are to be attached to the sides of the כַּפֹּרֶת
(1.5 cubits high and 2.5 cubits long, according to Ex 25:17), the writer
cannot have envisaged them to be large statues, such as those of the
Solomonic temple (1 Kgs 6–8). As smaller figurines or relief work, they
are most likely imagined as carved from pure gold (Haran 1978: 159).
Although verse 18 does not specify that the cherubim were to be made
of pure gold, it is likely that this is what is envisaged. Haran notes that
the phrase זָהָב טָהוֹר, 'pure gold', is only used to describe the inner furniture of the tabernacle. For example, the term 'pure gold' is not used
with regard to the tabernacle's planks and pillars which, he argues,
shows that they were considered to be inferior to the inner fixtures
(Haran 1978: 163). However, as regards the cherubim statues, although
the term "pure" is not used in connection with them, Haran argues that
they were, nevertheless, to be made of pure gold. He observes that the
phrase זָהָב טָהוֹר is only used at the beginning of each description of a
particular fixture. By employing the phrase in this way, Haran argues,
the writer is indicating that all the gold used for that fixture is pure,
thereby preventing the need to repeat the adjective טָהוֹר each time. The
description of the cherubim actually belongs to the כַּפֹּרֶת section, which
begins in verse 17 and does include the phrase "pure gold". In this
way, the cherubim are not to be regarded as inferior objects because the
writer describes them as "gold" rather than "pure gold".

The end of verse 18 reads: מִשְּׁנֵי קְצוֹת הַכַּפֹּרֶת. It is difficult to know
how to understand the preposition מִן here and in מִן־הַכַּפֹּרֶת תַּעֲשׂוּ of
verse 19. The BDB (579–581) includes verse 19 as an example of the

---

37 καὶ ποιήσεις δύο χερουβιμ χρυσᾶ τορευτὰ καὶ ἐπιθήσεις αὐτὰ ἐξ ἀμφοτέρων τῶν κλιτῶν
     τοῦ ἱλαστηρίου

partitive use of מִן, in which case the phrase should be translated, "a part of the כַּפֹּרֶת you are to make (the cherubim)." A similar rendering can be given for verse 18: "at the two ends of the כַּפֹּרֶת". That the cherubim form one entity with the כַּפֹּרֶת is emphasised by a midrash in TPsJ 37:8 (see Houtman 2000: 386). Whether they are made of the same sheet of gold as the כַּפֹּרֶת or whether they are joined to the כַּפֹּרֶת after their construction is unclear. If joined, presumably they are thought to be hammered or welded together in some way.

Hyatt (1971: 267) has suggested that the cherubim might not be statues (as is commonly thought); indeed, the text never specifies that they are. Instead, he asks whether they might be carved in shallow relief onto the כַּפֹּרֶת. Although this is conceivable, the fact that the cherubim "cover over" the כַּפֹּרֶת (Ex 25:20), together with the fact that Yahweh speaks to Moses from *above* the כַּפֹּרֶת but *between* the cherubim (Ex 25:22), implies that they are appendages to the כַּפֹּרֶת rather than decoration on it. Further evidence that the cherubim are envisaged as statues comes from the versions. In the Vulgate (Ex 37:7, 8) and the LXX, the cherubim are regarded as entirely separate from the כַּפֹּרֶת. The LXX has καὶ ἐπιθήσεις, "and you shall place", suggesting that the cherubim and the כַּפֹּרֶת are not made of one sheet of gold (see Houtman 2000: 386 but against Cassuto 1967: 332).

Verse 20 divulges the most information in this section regarding the physical form of the cherubim. Anatomical features (כְּנָפַיִם and פָּנִים) confirm that the cherubim statues depict some form of creature or being.[38] Nevertheless, the verse (as indeed the entire section) is still frustratingly laconic concerning any other physical attribute of the cherubim. At best, we can postulate that the cherubim are winged beings. The use of the dual form in Ex 25:20 confirms that the cherubim statues have two wings.[39]

Ex 25:20 stipulates that the cherubim are to be fashioned with their wings spread out upwards (פֹּרְשֵׂי כְנָפַיִם לְמַעְלָה), "covering over" the כַּפֹּרֶת (סֹכְכִים בְּכַנְפֵיהֶם עַל־הַכַּפֹּרֶת). The exact position and function of the

---

38 The combination of "face" and "wing" may be an indication that the cherubim were conceived as hybrid beings. Although an odd feature to be ascribed to a bird, the phrase פְּנֵי־נֶשֶׁר occurs in Ezek 1:10. That the cherubim had the form of birds might be the logical inference if one had only read Ex 25:20. Yet Ezek 1:10 is describing a hybrid creature and hence the strange combination may be due to the fact that the author is describing a supernatural being.

39 This is in contrast to the description of the cherubim in Ezek 10:21 (see § 1.3.4).

wings has been debated. At the heart of the problem is the meaning of the term סֹכְכִים. The qal participle of סכך is most often used in connection with cherubim (Ex 25:20; 37:9; 1 Kgs 8:7; 1 Chr 28:18; Ezek 28:14,16) and seems to mean "cover" or "screen". In poetic texts, forms of סכך are used to describe protection in battle or against evil (e.g. Ps 91:4; Ps 140:8; Nah 2:6) and have the sense of "shield". In Ex 40:3 and 21, the verb is used in relation to the פָּרֹכֶת veil, which screens the ark from view. In Ex 25:20, it is stated that the cherubim "cover above/over" the כַּפֹּרֶת with their wings, whereas in 1 Kgs 8:7 it is the ark that is "covered above/over".

There are two main arguments concerning what exactly the "covering" of the כַּפֹּרֶת and ark entails. First, there are those (e.g. Houtman 2000: 385) who view the primary function of the cherubim in both the tabernacle and temple as apotropaic. Following this assumption, the action of "covering" is protective in nature and, consequently, the cherubim are shielding the holy object (כַּפֹּרֶת or ark) or space above it (place of the divine presence) with their wings.[40] Second, Haran argues that the verb is meant only to specify the position of the wings of the cherubim in relation to the כַּפֹּרֶת. He contends, "The verb *skk* used in this context should not mislead us. The symbol is not that of a covering but of a throne formed by the outstretched wings" (Haran 1978: 253). Haran corroborates this by referring to the use of the term לְמַעְלָה, "upwards", in the first clause of 25:20. He argues that the term means "above the trunk up to the shoulders" (rather than above the shoulders). In his view, the wings are therefore horizontal. Yet Haran's understanding of a cherubim throne is dependent on the flawed rendering of the cherubim formula as "enthroned upon the cherubim" (see § 1.1). The wings can still be stretched out above the כַּפֹּרֶת and, also, have a protective function. It is not the case that the wings can only have a protective function if draped over the כַּפֹּרֶת. Indeed, it may be that it is neither the כַּפֹּרֶת nor the ark that is being "covered", but rather the space above the objects, between the cherubim. This would concur with the idea that it is above the כַּפֹּרֶת and between the cherubim that Yahweh manifests himself (Ex 25:22//Num 7:89). The description of the

---

40   The figurative association of wings with protective power is known throughout the ancient Near East. Kings are enfolded in the wings of deities in Egyptian iconography and wings have shielding properties in poetic texts (e.g. Ps 17:8; 36:8 and, especially, 91:4, where the verb סכך is used).

cherubim in Ex 25:20 seems to run counter to the idea that the cherubim formed Yahweh's throne, as the function of the wings is specifically said to be to "cover over/above" the כַּפֹּרֶת. Indeed, there is no mention of Yahweh's throne at all (a fact entirely neglected by Haran 1978: 247–249 and Mettinger 1982a: 112). Thus Haran's argument (that סֹכְכִים in verse 20 merely refers to the wings' position and not function) conveniently supports his 'cherubim throne' thesis. According to Haran, the divine presence can still be located above the cherubim and is not protected between or beneath the wings of the cherubim. Yet, if one attends simply to the text, without importing the idea of a cherubim throne (of which the text says nothing), then we are free to read the term סֹכְכִים in this verse as having its usual protective sense of "screen" or "shield".[41]

At first glance, the last two clauses of verse 20 seem to be contradictory. They read:

וּפְנֵיהֶם אִישׁ אֶל־אָחִיו אֶל־הַכַּפֹּרֶת יִהְיוּ פְּנֵי הַכְּרֻבִים׃

This can be rendered, "And their faces were each to his brother, to the כַּפֹּרֶת were the faces of the cherubim." However, it seems most logical that the first clause signifies that the cherubim are to face one another. In this way, it is only the second clause that describes the exact direction their faces are to point. The first clause merely indicates the position of the two cherubim in relation to one another. They are imagined as opposite each other.

Although the significance of the position of their faces towards the כַּפֹּרֶת is not made explicit in the text, it has been the subject of speculation for several scholars. Cassuto (1967: 335) and Haran (1978: 153) both argue that they turn their heads away from the divine presence that is enthroned above them, out of respect. Cassuto compares this to the action of the seraphim in Isa 6:2, who cover their faces with one set of wings, and to Moses who hides his face for fear of looking at God (Ex 3:6). In their role as guardians, Houtman (2000: 388) thinks that the faces of the cherubim are trained on/above the כַּפֹּרֶת, which is where the

---

41 The protective sense of סָכַךְ is explicit in poetic texts such as Ps 91:4, Ps 140:8 and Nah 2:6. The use of the term with reference to sacred space is interesting. It is employed with reference to the פָּרֹכֶת veil (in Ex 40:3, 21) as well as the cherubim. It is arguable therefore that it does not have a generic sense of "covering" but a more powerful and significant sense of "blocking off" or "shielding" the sacred from the profane.

divine presence rests. Houtman's reading does the greatest justice to what the text actually says (given the protective sense of the verb סכך) and is thus preferable to the other options. In verse 22, the significance of the whole ark/כַּפֹּרֶת/cherubim structure is revealed. It is here, above the כַּפֹּרֶת and between the cherubim, that Yahweh will manifest himself in order to speak with Moses and disclose his commandments for his people.

§ 1.2.1.2 The Inspiration for the Golden Cherubim

The view that the tabernacle depicted in Exodus 25 and 37 was largely invented by priestly writers has been prevalent since the 19th Century.[42] Although it has been demonstrated that tent-shrines (such as that described in Exodus) were likely known and used in pre-exilic Israel (Morgenstern 1942: 153–266), the opulent materials and the highly skilled craftsmanship needed to construct the tabernacle do not fit with the idea that the Israelites were refugees, who barely had the provisions to eat (Ex 16:3). This has caused most scholars to doubt the historicity of the text and propose new explanations for why the writers imagined the tent shrine as they did.

The dominant view is that, although the tabernacle never actually existed, it does reflect real elements of Jerusalem cultic furniture and thus contains, to some degree, "a nucleus of historical truth" (Haran 1978: 203). Houtman (2000: 329) is an exponent of this position when he argues:

> The writer talks about the past from the perspective of his own time. Only by 'colouring in' the past with images and information his readers are familiar with, can they know what he is talking about. That makes it likely that for his description he availed himself of a temple type the readers/hearers were familiar with.

For Houtman, this temple was the Solomonic temple on Mt Zion.

It follows from this that the inspiration for the golden cherubim of the tabernacle was the pair of cherubim statues in the דְּבִיר of the Solomonic temple. When Solomon brings the ark into the temple in 1 Kings 8, he places it under the wings of the immense cherubim statues that he has fashioned for the temple (1 Kgs 6:23–28). 1 Kgs 8:6–7 reads:

---

42   One of the first major exponents of this view was Wellhausen (1883).

⁶ וַיָּבִאוּ הַכֹּהֲנִים אֶת־אֲרוֹן בְּרִית־יְהוָה אֶל־מְקוֹמוֹ אֶל־דְּבִיר הַבַּיִת

אֶל־קֹדֶשׁ הַקֳּדָשִׁים אֶל־תַּחַת כַּנְפֵי הַכְּרוּבִים:

⁷ כִּי הַכְּרוּבִים פֹּרְשִׂים כְּנָפַיִם אֶל־מְקוֹם הָאָרוֹן וַיָּסֹכּוּ

הַכְּרֻבִים עַל־הָאָרוֹן וְעַל־בַּדָּיו מִלְמָעְלָה:

The wings of the cherubim spread out over the place of the ark and the wings "screen" (√ סכך) the ark and its poles "from above".

Verse 7 is remarkably similar to Ex 25:20 and may show how closely the writer is adhering to the temple tradition in his description of the tabernacle. Ex 25: 20 reads:

וְהָיוּ הַכְּרֻבִים פֹּרְשֵׂי כְנָפַיִם לְמַעְלָה סֹכְכִים בְּכַנְפֵיהֶם

עַל־הַכַּפֹּרֶת וּפְנֵיהֶם אִישׁ אֶל־אָחִיו אֶל־הַכַּפֹּרֶת יִהְיוּ פְּנֵי הַכְּרֻבִים

The author of Ex 25:20 (Ex 37:9) appears to draw directly upon the tradition contained in 1 Kgs 8:6–7. In 1 Kgs 8:7, the term מִלְמָעְלָה is used to describe the direction of the "screening". The cherubim screen off the ark and its poles "from above". In Ex 25:20, however, it is stated that the cherubim spread out their wings "upwards" (לְמַעְלָה). Haran (1978: 252) proposes that the use of this term is evidence that the function of the wings is to form the seat of the throne of Yahweh. Yet, if the direction of influence is from the Kings text to the Exodus text, then the function of the wings as described in Kings precedes that described in Exodus. Hence, it is likely that the term מִלְמָעְלָה in 1 Kgs 8:7 occasions the use of the term לְמַעְלָה in Ex 25:20, rather than the other way around. If this is the case, the earlier idea is not that the wings are outstretched "upwards" (perhaps to form a throne, as Haran argues) but that they screen the sacred space "from above".

A close reading of Ex 25:20 with 1 Kgs 8:7 thus shows that the earlier function of the cherubim in the Holy of Holies was to "block off" or "screen" (skk) the space above/over the ark/כַּפֹּרֶת.[43] This is the space where Yahweh will manifest himself (Ex 25:22; Num 7:89). Haran's argument that the verb סכך only relates to the position of the wings, and not their function, is unconvincing. The reason that he reads the text in the way that he does is transparent: to bolster his "cherubim throne" thesis. It is worth taking a closer look at the arguments for a

---

43   This is against Keel 1977: 28–29, who argues that the apotropaic function of the cherubim in 1 Kings 8 is secondary to the idea that they formed Yahweh's throne.

cherubim throne in order to weigh up the evidence for the existence of such a concept in the Hebrew Bible.

§ 1.2.1.3 Do the Cherubim Statues Form a Throne?

As noted above, the throne interpretation of the cherubim statues has its supporters and detractors. Those opposed to the throne interpretation tend to argue for an apotropaic function for the cherubim, based on 1 Kgs 8:6–7 and Ex 25:20//Num 7:89 (e.g. Houtman 2000: 384–385). Advocates of the throne interpretation tend to view this apotropaic function as secondary (e.g. Keel 1977: 28–29). These arguments require further examination.

The divine epithet יֹשֵׁב הַכְּרֻבִים, together with archaeological evidence and the textual data pertaining to the position of the cherubim within the sanctuary, has given rise to the idea that Yahweh's throne was formed by two cherubim with outstretched wings (see Keel 1977: 152–155). The first major proponent of the throne interpretation was Dibelius (1906). He was followed by Von Rad (1958: 109–129) and, later, to some extent, by Haran. Although each scholar differs slightly in how they imagine the throne to be conceived, they each share the idea that Yahweh is envisaged enthroned between or upon the cherubim. Yet, neither the 1 Kings account nor the description of the tabernacle in Exodus, gives any explicit indication that this is how the cherubim, or the shrine in general, were imagined.

Dibelius and Keel both argue that the function of the statues implied by 1 Kgs 8:6–7 (cited above) is secondary and that their original role was that of throne-bearers. That the cherubim were not originally associated with the shrine (Deut 10:1–5, 8) is supposed to support this idea as they are not connected with a sacred place which they must protect (Keel 1977: 28–29). Instead, the cherubim were originally creatures whose function was to carry the throne (or form the throne) of the deity.[44] Haran (1978: 257) maintains that, despite their size, the two golden cherubim of the כַּפֹּרֶת form a seat. He cites Ex 25:22 (//Num 7:89) as evidence for this, as it is between the wings of the cherubim that Yahweh will speak with Moses and reveal his commands.

---

44   Cassuto (1967:334–335) argues that the cherubim both symbolise the empty throne of Yahweh and protect and guard the כַּפֹּרֶת.

Houtman has criticized this view. He argues that the cherubim in 1 Kgs 8:6–7 and Ex 25:18–22 guard and protect the space above the כַּפֹּרֶת[45] in which Yahweh will manifest himself. In this way their function is apotropaic. Moreover, Houtman maintains that, as hybrid beings (a detail not made explicit in the 1 Kings or Exodus accounts), the cherubim incorporate the superlative features of powerful animals and are thus ideally suited as guardians. He translates יֹשֵׁב הַכְּרֻבִים as "who is enthroned amidst the cherubim," which he regards as indicating that Yahweh is surrounded by these supernatural guardians, who protect him and help him in battle (Houtman 2000: 385).[46]

Houtman's view is preferable to the idea of a cherubim throne. Those who argue that the cherubim statues in the tabernacle and temple form the throne of Yahweh are simply rewriting the Bible. There is no evidence in 1 Kgs 8:6–7 or Ex 25:18–22; 37:7–9 to support the idea. Indeed, in order to accept the cherubim throne theory, one must ignore (or at least downplay) the significance of the verb סָכַךְ in these texts. The biblical passages specifically state that the function of the cherubim is to "shield" the sacred space with their wings. In 1 Kgs 8:7, Ex 25:20 and 37:9, the cherubim are the subject of the verb סָכַךְ and not the wings (which are feminine). Thus it is the role of the cherubim themselves to "block off" the sacred space. This "blocking off" is not a side-effect of the spreading out of the wings to form a throne (as Haran 1978: 252–253 would have us believe) but is the fundamental reason for the presence of the cherubim. The texts say nothing of forming a throne for the deity. As already noted, the only text to link the cherubim to the throne of Yahweh is Ezekiel 10, a very difficult text. Even in this text though, the idea that the cherubim form the throne of Yahweh is entirely absent. The throne is a completely separate entity to the cherubim (Ezek 10:1). In the descriptions of the cherubim statues, it is the apotropaic role of the cherubim that comes to the fore. The space above the ark/כַּפֹּרֶת, between the cherubim, is where Yahweh will manifest himself (Ex 25:22//Num 7:89). Thus shielding the presence of the deity is the primary function of the golden cherubim statues.

---

45 Houtman stresses that the cherubim do not protect the ark or כַּפֹּרֶת but rather the space above them (Ex 25:22//Num 7:89). It is this space where Yahweh reveals himself and hence this is what is to be protected (not the contents of the ark, or the ark itself).

46 Houtman sees the connection between this epithet and "Yahweh Sabaoth" as evidence that Yahweh's host consisted of cherubim.

§ 1.2.1.4 The Cherubim Decoration on the פָּרֹכֶת Veil and Tabernacle Curtains

As stated in the introduction to this section, the cherubim do not only occur as appendages to the כַּפֹּרֶת, they also feature as decoration on the פָּרֹכֶת veil and the ten inner tabernacle curtains (Ex 26:1, 31; 36:8, 35). Haran (1978: 161–163) has shown how his principle of "material gradation" applies to the cherubim embroidered onto the tabernacle's fabric. Cherubim only feature on the fabric needed for the most important curtains (those of the פָּרֹכֶת veil and the inner tabernacle) and do not feature on the outer veil of the tabernacle, the court's screen (Ex 26:26; 27:16; 36:37; 38:18), or the outer tent curtains (26:7; 36:14).

The text identifies three weaving techniques: חֹשֵׁב, רֹקֵם and אֹרֵג. The cherubim are always said to be made using the חֹשֵׁב method (Ex 26:1, 31; 36:8, 35) and, according to Haran, this indicates that this type of weaving included figures, as opposed to a simple mixture of colours. He argues that because superior technique was needed to fashion these details, the cherubim only appear on the most important fabrics (Haran 1978: 160–161). Similarly, three types of material are used: goats' hair (which is not dyed), the more expensive dyed wool and שֵׁשׁ, which was a type of fine linen. The latter two are what are used for the ten curtains of the tabernacle and the פָּרֹכֶת veil (Ex 26:1, 31; 36:8, 35).

Accordingly, the פָּרֹכֶת veil is the most important of the textiles in the tabernacle. It is what separates the holy place from the holy of holies (Ex 26:33). It is made of a wool-linen mixture and decorated with cherubim, using חֹשֵׁב craftsmanship. Next in importance are the ten tabernacle curtains, which are designed to shield the outer sanctum. They are made from the same wool-linen mixture as the tabernacle curtains[47] and are also embroidered with cherubim of חֹשֵׁב craftsmanship.

Haran's observation concerning the material gradation of the textiles shows that the cherubim are, again, associated with the most holy areas of the tabernacle. Concerning their function, however, the text is again silent. Yet it may be possible that they have a similar apotropaic function to the golden cherubim. The verb סכך, used of the golden

---

47   Although, according to Haran, the fact that the list of fabrics is inverted shows that the פָּרֹכֶת veil is more important as the linen is mentioned last and the blue wool first (whereas the inverse is true for the curtains). He argues that the proportions used are relative to the importance of the fabric (1978:162).

cherubim statues in Ex 25:20, is also used to refer to the function of the פָּרֹכֶת veil in Ex 40:3 and 21. Both the cherubim statues and the veil "shield over/ above" the ark/כַּפֹּרֶת (Ex 25:18; 40:21). Hence the cherubim on the פָּרֹכֶת veil may help to strengthen the religious function of the veil. The cherubim figures on the curtains and פָּרֹכֶת veil are similar to those that appear on the walls and doors of the inner sanctum of the Solomonic temple (1 Kgs 6:32), although in the temple they are featured with palm trees and open flowers. It is possible that these plants are symbolic of the threshold between sacred and profane space (see Stordalen 2000: 137, 161, 284). If this is the case, then the cherubim depicted on the walls of the temple may represent guardian figures that protect the sacred space from contamination. This idea is corroborated by the use of the verb שׁמר in connection with the cherubim who guard the way to the Tree of Life in Genesis 3:24. If the cherubim on the curtains and veil of the tabernacle are equivalent to the cherubim friezes on the temple walls and doors, then they too may have this function.

§ 1.2.1.5 Summary

We have noted in our analysis of the cherubim of the tabernacle in Exodus that the text is remarkably silent about their exact form and function. About their form, the text only reveals that they are some sort of creature or being with two wings and one head/face (Ex 25:20). As to their function, a close analysis of the text seems to suggest that they have an apotropaic or guardian role, protecting the most holy space. This is not, as has been argued, a secondary function of the cherubim. Contrary to the views of most scholars (e.g. Haran), the text says nothing of a throne-bearing function of the cherubim. The description of the cherubim in the Solomonic temple, which inspired the authors of the Exodus accounts, mentions nothing of a cherubim throne either. Thus the primary function of the tabernacle cherubim seems to be to shield the most sacred space, where Yahweh will manifest himself.

§ 1.2.2 The Cherubim in the Solomonic Temple

Cherubim are said to have adorned many of the architectural features in the Solomonic temple: the walls (1 Kgs 6:29), the doors to the inner sanctuary and the nave (1 Kgs 6:32–35), and the wheeled lavers in the outer court (1 Kgs 7:29). Additionally, and perhaps most importantly, they appear as architectural features in their own right, in the form of the two large statues in the דְּבִיר (1 Kgs 6:23–28; 8:6–7; 2 Chr 3:10–13; 5:7–8). The author of the 1 Kings account appears most interested in the dimensions of the architecture and the materials used, and less interested in giving information regarding the religious significance of the design. The reason for this and its possible implications for our understanding of the cherubim will need to be investigated. Additionally, the marked divergences of the 2 Chronicles account from that of 1 Kings 6–8 require consideration.

§ 1.2.2.1 The Cherubim Statues in the דְּבִיר

Although the proportions of the cherubim statues are described in some detail, their ideological purpose is not mentioned. Nevertheless, as already noted, 1 Kgs 8:6–7 allude to the protective function of the cherubim.[48] 1 Kgs 6:23–29 (2 Chr 3:10–13) describes how the statues were made. It is useful to look closely at these verses in order to discern just how much information about the cherubim the author concedes.

Like the golden figurines of the tabernacle, the two cherubim statues are positioned centre stage in the sanctuary, in the דְּבִיר (1 Kgs 6:23). The Vulgate has *oraculum* in place of Hebrew דְּבִיר and this prompted some older English translations to render the word as "oracle". Yet this stems from the erroneous idea that the word derived from the Hebrew root דבר, meaning "to speak". It has since been argued (BDB) that דְּבִיר is etymologically related to Arabic *dub[u]r* and Akkadian *dabāru* "to push back." It would thus have the meaning "inner recess" or "inner chamber". However, most recently, scholars have suggested that דְּבִיר is derived from Egyptian *dbr*, which denotes a wooden item, made by a carpenter. Hurowitz (2005: 73) suggests that it refers to a wooden cubical structure, measuring 20 x 20 cubits. In 2 Chr 3:10, the cherubim are made בְּבֵית־קֹדֶשׁ הַקֳּדָשִׁים, "in the house of the holy of holies", a term pe-

---

48 The idea that the large cherubim statues in the temple formed a giant throne for Yahweh has been assumed by many scholars (see above). The same arguments apply to these statues as apply to the smaller statues of the tabernacle and they shall not be repeated in this section. There is no evidence that the larger statues were thought to constitute a divine throne any more than the tabernacle statues.

culiar to the Chronicler but which incorporates the priestly term "holy of holies". This phrase (occurring here and in verse 8), with its use of the word "house", appears to set the space apart as a separate shrine (see Japhet 1993: 556).

The material from which the cherubim are carved is עֲצֵי־שָׁמֶן (1 Kgs 6:23). Literally meaning "wood of oil", this phrase is commonly translated as "olivewood". Hurowitz (2005: 75) connects שֶׁמֶן with the Akkadian term *šamnu*, meaning 'sap', and argues that עֲצֵי־שָׁמֶן refers to wood from any tree that drips sap. Trees of this type may have been advantageous for building because excreted resin renders the wood less susceptible to damage from insects. Although this point is not mentioned by Hurowitz, he does argue that עֲצֵי־שָׁמֶן was a valuable wood, more costly than cypress, which is used for the doors of the הֵיכָל (Hurowitz 2005: 89). If this is the case, the materials used are consistent with Haran's principle of material gradation (see Haran 1978: 158–174) and the cherubim are made from the most expensive wood.

1 Kgs 6:28 observes that the statues are to be overlaid with gold and not beaten from it, like the smaller statues of the Exodus tabernacle. This is presumably because of the size of the temple statues. Chronicles again diverges from the 1 Kings account. 2 Chr 3:10 states that the cherubim are מַעֲשֵׂה צַעֲצֻעִים. The meaning of צַעֲצֻעִים, a *hapax legomenon*, is unclear. The LXX identifies the term as עֵצִים, "trees, wood" and the Vulgate has "images". By analogy with an Arabic cognate, meaning "to form, fashion", the latter is probably better and thus we can render it "carvings", or something similar.

In verse 23b, the statues are said to be ten cubits high (around 5.3m). It is widely maintained that verse 26 is displaced, its original position being between 23a and 23b (see e.g. Gray 1970: 170 and Montgomery and Gehman 1960: 154). This is corroborated by the singular pronominal suffix in קוֹמָתוֹ, which is awkward in the existing sequence, as it requires a singular antecedent, הַכְּרוּב הַשֵּׁנִי (verse 26), rather than the plural כְּרֻבִים, as in verse 23. According to Bloch-Smith (1997: 85), their immense height "attests to the Israelite vision of the deity as superhuman in size." She compares the cosmic dimensions of the Solomonic temple to the superhuman distances travelled by the gods in the Ugaritic myths. Likewise, the metre-long footsteps carved into the alcove of the temple at 'Ain Dara are also indicative of the supernatural size of the goddess Ishtar, to whom the shrine is dedicated. 2 Chr 3:10–13 omits any reference to the height of the statues, a detail repeated emphatically in the Kings account (6:23, 26). This, according to Japhet (1993: 556), is consistent with the Chronicler's omissions elsewhere (e.g. 2 Chr 3:8).

1 Kgs 6:24–25 describes the size of their wings. Each wing being 5 cubits, the wing span was ten cubits (5.3m). This means that the width of the statues is the same measurement as their height. Apart from the reference to wings, no anatomical features of the cherubim are mentioned in 1 Kgs 6:23–28. Thus even more than Ex 25:20, the text is remarkably silent as to the physical form of the statues. By contrast, the author of 2 Chronicles 3 makes fleeting references to their "their feet", רַגְלֵיהֶם, and to "their faces", פְּנֵיהֶם (2 Chr 3:13). Whether this is significant will be discussed later.

Some scholars view 1 Kgs 6:27 as secondary. The main reason for this is the apparent contradiction with verse 23. Here, Solomon is said to have "made" (וַיַּעַשׂ) the cherubim statues "in the *debhir*" (בַּדְּבִיר), whereas, in verse 27, Solomon "places" (וַיִּתֵּן) the cherubim in the "innermost part of the house" (בְּתוֹךְ הַבַּיִת הַפְּנִימִי). The idea that Solomon needs to place the cherubim in the inner sanctuary after making them there seems illogical.[49] Furthermore, the phrase בְּתוֹךְ הַבַּיִת הַפְּנִימִי is only otherwise used in Ezek 41:17, which may suggest a late dating for the first half of the verse. Thus an editor may want to avoid the idea that the statues were made in the דְּבִיר, perhaps because this was thought to be irreverent. The problems in verse 27 are limited to the first half of the verse and, contrary to some commentators,[50] it seems unnecessary to excise the second half. 2 Chr 3:11–12 knows a similar tradition to that of verse 27b. The central idea seems to be that the wings are outstretched and touch either wall of the sanctuary, thus filling the entire room.

Both the Kings and Chronicles accounts agree that the cherubim are gilded with gold. However, their placement of this information is different. The author of the Kings account postpones this detail until the end of his description (1 Kgs 6:28), whereas the author of Chronicles includes it among the first specifications. Montgomery and Gehman (1960: 156) maintain that the gold overlay is an "extravagant" detail which, as it would have been better placed in verse 23, is dependent on

---

49   However, it may be that נתן, here, means "set up" or "erected". Thus, the text may
      suggest that the statues have been carved in the דְּבִיר and then moved and placed *in
      situ*. However, the sheer size of the statues makes this unlikely.

50   E.g. Gray (1970:171), but with Montgomery and Gehman (1960:155)

the golden cherubim of Ex 25:18. However, it has since been argued convincingly[51] that the reverse is more likely.

§ 1.2.2.2 Cherubim relief (1 Kgs 6:29–35)

Solomon carved פִּתּוּחֵי מִקְלְעוֹת ("carved engravings"?) of cherubim, palms and calyxes on כָּל־קִירוֹת הַבַּיִת, as well as on the doors to the דְּבִיר and to the nave, on both sides (1 Kgs 6:29, 32, 35). The meaning of כָּל־קִירוֹת הַבַּיִת has been disputed. Some commentators have taken the phrase to mean "all the walls of the temple." However, according to Hurowitz (2005: 74), it refers only to the walls of the דְּבִיר. He regards the reference to the cherubim on the walls of the outer sanctum in 2 Chr 3:7 as anachronistic (Hurowitz 2005: 67). If this is the case, cherubim only occur on the walls of the most sacred space within the temple. This would accord with Haran's principle of material gradation within the tabernacle, where cherubim only feature on the curtains in closest proximity to the divine presence (Haran 1978: 161–163). Indeed, Hurowitz implies that just such symbolism is intended. Where, on the walls of the הֵיכָל, gourds and calyxes are carved (1 Kgs 6:18), on the walls of the דְּבִיר, palm trees replace the gourds and cherubim are added to the decoration. (Hurowitz 2005: 74). Thus the ornamentation of the דְּבִיר is more elaborate than that of the הֵיכָל .

Again, the ideological motivation behind the connection of the cherubim with the palms and calyxes is not made explicit in the text. Apart from 1 Kings 6–7, 2 Chronicles 3–4 and Ezek 41:18–25, there are two other passages which link the cherubim to vegetation, Gen 3:24 and Ezekiel 28. These two passages are significant because they refer to cherubim as real heavenly beings, rather than cultic images. In Gen 3:24, the cherubim are placed to the east (or in front) of the Garden of Eden, to guard the way to the Tree of Life. In Ezekiel 28, a cherub occurs in another Garden of Eden passage (Ezek 28:13–14). It is interesting that, in the temple complex, cherubim appear with vegetation on doors and walls. Stordalen (2000: 137, 161, 284–286) has argued that such vegetation is representative of the boundary between sacred and

---

51   By e.g. Noth (1962:203); Hyatt (1971:265–266), Haran (1978: 189)

profane space. If this is the case, the cherubim may feature here as sentinels, protecting the divine abode from evil.

§ 1.2.2.3 The Wheeled Lavers (1 Kgs 7:27–39)

The account of the cult stands in 2 Chr 4:14 is brief. By contrast, the author of 1 Kings 7 includes elaborate details concerning their measurements, design and ornamentation. The ten cult stands in 1 Kgs 7:27–39 consist of a wheeled frame (מְכוֹנָה), which supported a basin (כִּיוֹר). In 1 Sam 2:12–16, a כִּיוֹר is used in connection with the boiling of sacrificial meat and, in 2 Chr 4:6, the function of the ten כִּיוֹרִים is to wash the burnt offering. In Lev 1:9, 13 it is stipulated that the innards and hindquarters of sacrificial animals are to be washed in water. Albright (1969: 144–145) has compared the stands to *egubbû* vessels, which were used to carry water in Mesopotamian purification rituals. Although these rituals usually involve the purification of human beings or divine statues, one text describes the use of the *egubbû* vessels to wash portions of sacrificial meat.[52]

However, the information in 2 Chr 4:6 has no counterpart in Kings. Van Seters (1997b: 296) argues that we cannot view this statement as evidence of the original function of the lavers. He contends that the author of 2 Chr 4:6 has interpreted the function of the vessels by means of the bronze laver mentioned in the description of the tabernacle (Ex 30:17–21). Here, the laver is situated between the altar and the tabernacle and used for washing by the priests. Thus the author has understood Solomon's lavers in a similar light. Whether or not their original function was to wash sacrifices, the author purposefully omits the reference to the location of the vessels. In Kings, they are situated in the nave. However, according to Van Seters (1997b: 297), this is in breach of the Mosaic Law which states that washing must precede entry into the tabernacle. It is for this reason that the author of 2 Chr 4:6 makes little reference to the position of the lavers.

Some scholars have argued that the size of the lavers (4 cubits square and 7 cubits high, equivalent to $2.1m^2$ by 3.7m) would make any

---

52   Thureau-Dangin 1975: 5.iii 21

cultic function, such as washing, impractical, if not impossible.[53] Montgomery and Gehman (1960: 178), on the other hand, although conced-
ing the cumbersome nature of the objects, contend that the creation of
such large objects with no practical purpose would be senseless. Bloch-
Smith (1997: 83) maintains that the ten carts, five positioned at each side
of the temple entrance, are similar to the five lamp stands at either side
of the entrance to the holy of holies. She suggests that the ten carts represent the ten tribes, in accordance with the pre-monarchic amphic-
tyony recorded in the Song of Deborah (Judges 5). In this way, each
tribe or group has a basin within which it would present or prepare its
offering. Whether or not they are envisaged to be actively functional or
emblematic of such a function is unclear. Bloch-Smith (1997: 85) suggests that the dimensions of the lavers are again reflective of the superhuman size of the deity.

The cherubim are carved on borders or panels between the frames.
They feature in verse 29 with lions and cattle. Although these borders
may be merely decorative, this grouping might be significant with regard to the qualities ascribed to each creature. Elsewhere in the Hebrew
Bible, lions are associated with strength (Judg 14:18) and ferociousness
(Ps 7:2). They were an established feature of ancient Near Eastern temple iconography. They represented deities (e.g. Ishtar) and could also
act as sentinels to protect a sanctuary from evil. They were common at
gateways and on outer walls. Prov 14:4 states that cattle are among the
most valuable animals both for their labour and for their meat, according to Prov 14:4. They are also said to be important sacrificial animals
(Deut 17:1; Lev 22:23; Lev 4:3, 14). If the function of the lavers is to carry
sacrificial offerings, or indeed to represent such offerings, then the cattle that decorate them underscore this. The cherubim are perhaps included here to set apart and protect the sacred space which contained
the sacrifice.

Hurowitz makes an alternative suggestion concerning the religious
significance of the stands. He argues that Ezekiel's vision of the future
city and temple offers inner-biblical evidence for the symbolism of the
cult stands. Ezekiel does not mention explicitly any of the bronze vessels of the outer court. Nevertheless, in place of the bronze sea, stands
and basins, he envisages water, flowing from south of the altar (Ezek

---

53   Kittel, for example, argues that the stands are merely symbolic, representative of the
     divine provision of water (See Montgomery and Gehman, 1960: 178).

47:1–2). Hurowitz (2005: 81) compares the waters flowing from Ezekiel's temple to those streaming from the Garden of Eden. He contends that, "since the envisioned water replaces the Sea and basins that Solomon made, it becomes clear that these bronze vessels symbolize the river that flowed from the Garden of Eden" (Gen 2:10).[54] Moreover, this symbolism is augmented by the ornamentation on the stands. Hurowitz compares the combination of lions (wild animals), cattle (domestic animals) and cherubim (*Mischwesen*) to passages such as Isa 11:6–9, which reads:

> The wolf shall live with the lamb, the leopard shall lie down with the kid, the calf and the lion and the fatling together, and a little child shall lead them. The cow and the bear shall graze, their young shall lie down together; and the lion shall eat straw like the ox… They will not hurt or destroy on all my holy mountain; for the earth will be full of the knowledge of the LORD as the waters cover the sea. (NRSV)

The cult stands, made for bearing water, represent the life-giving water which flows from the deity. Concomitantly, the decoration on the stands represents the harmony of creation that is to be found on the holy mountain, upon which is situated the garden and the dwelling-place of the deity.[55]

In 1 Kgs 6:36, cherubim feature again as carvings on the cult stands' panels. This time, however, the cattle are omitted and the cherubim occur with lions and palm trees. According to Montgomery and Gehman, this seemingly unnecessary repetition of the decoration of the stand shows that verse 36 should be excised as secondary. However, the panels mentioned in verse 29 appear between the frames of the stand, whereas the panels in verse 36 are at the top of the stand (verse 35). Thus, it is better to view verses 29 and 36 as referring to two separate types of panelling. Hence the cherubim appear with palms and lions at the top of the base, and with lions and cattle between the frames. Their depiction with palms, as well as lions and cattle, is consistent with Hurowitz's suggestion that the decoration is symbolic of the Garden of Eden, or similar traditions concerning sacred space.

---

54 This could be seen to run counter to the idea that the bronze sea represents the cosmic deep (see Van Seters 1997, 297). Perhaps the emphasis is on creation symbolism in general.

55 The garden can be imagined as the periphery/threshold of the divine dwelling-place (see Stordalen 2000: 161).

§ 1.2.2.4 The Source of the 1 Kings Account

It is generally accepted that the 2 Chronicles account of the construction of the Solomonic temple is an abridged version of the 1 Kings description (see Japhet 1993: 549).[56] Yet the source and history of the 1 Kings account are uncertain. It is notable that the author seems to take an undue interest in the measurements and materials of the temple and its vessels, at the expense of specifying their cultic function and religious significance. This is in contrast to temple building accounts elsewhere in the ancient Near East, where little detail is given about the building and vessels but the religious and political significance of their construction is emphasised (Hurowitz 1992: 249).

The apparently unique style of the 1 Kings account amid the literature of the ancient Near East caused Van Seters (1983: 109–110) to presume a late date for the text. He compares the biblical description to stylistically similar accounts in the works of Herodotus and Josephus, which refer to a building that was destroyed long before the time of the author. The similarities between these texts lead Van Seters to deduce that the biblical account did not date to the time of the actual construction of the temple, but rather to a time much later, when it was necessary that the building needed to be remembered, a time when the building had been destroyed. In his estimation, this was during the exilic period when Deuteronomistic scribes wished to safeguard the memory of the temple.

This late dating for the temple account is challenged by Hurowitz (1992: 249), who, by a comparison with certain Neo-Assyrian inscriptions, argues that the literary style of the biblical description is not evidence of an exilic date. He highlights texts such as 'Palace without a Rival' from the reign of Sennacherib, which are written in a similar "visual" style to that of the biblical account. If such a style can be found in early texts, then there is no need to presume a late date for the biblical temple description.

Noth (1968: 104–106) suggested that the detailed descriptions of the temple architecture and appurtenances were an indication that the account derives from the actual building of the temple. He claimed that the specifications of measurement and design were evidence that the

---

56 The scholarly consensus that the books of Chronicles are entirely derived from the books of Samuel-Kings is challenged by Auld (1994).

written description in 1 Kings is based on the oral instructions for the temple builders and artisans. Eissfeldt (1966: 289), on the other hand, argued that it is rooted in written documents from the temple archives.

Hurowitz (1992: 259 and 2005: 65) refines Eissfeldt's theory, arguing that the term "archival" is not a sufficient title for a literary genre. Instead, he argues that we should use the term "administrative" on the basis of parallels in other ancient Near Eastern literature, which document the structural or design specifications for various buildings or cultic furnishings. The view that the temple account derives from administrative documents is preferable to Van Seters' argument that the account is entirely an exilic composition. Although the account may have undergone a long editorial process, there is some information that may reflect the historical reality of the temple. For example, the traditions of Phoenician input into the building of the temple are less prominent in the Chronicles account and seem to go against the grain of the ideology of the book of Kings as a whole. Hence the inclusion of these traditions in the 1 Kings account may be indicative of their historicity.[57]

If we accept Hurowitz's view that the temple account derives from administrative records, then the absence of any theological or ideological interpretation of the cherubim in 1 Kings is not remarkable. The records from which the compiler of the 1 Kings account was working may not have included any detailed information about the religious significance of the golden statues or the cherubim decoration. Moreover, the symbolism of the cherubim may have been so widely known that it was deemed unnecessary to include such information for the intended reader/audience.

§ 1.2.2.5 The Account of the Temple Cherubim in Chronicles

There are several problems that arise when we compare the depiction of the temple cherubim in Chronicles to that of 1 Kings. There are three main differences which need to be noted and carefully examined. First, the cherubim are mentioned in 1 Chr 28:18 in a passage which describes Yahweh's plan for the temple (1 Chr 28:11–21). This is one of the few instances when the writer of Chronicles alludes to an issue, present in the Samuel/Kings narrative, without making any use of the informa-

---

57   For further discussion of such issues see Millard 1997.

tion existing there (Japhet 1993: 483). Moreover, the writer uses unique vocabulary in relation to the temple cherubim. He includes the word הַמֶּרְכָּבָה, a term never used in connection with the cherubim elsewhere in the Hebrew Bible. Second, in 2 Chr 3:13, the writer inserts material concerning the cherubim that is absent in the 1 Kings account. He states that the cherubim "stood on their feet" with "their faces towards the house". Whether this addition is significant needs to be investigated. Third, in the following verse (2 Chr 3:14), it is stated that cherubim were embroidered onto the פָּרֹכֶת veil. This veil is not mentioned in the 1 Kings account, where a pair of doors screen off the דְּבִיר. The reference to the פָּרֹכֶת veil evokes the description of the tabernacle in Exodus (Ex 26:33), where the cherubim adorn the veil that separates the holy place from the holy of holies. Whether this tells us anything about the inspiration for the Chronicles account needs to be investigated further.

§ 1.2.2.5.1 1 Chronicles 28:18

1 Chr 28:18 reads:

וּלְמִזְבַּח הַקְּטֹרֶת זָהָב מְזֻקָּק בַּמִּשְׁקָל וּלְתַבְנִית
הַמֶּרְכָּבָה הַכְּרֻבִים זָהָב לְפֹרְשִׂים וְסֹכְכִים עַל־אֲרוֹן
בְּרִית־יהוה:

The verse occurs in the wider literary unit of 1 Chr 28:11–21, which describes Yahweh's plan for the temple. In contrast to the 1 Kings 6–7 account, where Solomon and even Hiram (a foreigner) are the chief architects of the temple, in 1 Chronicles 28, it is God. Thus, the writer's theological agenda in this unit seems to be to emphasise the divine endorsement of the temple (see Japhet 1993: 493).

In verse 18, הַמֶּרְכָּבָה הַכְּרֻבִים and the altar of incense are highlighted as being of particular importance. This is suggested, first, by the fact that these objects occur at the end of the catalogue of vessels (vv14–18) and, second, by the fact that they are single objects, as opposed to the collections of objects that have preceded them (see Japhet 1993: 496). Third, the phrase זָהָב מְזֻקָּק, "refined gold," used in connection with the altar, does not recur in Chronicles and seems to underscore the value of the object. Finally, הַמֶּרְכָּבָה הַכְּרֻבִים is described in detail and its significance is enhanced by the use of the term תַּבְנִית, "pattern", which emphasises the divine authority behind its construction.

The use of the term הַמֶּרְכָּבָה in relation to the cherubim is unique to this passage in the Hebrew Bible. In the Pentateuch, מֶרְכָּבָה refers to a type of chariot used by foreign nations (e.g. Gen 41:43; Ex 14:25). In the books of Samuel and Kings, it refers to a type of chariot owned by Israelite and Judahite kings (e.g. 1 Kgs 22:35; 1 Sam 8:11). The only other occurrence of the term with a cultic connection is in 2 Kgs 23:11, where Josiah destroys the chariots of the sun.[58] It is clear from this passage that the appearance of a chariot amid the cultic furniture of the temple was not something surprising.

Nevertheless, a cherubim chariot is not mentioned in the 1 Kings account. The idea that a single cherub could transport the deity is something alluded to in the MT of Ps 18:11 = 2 Sam 22:11.[59] The final form of Ezekiel 10 also links cherubim to the transportation of the deity. Yet what is the מֶרְכָּבָה in 1 Chr 28:18? Is it separate from the cherubim or do the cherubim actually form it? The use of the technical term elsewhere in the Bible seems to denote a particular type of chariot, used for war. This would suggest that the chariot cannot be the cherubim themselves. The syntax of the whole phrase, הַמֶּרְכָּבָה הַכְּרֻבִים זָהָב, is difficult.[60] The two nouns appear to be in apposition with one another. This would suggest that one noun is a secondary explanation of the other. The clause thus seems to be structured in either of the two following ways: "... and for the pattern/model of the chariot (the cherubim), gold – for those spreading and covering over ..." or "... and for the pattern/model of (the chariot) the cherubim, gold – for those spreading and shielding above ..." The subsequent relative clause, "who spread out and shield above the ark of the covenant of Yahweh," cannot refer to the chariot but only to the cherubim. [61] Thus we are better to view the structure of the clause in accordance with the second arrangement.

---

58 Johnstone (1997: 281) asks whether 1 Chr 28:18 is a polemical allusion to this incident in 2 Kings, which is not recorded by the Chronicles writer in the parallel account (2 Chr 34:31).

59 The versions reflect a plural form. See §1.2.3.

60 The LXX has no reflex for זָהָב, which may indicate that זָהָב has crept into the second half of the verse under the influence of its use in the first. Alternatively, the LXX may have attempted to tidy up the awkward syntax of the MT.

61 Not only the use of the plural rather than the singular but also the similarities between this verse and 1 Kgs 8:7 and Ex 25:20 confirm this.

A further problem still is how the author of 1 Chronicles 28 envisages the cherubim to be related to the ark. Is it the two giant cherubim, built independently of the ark (1 Kgs 6:23–29; 2 Chr 3:10–13), that are envisaged here, or is it the small pair of cherubim that are attached to the כַּפֹּרֶת on the ark (Ex 25:18–22; 37:7–9)? There is evidence that, in his description of Yahweh's plan for the temple, the author of 1 Chronicles 28 viewed the ark through the lens of the Exodus tabernacle tradition. For example, in 1 Chr 28:11, the holy of holies is called the בֵּית הַכַּפֹּרֶת, "house of the כַּפֹּרֶת" (one of only two incidences of the term כַּפֹּרֶת outside Exodus and Leviticus).[62] Japhet (1993: 497) argues that the author, in his understanding of the cherubim in this verse, has been influenced by the description of the tabernacle in Exodus and thus views the cherubim as physically connected to the ark. However, the second half of verse 18 recalls not the cherubim attached to the כַּפֹּרֶת but the cherubim as described in 1 Kgs 8:6–7 and 2 Chr 5:7–8. In these passages, the ark is initially separate from the cherubim statues but is subsequently placed under them and is overshadowed by their wings. This appears to be evidence against Japhet's interpretation. Indeed, the probability that, for the author of 1 Chronicles, the ark's cherubim were made in the wilderness would preclude the idea that the cherubim chariot is identical with the Mosaic cherubim.[63]

Whether the author is referring to the two large free-standing statues or the small statues of the כַּפֹּרֶת, we still need to decide why he uses the unique term מֶרְכָּבָה to describe them. As stated previously, the locomotive power of the cherubim is alluded to in a few biblical passages and it may be that the author merely uses this term arbitrarily, to refer to one of the functions of the cherubim. Yet the importance of the term הַמֶּרְכָּבָה in connection with the cherubim in post-biblical literature compels us to ask whether the writer's inclusion of it here is perhaps of deeper significance.

The post-biblical theology of *merkābāh* mysticism was predominantly based on Ezekiel's visions (Ezekiel 1; 10). These visions picture the deity as transported through the sky by four hybrid beings (called cherubim in Ezek 10:15, 20). However, the term מֶרְכָּבָה never occurs in either vision. Instead, it was later interpreters of the visions that identi-

---

62 The only other instance is Num 7:89, which is parallel to Ex 25:22.
63 This would be the case if the author of 1 Chronicles knew the Exodus tradition, which is more than likely.

fied the cherubim and the wheels as a "chariot". Thus, it may be that we can view the unique occurrence of the term מֶרְכָּבָה in connection with the cherubim in 1 Chr 28:18 as a precursor to this type of interpretation. We may acknowledge that the locomotive function of the cherubim is a very ancient one but still doubt the existence of a cherubim chariot in pre-exilic thought. Indeed, it is only in Ezekiel's visions that cherubim are associated with wheels, an essential component of a chariot. Hence, what we may have in 1 Chr 28:18 is an innovation, based on the depiction of cherubim in Ezekiel's visions.[64] If the cherubim transport the deity using wheels, as is suggested by Ezekiel's visions, then they naturally form a chariot. Hence, although speculative, we may have, in 1 Chr 28:18, a first step towards a *merkābāh* theology.[65]

§ 1.2.2.5.2 2 Chronicles 3:13

Chronicles' second major divergence from the Kings account, with respect to the presentation of the cherubim, occurs in 2 Chr 3:13, which reads:

כַּנְפֵי הַכְּרוּבִים הָאֵלֶּה פֹּרְשִׂים אַמּוֹת עֶשְׂרִים וְהֵם
עֹמְדִים עַל־רַגְלֵיהֶם וּפְנֵיהֶם לַבָּיִת

First, it is stated that the wings of the cherubim spread out over twenty cubits. This, although differently worded to the 1 Kings account, is not inconsistent with it. 1 Kgs 6:24–25 asserts that each wing of each cherub was five cubits and thus the wingspan of both together would be twenty cubits. It is the second half of 2 Chr 3:13 which offers completely new material. The cherubim are said to stand on their feet with their faces towards the house.

According to Japhet, the latter half of the verse is included by the author in order to differentiate between the small pair of cherubim affixed to the כַּפֹּרֶת on the ark and the larger, free-standing statues. As stated previously, the author knew the Exodus tradition and, in his presentation of the temple building and its vessels, seems to want to

---

64   Chronicles uses several innovative terms in relation to the cultic furniture, for example, the phrase "footstool of our God" (1 Chr 28:2) with reference to the ark.

65   The fact that מֶרְכָּבָה and כְּרֻבִים share the same root letters probably helped to give rise to the inclusion of the term מֶרְכָּבָה in the Chronicles account.

bring the Solomonic temple into line with the tabernacle.[66] Thus, for Japhet, the writer is imagining two pairs of cherubim: one joined to the כַּפֹּרֶת, the other free-standing. Yet, as mentioned earlier, Japhet argues that, in 1 Chr 28:18, the cherubim chariot refers to the cherubim on the ark. This is doubtful as the Chronicler would then be imagining two sets of cherubim that both perform the same function: they spread out and shield above the ark with their wings (1 Chr 28:18; 2 Chr 5:8). Instead, it seems more likely that the author is referring, both times, to the two larger statue. Although it does seem that the writer is attempting to harmonize the Solomonic temple with the Exodus tabernacle in his description of the temple, he does not specify how the new cherubim statues would relate to the cherubim on the ark. In 2 Chr 5:8, when the ark is positioned under the giant cherubim statues in the holy of holies, the author merely duplicates the material in 1 Kgs 8:6.

The writer's inclusion of anatomical features that are absent in the 1 Kings account may be of further significance. The omission of such detail in 1 Kings can be attributed to the fact that the author is working from administrative records which do not include specifications of the exact form of the cherubim. However, it seems odd that the author of Chronicles, whose account is based on 1 Kings, should know more. It may be that the author of Chronicles knew exactly what the cherubim were and how the two large statues were initially positioned. Nevertheless, it may also be possible that the author has gleaned this extra information about the anatomy of the cherubim not only from the Exodus tradition (which includes references to the "faces" of the cherubim) but also from Ezekiel's visions (which mention both "faces" and "feet").[67] If we are right in thinking that the reference to the cherubim chariot in 1 Chr 28:18 is partly inspired by Ezekiel's visions, these extra

---

66   That the temple building and vessels constitute a "continuity theme" for the author(s) of Chronicles is something stressed by Ackroyd (1972:166–181). Van Seters has argued that the writer does not only wish to bring the Solomonic temple and the Exodus tabernacle into alignment, but also sees the temple of his own time as part of the continuity motif (1997:285).

67   Each creature has four faces (Ezek 1:6; 10:14). Feet are mentioned in 1:7 but are not mentioned in the second vision account of chapter 10. According to Halperin (1988), the feet are not mentioned in the later, highly edited vision of chapter 10 because they are said to be like calves' feet (Ezek 1:7), which is reminiscent of the apostasy of the golden calf episode. Consequently, the later editor of chapter 10 has purposefully omitted the reference to the bovine features of the beast/cherub.

details concerning the anatomy of the cherubim may be derived from the same source.

§ 1.2.2.5.3 The פָּרֹכֶת veil

Again, Chronicles diverges from the 1 Kings account of the temple when it refers to the פָּרֹכֶת veil at the entrance to the holy of holies (2 Chr 3:14). In 1 Kgs 6:31–32, Solomon makes two oil-wood doors for the entrance to the inner sanctuary. The פָּרֹכֶת veil is made as a screen between the inner sanctuary and the main chamber of the Exodus tabernacle in Ex 26:31–33. It may be that the author of 2 Chr 3:14 is again trying to bring Solomon's temple into alignment with the desert tabernacle by incorporating the veil instead of the doors. Van Seters (1997b: 293) argues that, "The veil was included in Chr's treatment of Solomon's temple, because it established an important continuity between the tabernacle of Moses and Solomon's temple." He maintains that the veil was symbolic of the desert tabernacle in its entirety and was connected with the most important ritual on the Day of Atonement (Leviticus 16). In this way, the religious significance of the veil was too profound for the author not to include it in the description of the Solomonic temple. Yet, it is also possible that the author had the temple of his own day in mind when including the veil. Josephus[68] notes that the second temple had a veil and it may be that it is this veil that the writer is describing anachronistically (see Japhet 1993: 557). As Van Seters (1997b: 284; 293) asserts, the veil is one element in the writer's description of the temple that forms a "continuity theme," emphasising the divine authority behind the construction of the tabernacle and the first and second temples. In this way, the author of 2 Chr 3:14 not only draws on information from the priestly tradition but also from the temple of his own day in his description of the Solomonic temple. This has the inevitable corollary of harmonising all three sanctuaries in order to accentuate the divine plan underlying each of them.

---

68   *Jewish War* V, 5, 5

§ 1.2.2.6 Summary

The 1 Kings account of the Solomonic temple is probably based on administrative records of the construction of the temple and its vessels. This is the most plausible reason for the lack of information regarding the cultic and religious significance of the cherubim. Nevertheless, we can make several inferences regarding the cherubim based on their description in 1 Kings. First, they are connected with the most holy space within the sanctuary. Second, they feature at thresholds and on walls, which is suggestive of an apotropaic function. 1 Kgs 8:6–7 and 2 Chr 5:7–8 also point in this direction as does the appearance of the cherubim on the wheeled lavers. Their association with vegetation may also be indicative of their role as guardians because gardens are often associated with border areas between the divine and human realms in ancient Near Eastern myth (see Stordalen 2000: 161). This connection may also suggest that the cherubim are sentinels of the garden of God, of which the outer temple is the earthly form. This interpretation can be strengthened by reading the 1 Kings account with texts such as Genesis 2–3 and Ezek 28:11–19. Third, the locomotive power of the cherubim, coupled with later interpretations of Ezekiel's visions, may have caused the author of Chronicles to view the cherubim statues as a chariot, which transported the throne of Yahweh.

The Chronicles version of the building of the temple is largely extracted from the material in 1 Kings. Nevertheless, the desire of the author to create a "continuity theme" with reference to the temple means that he has also used information from the tabernacle tradition as well as his knowledge of the second temple. In his allusion to the cherubim chariot and to the "feet" and "faces" of the cherubim, the author of 2 Chronicles 3 may also have had Ezekiel's visions in mind when describing the statues.

1.2.3 Ezekiel 41:18–25

In Ezekiel's vision of the new temple (Ezek 40:1–42:20), the author includes several references to cherubim as decoration on walls and doors (Ezek 41:18–25). While there are some similarities between the description of the new temple and the description of the Solomonic temple in Kings and Chronicles, there are major differences. The text says nothing of the interior of the holy of holies, only its measurements are described (Ezek 41:4). Hence there is no mention of the pair of free-standing cherubim statues that feature in the דְּבִיר in 1 Kgs 6:23–29 (2 Chr 3:10–13). Similarly, there is no description of the bronze vessels in Ezekiel and hence the cherubim on the lavers are absent.

As in the Kings account, the author of Ezek 41:18–25 describes cherubim, together with palm trees, carved onto the walls and doors of the temple. But the author of the Ezekiel text gives a much fuller account of the form and position of the cherubim. A palm tree appears between each pair of cherubim. The cherubim have two faces, one human, and the other leonine (v 18). Each face is turned towards the palm tree closest to it, so that the two faces look in opposite directions (v 19). The two faces and their configuration in relation to the palm trees is not mentioned in the Kings description.

If we look at the portrayal of the cherubim in the Hebrew Bible as a whole, we notice that the only descriptions of cherubim with more than one face occur in the book of Ezekiel. Consequently, the attribution of two faces to the cherubim in Ezek 41:18–22 may be dependent on the physical descriptions of the cherubim in Ezekiel 1–11 rather than the description of cherubim decoration in the 1 Kings account. Block (1998: 558) suggests that the reason that the cherubim are described with two faces in Ezek 41:18 is because the relief was two dimensional. It is well known that ancient Near Eastern artisans found it difficult to depict three-dimensional features on relief work (as opposed to free-standing statues). Often they would portray the faces of humans, gods and animals in profile in order to achieve a comprehensible likeness. This is what Block envisages here. The cherubim could not be depicted with four faces, as they occur in Ezekiel's visions, because the author knows that this would be too difficult to represent in a two-dimensional format. Thus, although the author of Ezek 41:18–22 conceived of the cherubim as having four faces, for artistic purposes, in the relief, they only have two.[69]

Multi-faced winged creatures do exist in the iconography of the ancient Near East (particularly in that from Mesopotamia). However, no creature is represented in the configuration described in Ezek 41:18–25.

§ 1.3 כְּרֻבִים as Heavenly Beings

In addition to the biblical texts that refer to cherubim as cultic images in the temple and tabernacle, there are a few passages which refer to them as real heavenly beings (Gen 3:24; 2 Sam 22:11 = Ps 18:11; Ezekiel 9–11; 28:11–19). Various types of heavenly beings are mentioned in the Hebrew Bible and the cherubim are just one of these types (see Olyan 1993: 15–18). Most often these beings escort Yahweh in his theophanies (e.g. Deut 33:2) or attend his divine council (e.g. 1 Kgs 22:19–22). They function as divine warriors (e.g. Judg 5:20), servants (e.g. Ps 104:4) or agents of praise (e.g. Isaiah 6; Ps 148:2). What status the cherubim had in relation to the other types of heavenly beings is never explicitly stated. 2 Sam 22:11//Ps 18:11 suggests that a cherub could accompany Yahweh in his theophanies and the divine epithet יהוה צְבָאוֹת יֹשֵׁב הַכְּרֻבִים may imply that the cherubim were considered to be members of Yahweh's heavenly army (although see § 1.1.2). If this is the case, they may have had a similar ideological function to some of the other classes of heavenly beings. In order to investigate this further, we shall have to look at each text in detail.

§ 1.3.1 Genesis 3:24

It is interesting that the first of the texts that speak of cherubim as heavenly beings occurs in the primeval history (Genesis 1–11), which, in a number of places, alludes to inhabitants of the divine world other than Yahweh (Gen 1:26; 3:22; 6:1–4; 11:7). Genesis 3:24 is the final verse of the Eden narrative (Gen 2:4b–3:24) and within it is the first canonical reference to cherubim as heavenly beings. The MT reads:

וַיְגָרֶשׁ אֶת־הָאָדָם וַיַּשְׁכֵּן מִקֶּדֶם לְגַן־עֵדֶן אֶת־הַכְּרֻבִים

וְאֵת לַהַט הַחֶרֶב הַמִּתְהַפֶּכֶת לִשְׁמֹר אֶת־דֶּרֶךְ עֵץ

הַחַיִּים:

The LXX provides a variant reading in the second clause. It presents the man, and not the cherubim and 'flame', as direct object of the verb שׁכן, offering: καὶ κατῴκισεν αὐτὸν ἀπέναντι τοῦ παραδείσου τῆς τρυφῆς καὶ ἔταξεν τὰ χερουβιμ. The Greek implies that it is Adam that is placed ἀπέναντι ('over against') the garden, and not the guardian figures. The cherubim and 'flame' are only introduced in the final clause and no reference is made to their exact location. Wevers notes that the LXX translator divided the first half of MT Gen 3:24 into two clauses. This "leaves the two אֵת phrases up in the air, and so the translator gratuitously introduced καὶ ἔταξεν" (Wevers 1993: 49). Therefore, it is likely that the MT preserves the more ancient tradition.

In the MT, the cherubim and the 'flame' are stationed "to the east" or "opposite" the Garden of Eden (3:24), in order to guard the way to the Tree of Life so that the humans cannot reach it (3:22). Stordalen has observed, in his detailed analysis of the meanings and uses of the Hebrew מִקֶּדֶם, that there are fifty-five occurrences of the construction מִן plus geographic locator followed by לְ and a topographic name (2000: 264). In each occurrence, the מִן serves a partitive function. Thus, he argues, the syntax of the phrase מִקֶּדֶם לְגַן־עֵדֶן belongs to "firm linguistic convention" and hence the meaning is unquestionably, "to the east of the Garden of Eden." Consequently, in this verse, מִקֶּדֶם cannot have a relative perspective, "in front of", or temporal significance, "in the olden days" (as it does in Gen 2:8; see Stordalen, 2000: 262–270). If the Garden of Eden is to be equated with a sanctuary, as several scholars have noted,[70] then the east of the garden would be where the entrance was thought to be located. Thus the cherubim and the 'flame' guard the entrance to the garden.[71]

Wenham notes that the use of the verb שׁכן in Gen 3:24 may also be significant with regard to the identification of the Garden of Eden as the archetypal sanctuary.[72] The *piel*, and sometimes the *hiphil* (as occurs here), are used in connection with Yahweh's residence in the tabernacle, in the midst of his people (e.g. Deut 12:11; Jer 7:3; Josh 18:1). Wenham observes that "the word's cultic overtones are further reinforced by the presence of the cherubim... the traditional guardians of sanctuaries in the Near East" (1987:86). Although this is an assumption, the

---

70 E.g. Wenham (1987: 86) and Stordalen (2000: 410–417)
71 Kapelrud (1950: 153) has argued that the concept of the Hebrew cherubim derived from the Sumerian door-god. He compares the god's task of admitting the just and barring the evil to the duty of the cherubim in Gen 3:24. However, the Hebrew text says nothing of such a role for the cherubim. They are to prevent man from eating the fruit of the Tree of Life, but nothing is said about them admitting the righteous.
72 The Garden of Eden is nowhere said to be Yahweh's dwelling place but in Ezek 28:13 Eden is described as גַּן־אֱלֹהִים. The vegetal decoration, which Bloch-Smith (2002: 87) connects with Eden traditions, may symbolize the threshold of divine space rather than the divine abode itself. It may follow, therefore, that the Garden of Eden should be located at the periphery of the divine locale.

cherubim do seem to be positioned by God at the entrance of the garden in order to protect the sacred space from being encroached upon
by man. This may well parallel the function of the cherubim in the
Exodus tabernacle and the Solomonic temple, where cherubim feature
as part of the most holy furnishings of the sanctuaries. Appearing with
sacred trees[73] (1 Kgs 6:29–35; 7:36; Ezek 41:18–25) on walls and doors,
the cherubim seem to mark and guard the boundary between the divine and human realms.

The significance of the pairing of the 'flame' with the cherubim requires a more detailed examination. The exact meaning of הַמִּתְהַפֶּכֶת
לַהַט הַחֶרֶב is difficult to ascertain. Although hitherto glossed as 'flame,'
the meaning of the three words and their syntactical relationship to
each other are obscure. The meaning of the first word, לַהַט, is, at first
glance, relatively uncomplicated. Although this noun does not appear
elsewhere in the Hebrew Bible, the verb לָהַט occurs quite frequently
and has the meaning 'burn'. It can refer to literal burning (e.g.
Ps 106:18) and, in poetic texts, it can be used figuratively, in connection
with God's judgment (e.g. Isa 42:25). Thus לַהַט probably has the meaning 'flame' or 'flaming'. Yet there could be an additional nuance attached to the word which can only be grasped by looking to the use of
the synonymous term לַהַב. This noun can mean 'flame' but it can also
refer to a 'blade' or 'tip' of a weapon, as it does in Judg 3:22, Job 39:23
and Nah 3:3. The semantic overlap is probably due to the similarity in
shape between a flame and a blade. The fact that such an overlap exists
in the synonym לַהַב, together with the fact that לַהַט occurs here in construct relationship with the noun חֶרֶב, obliges us to consider translating
לַהַט as 'blade.'

The second word, הַחֶרֶב ("the sword"), appears to be in construct relationship with לַהַט, and thus the two words together mean either "the
flame of the sword" or "the blade of the sword." At first blush, the second translation seems better, as "the flame of the sword" makes little
sense. Yet the natural elements (wind, fire, water etc) are often used as
weapons of Yahweh (e.g. in Ps 104:4; 148:8) and hence the idea of a
fiery sword may not be surprising in this context, where Yahweh-God
positions it with the cherubim to guard the way to the Tree of Life.[74]

---

73   The תְּמֹרָה ("palm tree" – 1 Kgs 6:29–35, 7:36; Ezek 41:18–25) had sacred significance
      throughout the ancient Near East (see Lambert 2002: 321–326).
74   This is how the LXX translator, who offers τὴν φλογίνην ῥομφαίαν τὴν στρεφομένην,
      understood the phrase.

More evidence to support the 'flame' translation comes from two texts, one Ugaritic and the other Akkadian, which seem to present 'fire' and 'flames' as divine beings with weapons. First, in KTU 1.2 i 32–33, two messengers of Yamm arrive at the council of El:

> (32)ʾišt ʾištm yʾitmr
> ḥrb lṭšt (33) [bym/lš]nhm
> A flame, two flames they appear,
> Sharpened sword(s) their tongue/in their right hand[75]

However we restore the beginning of line 33, it is clear that the messengers of Yamm appear as flames and are either likened to swords in some way[76] or have swords as weapons. The idea of a deity's messengers as flames, together with their connection with a sword, strengthens the argument for the translation "flame of the sword" in Gen 3:24. A second Ugaritic text is also relevant. KTU 1.3 iii 45–46 mentions "fire" and "flame" among Anat's list of monsters which she had slain:

> m ḫšt klbt ilm išt
> klt bt il ḏbb
> I smote the bitch of El, fire
> I destroyed the daughter of El, "Flame."[77]

Again, it seems that supernatural beings (in this case the daughters of El) could be conceived of as flames. The fact that Anat has killed them reinforces the idea that "fire" is a deadly enemy.

An Akkadian text is also significant with respect to the translation of לַהַט הַחֶרֶב in Gen 3:24. It describes a divine being, "Fire", in a similar way to KTU 1.2 i 32–33 above:

> ᵈIšum ṭābiḫu naʾdu
> ša ana našê kakkīšu ezzūti
> qātāšu asmā
> u ana šubruq ulmēšu šērūti

---

75   There is a gap at the beginning of line 33. lšnhm, "their tongue," is restored by Cross (1973:190, n. 187) and bymnhm, "in their right hand," by Gaster (1950:139). According to Hendel (1985:674, n. 19), there is room for two or three signs, whereas Miller (1965:257, n. 8) argues that there is only room for two.

76   Given the context, "their tongue" (if that is the correct restoration) is perhaps not literal but refers to the shape of the flames (cf. Isa 5:24). Thus their form is like a sharpened sword. This image would connote the menacing nature of Yamm's messengers.

77   The meaning of ḏbb is unclear but the parallelism suggests the translation "flame." Whether both lines refer to the same monster or to a pair of monsters is also uncertain.

Fire, the famous slayer,
Whose hands are suited
To wield his terrible weapons
And to make his fierce swords flash.[78]

Again, fire is depicted as a divine being[79], whose weapons are swords. "Swords" may not refer to literal weapons here but to the sword-shaped flames of fire. This makes an interesting parallel to Gen 3:24 and, although we should not let it guide our interpretation of the biblical verse completely, it does render the translation "the flame of the sword," for לַהַט הַחֶרֶב, more probable.

The third word in the phrase לַהַט הַחֶרֶב הַמִּתְהַפֶּכֶת is a feminine singular *hithpael* participle of the verb הָפַךְ, meaning "to turn, overturn." As a feminine, and with the definite article, it agrees with the previous word הַחֶרֶב and not לַהַט. Thus the participle modifies the sword and not the flame. The *hithpael* form may have a reflexive or an iterative function here. Most scholars tend to point to Judg 7:13, where the same verb is used to refer to the cake which "rolled" into the camp of Midian. A similar iterative meaning is perhaps conveyed by the same verb in Job 37:12. Consequently, most scholars translate "revolving" or "whirling".[80] Although this is the most likely sense of הַמִּתְהַפֶּכֶת, it is worth noting that the verb הָפַךְ is often used in connection with Yahweh's wrath (e.g. Gen 19:21, 25, 29; Deut 29:22; 2 Kgs 21:13; Is 13:19; Jer 20:16, 49:18, 50:40; Jonah 3:4). In these cases, it is generally used in relation to the destruction of cities and translated "overthrow" (so RSV). In Hag 2:22, it is used in parallel with שׁמד and, in Prov 12:7, it is used to describe the annihilation of "the wicked". It may be considered, therefore, that הַמִּתְהַפֶּכֶת possesses something of these more menacing connotations and may have the sense of "thrashing".

Thus the entire phrase can be translated quite confidently as "The flame of the revolving/thrashing sword." Yet, despite the conviction with which we can translate the words, what exactly is meant by the phrase remains elusive. There are two traditional interpretations of the image. The first understands it as depicting a lightning bolt, which is a common weapon in the hands of deities in the iconography of the ancient Near East.[81] However, such a naturalistic explanation reads too much into the text. Surely if a lightning bolt was meant, there would be

---

78 Text cited in Hendel (1985: 674)
79 Occurring, as it does, with the Akkadian *dingir* sign.
80 So Skinner (1910: 89) and Wenham (1987: 86)
81 E.g. Von Rad (1968: 97–98), Cassuto (1961:176) and Skinner (1910:89).

no reason not to state it more explicitly. The second interpretation takes
the phrase as referring to a magical weapon belonging to Yahweh.[82]
This explanation tends to view the לַהַט הַחֶרֶב as a weapon that is actually wielded by the cherubim.[83] Again, if this were the case, why does the
text not say this more openly? Indeed, as Hendel argues (1985:672), the
strength of the conjunction in the phrase אֶת־הַכְּרֻבִים וְאֵת לַהַט הַחֶרֶב implies that the fiery sword is separate from the cherubim. Yet, if it is
separate from the cherubim, how does it relate to them and why is it
coupled with them?

Both the above interpretations understand the לַהַט הַחֶרֶב to be a
weapon. There are several references in ancient Near Eastern myth to
weapons as animate beings. The obvious example here is in the Ugaritic text KTU 1.2 iv 10–25. In this passage, the god Kothar fashions two
maces, both of which are given names and spoken to by Kothar, and
both of which proceed to act autonomously. In a similar way, as noted
previously, the natural elements (wind and fire) are often used by
Yahweh as weapons and yet seem to have a certain degree of autonomy as divine agents (e.g. Ps 104:4, 1 Kgs 22:21 and perhaps also Gen
1:2). Could it be that it is an animate, supernatural weapon that is intended by לַהַט הַחֶרֶב in Gen 3:24? Certainly this would make a better
parallel to the cherubim, themselves animate supernatural beings.

Hendel (1985) has taken this idea one step further. He argues that the
לַהַט הַחֶרֶב is not merely an animate, supernatural weapon but is actually a
minor deity on a par with the cherubim. He compares the phrase to epithets of the West Semitic god, Reshep, whose name means 'flame'. In
three Phoenician inscriptions from the fourth century B.C.E, an altar and
two hearths are dedicated to ršp ḥf, "Reshep of the Arrow". According to
Hendel, this construction (divine name, 'flame,' in construct with a
weapon) corresponds exactly to לַהַט הַחֶרֶב, "flame of the sword". Thus
לַהַט may be a tutelary deity, equivalent to the cherubim, whose characteristic weapon is the "revolving" or "thrashing sword" just as the arrow
is Reshep's trademark weapon in the Phoenician texts.[84]

Although Hendel's argument has not gained much support among
other scholars,[85] it does solve the problem of the apparent asymmetry
in the pairing of the cherubim with a weapon. The cherubim, as por-

---

82   Gaster (1969:48–49) and Wenham (1987: 86)

83   Wenham (1987:86), Stordalen (2000:294) and Miller (1965:259)

84   For the arrow as the characteristic weapon of Reshep, see Hendel (1985:673, n. 16).

85   See e.g. Stordalen (2000:294) who dismisses Hendel's suggestion as "unsupported".

trayed elsewhere in the Hebrew Bible, are never depicted with weapons. Indeed, as we shall see in our discussion of Ps 18:11 = 2 Sam 22:11 (§ 1.3.3), a cherub may well have been conceived of as quadrupedal and therefore incapable of holding a sword. Hendel's idea, that it is the function of these supernatural figures that has caused them to be brought together in this text, makes much more sense. As Miller (1965) has shown, fire is one element that often forms part of Yahweh's heavenly host in his holy wars (e.g. in Num 21:27–30 and Amos 1–2). It could be that the cherubim also form part of Yahweh's heavenly host. The divine epithet יְהוָה צְבָאוֹת יֹשֵׁב הַכְּרֻבִים may point in this direction (although see § 1.1.2). If this is the case, the cherubim and the לַהַט הַחֶרֶב הַמִּתְהַפֶּכֶת are part of Yahweh's supernatural entourage, at his disposal to carry out his demands. Accordingly, they are positioned as menacing sentinels, barring the way to the Tree of Life.

More needs to be said concerning the Tree of Life,[86] the way to

---

86 It is often said that the Tree of Life is a common symbol or mythological concept in the literature and artwork of the ancient Near East (E.g. Skinner 1910: 59 and Westermann 1974: 290). Yet there is no expression "Tree of Life" in ancient Near Eastern literature outside the biblical books of Genesis and Proverbs. There are only two possible extra-biblical examples of a possible mythological Tree of Life in the ancient Near East: the "plant of rejuvenation" in *The Epic of Gilgamesh* and the *Kiškanu* tree, which appears in a bilingual (Sumerian/Akkadian) incantation text (see Widengren 1951: 5–6 for a translation). However, the "plant of rejuvenation" of the Gilgamesh epic is not identical with the Tree of Life in Genesis 2–3 as it is a much smaller plant (it is easily transported). Likewise, the *Kiškanu* tree has healing properties but does not have the more powerful life-giving properties which the Tree of Life has in Genesis 2–3. Widengren (1951) and Parpola (1997) both attempt to prove that the notion of a Tree of Life was a widespread and theologically significant concept in ancient Near Eastern religion. Both refer chiefly to iconographical evidence to support their arguments. However, sacred trees in ancient Near Eastern artwork are depicted in many different ways. Stordalen (2000: 289–291) notes that a tree could be an image of the life-giving power of the deity or the king and it could also represent cosmic order. Consequently, the trees in ancient Near Eastern iconography do not represent one particular mythological Tree of Life, which could bestow eternal life on the person who ate its fruit. Instead the image of a tree could have many different referents. Sjöberg strongly criticises the view that there is a Tree of Life in Mesopotamian literature or artwork. He argues: "There is no evidence that there was a Tree of Life in Mesopotamian myth and cult. The identification of different trees on Mesopotamian seals as a Tree of Life is a pure hypothesis, a product of pan-Babylonianism which wished to trace all Old Testament religious and mythological concepts back to Mesopotamia" (1984: 221). Although the connections between Genesis 1–11 and some of the themes in the Epic of Gilgamesh mean that the Tree of Life may have something in common with "the plant of rejuvenation", it is inadvisable to think of the Tree of Life in Genesis 2–3 as a popular ancient Near Eastern motif.

which is guarded by the cherubim. Why does the tree need guarding and why are the cherubim chosen to guard it? According to Gen 3:22, eating of the Tree of Life will result in human beings "living forever", a state of affairs which Yahweh-Elohim wishes to prevent. What this phrase means and the implications of humanity living forever have been much debated. In eating the fruit of the Tree of Knowledge, the human beings become "like the gods" (Gen 3:5, 22), knowing good and evil.[87] Although not explicitly stated, the narrative seems to suggest that "living forever" was also a divine quality. Arguably, the parallelism set up between the two trees is enough to indicate that this is what is meant.[88] Although immortality is not a developed theological idea in the Hebrew Bible, the expression "live forever" occurs several times. In Deut 32:40, Yahweh makes an oath using the phrase "As I live forever". The common oath formula is usually just "as I live" or "as the lord lives". It is interesting therefore that, at this point in the poem, when Yahweh is speaking of his divine legitimacy, this unique[89] formula occurs. Perhaps we can argue that Yahweh's power to "live forever" is purposefully emphasized in Deut 32:40 in order to stress his divine reality and legitimacy. Several times (e.g. in 1 Kgs 1:31 and Neh 2:3), "living forever" is something wished for a king by one of his subjects. This may be purely a matter of royal protocol and flattery but could also be connected with royal ideology and possibly the notion of divine

---

87   The use of the plural in Gen 3:22 indicates that the knowledge of good and evil is a divine quality in general and not just a quality of Yahweh-Elohim. The use of Elohim rather than Yahweh-Elohim in the conversations of the serpent and Eve in Gen 3:1–5 also support this. The exact sense of "knowing good and evil" is uncertain but is likely to do with rational and ethical discrimination (see Barr 1992: 61–63). It must be something that was considered a quality of divinity that was shared by humanity after the fruit was eaten. Therefore, it must also be something that distinguishes humans from animals. Barr (1992: 65) argues that the acquisition of the knowledge of good and evil was "a coming of consciousness of lines that must not be crossed, of rules that must be obeyed."

88   The inconsistencies within the story of Genesis 2–3 have caused most scholars (e.g. Westermann 1974: 288–292; Wenham 1987: 62) to argue that the narrative originally concerned only one tree. In Gen 3:3, the woman says that god only prohibited eating from the tree (singular) "in the midst of the garden", whereas in Gen 2:17 it is only the fruit of the Tree of Knowledge that is proscribed. In Gen 2:9, the phrasing is awkward but suggests that both trees were in the middle of the garden. It thus seems likely that the story initially involved one tree rather than two (see Barr 1982: 57–61). Whatever the history of the development of the narrative, the current arrangement does set up a parallelism between the two trees.

89   The formula also occurs in Dan 12:7, arguably a much later text.

kingship. It seems, therefore, that "living forever" was considered a divine quality which humanity should not be allowed to gain access to.

Stordalen (2000: 230–232) has argued that the first humans were allowed to eat from the Tree of Life before they disobeyed Yahweh-Elohim and ate from the Tree of Knowledge of Good and Evil. Yahweh-Elohim never prohibits eating from the Tree of Life (Gen 2:16–17) and it is only after the first humans have consumed the fruit of the forbidden tree that they must be prevented from eating the fruit of the other tree (Gen 3:22). Barr contends that the syntax of verse 22b shows categorically that the first humans had not previously eaten from the Tree of Life (Barr 1992b: 58). He follows Humbert (1940: 131) in surveying all 131 occurrences of Hebrew פֶּן and observing that in none of these cases is it used with the notion of continuity. Thus, the phrase, וְעַתָּה פֶּן־יִשְׁלַח יָדוֹ וְלָקַח גַּם מֵעֵץ הַחַיִּים, cannot mean, "And now, lest he continue to reach out his hand and take also from the Tree of Life". Instead, the phrase must indicate that the humans had not formerly eaten its fruit.

Stordalen has criticized Barr on this point. He notes several instances where פֶּן does in fact articulate continuity between what has happened previously and what should not ensue.[90] Thus he argues: "It seems clear that an imperfect verb negated with פ could indeed mean 'lest someone continue to do what they are already doing'" (2000: 231). He observes, "Being created from dust (2:7), humankind was mortal, but continued eating would result in the lasting delay of aging and death" (2000: 291). Moreover, Stordalen argues that, whether or not the humans did in fact eat from the tree prior to their disobedience, "the crucial point in Gen 3:22 is the potential new situation" (2000: 231). Thus, although we cannot tell whether the humans ate from the Tree of Life before they ate from the Tree of Knowledge, what is important is that, after they have eaten from the Tree of Knowledge, they must not eat from the Tree of Life.

If attaining the knowledge of good and evil takes humanity a step towards divinity (Gen 3:22), then it may be implied by the narrative that 'living forever' would do the same. The acquisition of the knowledge of good and evil significantly elevates the status and power of humanity. It distinguishes humankind from the animals (on this see Barr 1992b: 62–63) and gives them a divine quality. Following this gain, it becomes imperative for Yahweh-Elohim to prevent humanity from

---

90   He cites Gen 45:11; Ex 1:9–10, 33:3; 1 Sam 13:9; 2 Sam 12:27f

acquiring another (and perhaps the only other) divine quality that distinguishes humankind from divinity. As Barr (1982b: 89) argues, Gen 2–3 is somewhat aetiological, "It tells why man comes close to God in respect of knowledge but remains mortal... in spite of that nearness."

Following this interpretation, the cherubim and לַהַט הַחֶרֶב bar access to the Tree of Life in order to prevent humanity from gaining the divine quality of immortality. Prior to the disobedience of the first humans, Yahweh-God walks in the same domain as humanity (Gen 3:8). Such intimacy between creator and creatures is rarely described in the Hebrew Bible outside Genesis 1–11. The verb used is the *hithpael* of *hlk*, which is also used to describe Enoch and Noah walking "with God/the gods" in Gen 5:22, 24 and Gen 6:9.[91] Interestingly, Enoch does not die but is "taken" by God. In Gen 3:21, Yahweh-God personally makes garments for the humans and clothes them. This act has the same degree of intimacy as God walking in the garden but can be interpreted as a final paternal act before sending the humans out into the cursed land. After the humans have acquired the divine quality of knowing good and evil, the cherubim and לַהַט הַחֶרֶב are needed in order to prevent the humans from gaining the further quality of immortality. They thus serve as boundary markers and protectors of the proper order of creation. The phrasing of Gen 3:24 does not suggest that the cherubim and לַהַט הַחֶרֶב were created especially for the purpose of guarding the way to the Tree of Life. Rather, it implies that these were pre-existing subordinate divine beings that could be called upon by Yahweh-Elohim to carry out his commands. In this instance, their appointment is designed to safeguard the correct boundaries between humanity and divinity.

From our analysis of Gen 3:24, we can conclude that the cherubim have an apotropaic function. This is not only made explicit in the text by the fact that the cherubim are the subject of the verb שׁמר, but is also implicit in the pairing of the cherubim with the "flame", a menacing weapon or warrior of Yahweh-God. The cherubim prevent humanity from returning to their prior state of existence, when they lived in close contact with their creator. Their appointment represents a new state of

---

91   It is also used in relation to the King of Tyre, who "walked up and down" among the "fiery stones" on the holy mountain of god and in the Garden of Eden (Ezek 28:13–14). Thus, again, it is used in connection with human/divine relations and the divine locale.

affairs with regard to the relationship between God and humanity. Initially, the humans could exist in close proximity to their creator. Following their disobedience, however, the domain of God and the domain of humankind must become more distinct. The cherubim serve as the guardians of the boundary between the two realms. If we associate the Garden of Eden with the temple and tabernacle (each the holy domain of God), then we can compare the cherubim in Gen 3:24 to the cherubim that occur as architectural features of the temple. In each case, the cherubim are boundary markers and guardians of what is sacred.

§ 1.3.2 Ezekiel 28:11–19

The pericope of Ezekiel 28:11–19 is loaded with rare and difficult vocabulary, as well as unexpected forms and textual variants. These uncertainties within the text have led to an array of translations of the passage and several traditions concerning its overall interpretation. The oracle is introduced as a lament (verse 12) and, as is typical of the dirge style, can be separated into two sections, the first depicting former glory and the second describing present tragedy.[92] The first section of the passage (verses 12b–15) illustrates the past splendour of the king of Tyre, and the second section (verses 16–19) recounts the transgressions of the king and the subsequent judgement upon him.[93] The author[94] makes use of colourful images in order to convey the former majesty of the king. These images are complex and, at times, abstruse. The obscurity of the images has prompted scholars to look to certain mythological texts in order to shed light on their meaning. One of two putative Mesopotamian or Canaanite myths is usually assumed to underlie the

---

92 So Greenberg (1997: 587). Block (1998: 102), on the other hand, observes that "although hints of the 'once-now' scheme are evident," the fact that the whole oracle is communicated in the past tense means that certain scholars (e.g. Zimmerli, 1969b: 680) have seen a disintegration of the original lament form.

93 The lament formula is used satirically in the collections of "Oracles against the Nations". It is therefore probable that the first half of the pericope of Ezek 28:11–19, which appears to eulogize the splendour of the king of Tyre, is also intended to be understood ironically (see Williams 1976: 49–61, esp. 58).

94 It cannot be assumed that Ezekiel is the author of this pericope. Although some scholars (e.g. Greenberg) would argue that there is no reason to doubt the prophet's authorship, Fechter (1992) attributes almost none of the foreign nation oracles in Ezekiel to the hand of the prophet. Yet he does argue that the section which comes closest to the prophet's style is Ezek 28:1–19 (Fechter 1992: 192).

oracle: first, an 'Adamic' myth concerning a primal and royal figure (similar to that of the Eden story in Genesis 2–3)[95] or, second, a myth concerning a rebellious deity, vestiges of which are said to be found in the Ugaritic texts.[96]

One of the most obscure images in the passage is that of the cherub (appearing in verses 14 and 16). The main setback when trying to understand the image is the question of the cherub's identity. The syntax of verses 14 and 16 is awkward, and the MT and LXX differ significantly. The MT offers verse 14 as follows:

אַתְּ־כְּרוּב מִמְשַׁח הַסּוֹכֵךְ וּנְתַתִּיךָ בְּהַר קֹדֶשׁ אֱלֹהִים

הָיִיתָ בְּתוֹךְ אַבְנֵי־אֵשׁ הִתְהַלָּכְתָּ

The cherub is identified in the MT as the recipient of the oracle, the king of Tyre. However, if the text is read in its original form, without vowels, it is grammatically possible to give a second explanation for the cherub's identity. The consonants of the rare second person masculine singular pronoun, *'att*[97], attested by the MT, can also be read as *'et*, "with".[98] If this was the original reading of the text, the king of Tyre would no longer be identified as a cherub. Instead, the text would be introducing a wholly new and independent character, a supernatural being with whom the king of Tyre is placed by Yahweh. This second reading is that witnessed by the LXX and Syriac versions. The LXX reads, μετὰ τοῦ χερουβ ἔθηκά σε ἐν ὄρει ἁγίῳ θεοῦ ἐγενήθης ἐν μέσῳ λίθων πυρίνων, which can be translated as "with the cherub I placed you, on the holy mountain of God you were, in the middle of the fiery stones."[99]

---

95 Widengren (1958: 165–176); May (1962) and Neiman (1969: 109–124)

96 Pope (1955: 97–102) asserts that a myth about the deposition of the Canaanite god, El, lies beneath the Ezekiel passage. Also, see Morgenstern (1939: 29–126); Wyatt (1986: 424–429) and Page (1996: 157).

97 Usually feminine, but on two other occasions in the Hebrew Bible (Num 11:15 and Deut 5:24) *'att* has a masculine antecedent.

98 It is also grammatically possible to read אֵת as the direct object marker. If this were the case, we would then expect the cherub to be the object of the verb, yet the only suitable verb to hand is וּנְתַתִּיךָ and the syntax would be awkward, though not impossible.

99 The LXX offers a substantially shorter text, which either suggests that the LXX translator purposefully left out some of the more difficult vocabulary of the MT recension and smoothed out its syntax, or that the MT has subsequently expanded an originally shorter text.

In verse 16, the LXX continues to understand the cherub as entirely independent of the king of Tyre. Indeed, the Greek text even has the cherub inflicting punishment on the king, removing him from the midst of the fiery stones. The syntax of the MT in verse 16 is, like verse 14, extremely problematic. However, the Hebrew appears to read first person forms in the second half of the verse, thus understanding Yahweh to be the subject of the punishing. The reference to the cherub is then best read as a vocative, again identifying the cherub with the recipient of the oracle, the king of Tyre.

Hence, in this passage, the king of Tyre is depicted either *as* a cherub or *situated with* a cherub. As we shall see, the cherub's identity is vital for our understanding of why it appears in this text. Not only does the matter affect how we view the portrayal of the king of Tyre, but it also influences what we consider to be the main source of inspiration for the choice of imagery. If the MT is deemed superior to the LXX witness, then the depiction of the king *as* the cherub and not *with* the cherub radically weakens the grounds for supposing that the inspiration for Ezek 28:11–19 is an 'Adamic' myth concerning primal man, as the king is compared to a divine, not a human, being.

§ 1.3.2.1 Earlier Exegesis

As stated previously, the textual difficulties in Ezekiel 28:11–19 have prompted many scholars to interpret the passage in the light of a supposed mythological backdrop. Scholars usually fall into two camps on this matter: those who subscribe to the view that a primeval myth about the creation of the king/first man underlies the oracle, and those who consider a Canaanite myth about a rebellious god to be the main source of inspiration. Those who regard a primeval myth to lie beneath Ezekiel 28:11–19 tend to deem the LXX to be the superior witness in verses 14 and 16 and hence view the cherub as a supernatural being with whom the king of Tyre is placed. This harmonises well with the Eden story of Gen 2:4b–3:24, where the cherubim are entirely separate from אדם (Gen 3:22–24). Commentators who regard a myth about a god to be the inspiration for Ezekiel's oracle have explained the cherub in various ways, some identifying it with the king of Tyre and arguing that the king is purposefully presented as an insubordinate yet divine being in accordance with a rebellion myth.

§ 1.3.2.1.1 The Myth of a Rebel Deity

Morgenstern (1939: 111) conforms to the latter group of scholars, viewing the source of Ezek 28:11–19 to be a myth about a celestial being,
who rebelled against the high god, only to be expelled from heaven to
earth. He connects the oracle to passages such as Psalm 82 and Isa
14:12–14, both of which, like Ezek 28:11–19, give an account of the punishment of supernatural beings because of acts of pride and injustice.
Morgenstern argues that the king of Tyre is purposefully envisaged as
a divine being, the cherub, in order to draw on this widely known myth
about a rebel deity. In this way, the author intentionally compares the
fate of the king of Tyre to the fate of this legendary being.

The cherub in Ezekiel 28, according to Morgenstern, is no ordinary
cherub or divine being, but "one who had distinctive personality and
individuality and who held a special rank or discharged a particular
function in the service of the deity" (1939: 111).[100] The evidence he gives for this assumption is that the word כְּרוּב lacks the article in both
verses 14 and 16 and appears to be in a construct relationship with the
two following words, מִמְשַׁח הַסּוֹכֵךְ in verse 14.[101] Hence Morgenstern
views מִמְשַׁח הַסּוֹכֵךְ as qualifying כְּרוּב and thus helping to identify a
specific cherub. Accordingly, he views כְּרוּב מִמְשַׁח הַסּוֹכֵךְ as a character
from a popular story or myth, which played a distinct religious or ideological role within the Hebrew (or Phoenician) belief system.[102]

Pope draws on Morgenstern's theories regarding the mythological background of Ezek 28:11–19. Like Morgenstern, Pope argues that
the king of Tyre is being compared to a legendary divine being, who
rebelled against another deity but was himself deposed and exiled.
However, Pope has reservations about Morgenstern's identification
of the cherub with this rebel deity. Where Morgenstern regards
כְּרוּב מִמְשַׁח הַסּוֹכֵךְ (in verse 14) to be naming the rebel god, Pope (1955:
98, n. 72) maintains that this phrase is too obscure (and most likely cor-

---

100 Morgenstern regards Ezek 28:11–19 as containing elements of an original satanic
     myth.
101 In fact, there is no evidence that כְּרוּב is in a construct relationship with מִמְשַׁח or
     הַסּוֹכֵךְ. The meaning of מִמְשַׁח is uncertain and הַסּוֹכֵךְ may be in apposition with what
     has gone before. Thus there is no reason to view כְּרוּב as definite. The Greek witness
     of verse 14 reads "the cherub". The use of the definite article here is most likely due
     to the presence of the preposition preceding it.
102 Zimmerli (1969b: 675) asks whether כְּרוּב, without the article, has the quality of
     proper name.

rupt) to support Morgenstern's proposal. Indeed, he seems to doubt that the cherub was original to the oracle at all.[103] Instead of the cherub, he argues that the king of Tyre is compared to the Canaanite god El. El, according to Pope, was displaced by the more popular god Baal in Ugaritic religion and hence myths arose concerning his dethronement. Pope notes several indications in the text of Ezek 28:11–19 which suggest that the ousted god, to whom the king of Tyre is compared, is El.[104] First, he compares the precious stones mentioned in verse 13 to the jewels associated with the dwelling place of the Ugaritic god Baal, especially ברקת, which Pope associates with the Ugaritic *abn brq* ("stone of lightning"), a material used to build Baal's house.[105] Pope (1955:101) also interprets the reference to the "stones of fire" in Ezek 28:14 in the same light, suggesting that these stones are comparable to the silver and gold used in the construction of Baal's house, which were smelted in fire and out of which elements of the house were formed. He argues that because the ornamentation associated with the king of Tyre in Ezek 28:11–19 resembles that of Baal's abode in the Ugaritic texts (and hence also the decoration of El's house, prior to Baal usurping the throne) there is reason to believe that Ezekiel may well have exploited Ugaritic mythology concerning Baal and El in Ezek 28:11–19.[106]

Wyatt bridges the gap between those scholars who consider a myth of a rebellious deity to underlie Ezek 28:11–19 and those who understand a primeval myth to lie behind the pericope. He argues that passages such as Ezek 28:1–10; 11–19 and Isa 14:4–21 can be linked to Gen

---

103 However, that all versions of Ezekiel 28 attest "cherub" in verses 14 and 16 is strong evidence that the cherub is not a later editorial addition to Ezekiel 28, as Pope would have us believe.

104 Pope associates the second oracle against the king of Tyre in Ezekiel (28:11–19) with the preceding oracle (28:1–10) and uses the references to אל (El/a god) in the first oracle as further evidence that the entire chapter contains vestiges of the myth of El's dethronement.

105 Pope (1955: 99). Wyatt, on the other hand, interprets the expression *abn brq* entirely differently and there seems little reason for viewing the phrase as referring to a material used to build Baal's house (see Wyatt, 1998: 78).

106 Pope's identification of the jewels in Ezek 28:13 with the abode of Baal/El is not evidence enough to presume that Ezekiel is definitely exploiting this Canaanite mythology. There are a number of other, perhaps more cogent, explanations for the jewels. First, the jewel garden described in tablet IX of the *Epic of Gilgamesh* has been connected to the jewels mentioned in Gen 2:11–12. Second, certain scholars argue that Ezek 28:13 is dependent on the list of jewels forming the high priest's breastplate in Ex 28:17–20 and 39:10–13 (e.g. Stordalen 2000: 338) hence we may not even need to look beyond Hebrew tradition to explain the jewels in 28:13.

2:4b–3:24. In all four texts, a lesser deity or human being is situated (Ezek 28:13–14; Gen 2:8–9) or desires to be situated (Isa 14:13–14) in a sacred place, a place associated with the ruling deity (Yahweh-Elohim, El, or Elyon). Yet the overweening pride of the creatures (Isa 14:11; Ezek 28:2, 17) and their desire to be a god/the most high (Ezek 28:2, 6; Gen 3:5, 22; Isa 14:14) results in their expulsion from the sacred place. Where these passages seem to differ is that the mythic protagonist is a human being in Genesis, but may well be a divine being in Ezekiel 28 and Isaiah 14. However, the referent, who is compared to the mythic beings in Ezekiel 28 and Isaiah 14, is a king (the king of Babylon in Isaiah 14 and the king of Tyre in Ezekiel 28). Wyatt (1986: 424) argues that the oracles in Ezekiel 28 and Isa 14:4–21 actually contain vestiges of a kingship myth. Viewing the three oracles in the light of royal ideology then allows comparison with Gen 2:4b–3:24 as, according to many scholars (e.g. Engnell 1955:103–109), Adam is the prototype of the Hebrew king.

Wyatt interprets the identity of the cherub in accordance with the LXX. He translates verse 14 as follows: "With the Cherub I set you, on the holy mountain a god you were, in the midst of 'firestones' you walked" (1986:425). He thus reads against the Masoretic division of the verse and views the cherub as a creature with whom the king of Tyre is placed. His translation of the second line of the verse, "on the holy mountain a god you were," requires further discussion. In the second line of the verse, the MT reads the construct *beʰar* ('on the mountain of') and hence the whole phrase is usually translated "on the holy mountain *of* God/the gods". The LXX reads the genitive θεοῦ, 'of God' and, consequently, the clause is normally translated in a similar way to the Hebrew. Wyatt, however, reads the absolute form of the Hebrew בהר, *bāhār*, and thus sees no relationship between בהר and אלהים.[107] Although his translation does help with the syntax of the verse, he does not justify his translation of the clause but merely states that this is his preference (1986: 425, n. 25). On the basis of the ideas expressed elsewhere in his article, it would seem that Wyatt sees here a reference to the divinity of the king, a theme which he regards as common to all the passages that, he argues, contain vestiges of a kingship myth (Eze-

---

107   A similar translation of verse 14 was suggested previously by Widengren (1950: 94–97).

kiel 28, Isaiah 14 and Genesis 2–3). However, there are several reasons why he is wrong to translate verse 14 in the way that he does. First, there is strong evidence from the versions that the verse means "on the holy mountain *of* God/the gods". Second, the phrase "mountain of God" is relatively common in the Hebrew Bible.[108] Third, the phrase "holy mountain of God/the gods" in verse 14 seems to parallel "Eden, the garden of God/the gods" in verse 13 and Wyatt himself translates בְּעֵדֶן גַּן־אֱלֹהִים הָיִיתָ as "You were in Eden, the garden *of* God". Similarly, in verse 16, הַר and אֱלֹהִים appear together again and, this time, there is no doubt that the words are in construct relationship. Indeed, Wyatt translates, "I have thrown you down from the mountain *of* God". Surely, it cannot be methodologically sound to translate הַר and אֱלֹהִים as independent of each other in verse 14 but as in a construct relationship in verse 16. Thus it would seem that Wyatt is translating verse 14 in a way which would conveniently support his premise that Ezek 28:11–19 contains allusions to the divinity of the king.

Page is one of the most recent scholars to envisage a Canaanite myth about a rebel deity as underlying Ezek 28:11–19. Page (1996: 157) argues that the author is comparing the king of Tyre to one of Yahweh's/El's "trusted associates", who was unrivaled in the cosmos but was ultimately expelled because of his pride. He views this celestial being as a member of the divine council, which met on the assembly mount (בְּהַר קֹדֶשׁ אֱלֹהִים). According to Page (1996:149, n. 264; 154), the precious stones of verse 13 and the fiery stones of verse 14 are allusions to astral deities, who form the divine council, and with whom the divine being is placed. Following the syntax of the MT in verses 14 and 16, he maintains that the cherub is the rebel deity, to whom the king of Tyre is compared. He claims that there are three possible meanings of the term כְּרוּב. First, the term may be a divine name, which is also suggested by Zimmerli (1986: 94). Second, the word may be an epithet for a Canaanite, Mesopotamian or Israelite deity. Finally, כְּרוּב may be a "title or classification of beings with a functional significance" (Page 1996: 153). This third meaning accords with the presentation of the cherubim elsewhere in the Hebrew Bible, where they are presented as guardians of the divine sanctuary (see §§ 1.2–1.3.1 above). Page interprets כְּרוּב as having this third meaning in Ezek 28:14 and 16, and thus כְּרוּב designates a type of divine being with a definite theological function. Page

---

108   E.g. Ex 3:1; 18:5; 24:13 and Ps 48:3

argues that vestiges of the rebellion myth can be found in numerous
passages in the Hebrew Bible (e.g. Gen 6:1–4; Isaiah 14, Ezek 28:1–9, 11–
19, Psalm 82 and Job 38). He contends that the descriptions of the rebellious figures in these passages suggest that the rebel deity was an astral
god.[109]

The arguments of Morgenstern, Pope, Wyatt and Page are representative of the leading commentators who presume a 'rebellion' myth
to underlie Ezek 28:11–19. Having reviewed their arguments, it is apparent that the identity and function of the cherub are interpreted in
different ways. A reconstructed 'rebellion' myth does not seem to deal
adequately with questions concerning who or what the cherub is and
what role 'he' or 'it' plays as a poetic image.

§ 1.3.2.1.2 An 'Adamic' Myth

The majority of commentators on Ezek 28:11–19 have connected the
pericope in some way to Gen 2:4b–3:24. There are several reasons why
scholars have made this connection. First, a number of enigmatic images occur in both passages: the Garden of Eden, a list of jewels and a
cherub/cherubim. Second, the general plot developed in the passages is
similar. A creature is situated in a sacred place, the Garden of Eden,
and given special status. Yet, on account of certain deeds, the creature
is expelled from the garden. Finally, general themes such as creation
and wisdom are also present in each passage.

Traditionally, Ezek 28:11–19 is viewed as an older and "more
mythological" version of the story found in Genesis 2–3.[110] Gunkel, for
example, argues that Ezek 28:11–19 depicts the "first man" as a sort of
demigod. In his view, the author of Genesis 2–3 has demythologised
the primeval account and thus rid the occupant of the garden of supernatural qualities. He follows the LXX in regarding the cherub as entirely separate from the inhabitant of the garden, and he considers the
cherub to be the one expelling the demigod (king of Tyre) from among

---

109 Page (1996: 207). As we have already seen, Page notes that the references to the
precious stones and the stones of fire in Ezek 28:11–19 allude to astral deities. Similarly, Page asserts that the cherub's destruction by fire and reduction to ash also refers to the astral quality of the rebel deity.
110 See Gunkel (1910: 34), Cooke (1936: 315), Zimmerli (1969b: 281–282), Van Seters
(1989: 333–342)

the fiery stones in verse 16. This interpretation of the cherub concurs, to some degree, with the presentation of the cherubim in Gen 3:24, who are placed as guardians of the way to the Tree of Life, to the east of the Garden of Eden.[111]

Cooke also thinks that Ezekiel draws on a popular story about a creature's fall from paradise. He argues that this story belonged to the stock of myths prevalent in all Semitic cultures and is the basis for Ezek 28:11–19 and Genesis 2–3. However, although in Genesis the story has been "purged" of mythological allusions, in Ezekiel "the purifying process has not gone so far" (Cooke 1936: 315). Cooke maintains that "nothing can be made of" the MT version of 28:14. He states, "Obviously the denizen of the garden cannot be identical with the cherub" (1936:317). Instead, he deems the LXX to be the superior witness and translates, "With the cherub… I placed thee." He thus sees the cherub as the attendant or companion of the occupant of the garden.

The description of the cherub הַסּוֹכֵךְ ("the one covering") in Ezek 28:14 indicates, according to Cooke, that the "cherub of paradise has been assimilated to the cherubim of the ark" (1936: 318). Here, Cooke seems to suggest that the function of the cherubim as "shields" of the ark (as observed in Exodus 25:20 and 37:9) was originally separate from the function of the "cherub of paradise". However, who or what exactly this "cherub of paradise" is remains far from certain. Cooke implies that this cherub was a character found in what he calls the "paradise story". Yet, there is no evidence for the existence of a prevalent paradise myth in the ancient Near East. Even the Eden narrative in Genesis 2–3 cannot be described as a paradise story and it is arguable whether the Garden of Eden can be labelled a paradise at all (see Batto 1991: 33–66, esp. 51–55). Furthermore, the idea of *a cherub* (in the singular) dwelling in paradise or the Garden of Eden is not corroborated by any biblical or ancient Near Eastern text, other than Ezekiel 28:13–14. In Genesis 3:24, *cherubim* (in the plural) are made to dwell to the *east* of Eden. At no point, however, are the cherubim described as living *in* Eden and at no point is one cherub singled out as having a special function or said to dwell with primal man. The only link between a single cherub and

---

111 It is important to note, however, that the cherubim are only appointed as the guardians of the Tree of Life after the first humans have been evicted from the garden. Therefore, it does not provide a neat parallel with LXX Ezek 28:11–19 as, in this version, the King of Tyre is placed with the cherub in the garden.

the Garden of Eden is in Ezek 28:13–14. Thus Cooke's intimation that a "cherub of paradise" existed as a literary or mythological character in the ancient Near East is unsupported by the textual evidence. Moreover, the cherubim of Genesis 3:24 are placed to the east of Eden in order *to guard* the way to the Tree of Life. The function of the cherubim of the ark (mentioned in Ex 25:20 and 37:9) also seems to be to guard or "shield" (סכך) the space above the ark, either from profane space or from human (i.e. profane) eyes. Hence, the function of the cherubim of the ark and the function of the alleged "cherub of paradise" are actually very similar. The cherubim are always depicted as guardians of the divine locale.

Zimmerli, like Cooke, considers a common myth to underlie Genesis 2–3 and Ezek 28:11–19. Where Cooke argues that it is only implied in Ezek 28:11–19 that the main character in the story is the first man (1936:315), Zimmerli claims that the references to the creation of the individual in verses 13 and 15 support the notion that a myth about primeval man underlies Ezek 28:11–19. The phrase בְּיוֹם הִבָּרְאֲךָ (occurring in verses 13 and 15) has prompted much scholarly discussion. The verb ברא is principally used to denote creation by God in the Hebrew Bible, and seldom has any other than Yahweh, or Elohim, as its subject. Zimmerli describes the verb ברא as the *terminus technicus* of the Priestly creation story (1969b: 682). He, like many scholars, argues that the author purposefully uses the verb in order to allude to the Priestly creation account of primordial man in Genesis 1.[112] However, the chief ideas in Ezek 28:11–19 seem to have more in common with the "Yahwistic", rather than the "Priestly", creation story (see Petersen 1999: 490–500). The verb ברא is never used in Genesis 2–3.

In his interpretation of Ezek 28:11–19 in the light of a myth concerning primal man, Zimmerli questions the Masoretic association of the cherub with the principal character of the story. He argues that, owing to the independence of the cherubim and Adam in Genesis 2–3, we should follow the translation of the LXX in verses 14 and 16 rather than the MT. According to Zimmerli, the depiction of cherubim as guardians of Yahweh elsewhere in Ezekiel (e.g. 10:2) and in Exodus (25:20 and 37:9) suggests that here too the cherub guards the sanctuary of the god. He contends, "Das Heilige, das er 'absperrt' (סכך), ist, anders als in Ex

---

112   Callender (1998: 606–625) also sees a link between Ezekiel's description of the king of Tyre and the account of the creation of primal man in Gen 1:26–28.

25:20; 37:9, nicht die Deckplatte der Lade, über welcher Jahwe erscheint, sondern der hohe, der Menschennähe entrückte Bergwohnsitz Gottes" (1969b: 684). According to Zimmerli (1969b: 684), the magnificent first man is associated with the cherub in verse 14 in order to signify his admission to the dwelling place of the gods.

§ 1.3.2.2 The Significance of the Masoretic Text

From a survey of earlier scholarship, we can see that both the identity and function of the cherub in Ezek 28:11–19 have been construed in numerous ways. However, no myth yet reconstructed adequately deals with why the MT compares the king of Tyre to the cherub. Indeed, many of the arguments are somewhat circular, reconstructing an ancient Near Eastern myth from the biblical material and then interpreting the biblical material according to this reconstructed myth.[113] Even if we accept Zimmerli's association of the passage with a myth about primal man, we are still left wondering why the MT, in both verses 14 and 16, likens the king of Tyre to a cherub. It is possible that the MT is corrupt, but we still have to explain the reasons for this corruption. Surely, the fact that the MT identifies the king of Tyre with a cherub, not only once but twice, suggests that the cherub was an adequate or even appropriate image with which to represent the king of Tyre.

Furthermore, there are several compelling reasons why the MT may well preserve a superior reading to that of the LXX. Two scholars have put forward persuasive arguments for retaining the text and sense of the MT. First, Jeppesen (1991: 90–91) maintains that, if we emend the MT in order to read "with a cherub," there remains a problem with the translation of verse 16. Here, as in verse 14, the MT seems to equate the cherub with the king. Further emendation of the MT is thus required in order to preserve the independence of the cherub and the king. Some commentators have done this by reading וָאַבֶּדְךָ as the 3ms *qatal* form of אבד (rather than the 1cs *yiqtol* form represented in the MT) and translate, "So the guardian cherub destroyed you". This requires no emendation to the consonantal text of the MT. However, the syntax of the MT in verse 16 makes sense as it is. Although the full version of the 1cs *yiqtol* of אבד should be written with two *alephs*, the elision of the *aleph*,

---

113 This is particularly the case with Page's argumentation (Page 1996).

although unusual, is not impossible.[114] This omission of an *aleph* occasionally happens in the *piel*, for example in 2 Sam 22:40. Also, only earlier in Ezekiel 28:16 itself, the third person plural *qal qatal* of מלא is written without the third radical, *aleph*. Another point in favour of the MT in verse 16 is the fact that the subject of the previous verb, וָאֲחַלֶּלְךָ, is Yahweh. Arguably, the agent of punishment is Yahweh and thus he should be the subject of וָאַבֶּדְךָ and not the cherub.[115] Those scholars who amend the vocalization of וָאַבֶּדְךָ to read the third person form are thus harmonizing the text in order to preserve the independence of the cherub and the king and create a better parallel between Ezek 28 and Gen 2–3. Hence, Jeppesen is right to argue that we should read with the MT (as *lectio difficilior*) in verses 14 and 16.

Second, Barr (1992a: 213–223) has pointed to another textual difficulty that arises if we emend the Masoretic vocalization of את to mean "with" in verse 14. The LXX supplies a simple reading, "With the cherub I placed you". However, after אַתְּ־כְּרוּב, the MT has two other descriptive words which the LXX omits. Following these words in the MT is the verb "I appointed you", yet this is separated from the previous verbless clause by the conjunction "and", thus וּנְתַתִּיךָ. The LXX does not represent this conjunction. Barr argues that the syntax of the MT necessitates two clauses, the nominal clause, "You are the cherub", and the verbal clause, "and I appointed you."[116] However, the LXX translator, not understanding the rare 2ms pronoun אַתְּ, reads אֵת ('with'). In doing this, the Greek translator is then forced to read one clause instead of two. The LXX does not supply anything in place of the Hebrew הִתְהַלָּכְתָּ in the third clause. הִתְהַלָּכְתָּ would be a completely unnecessary later addition to the Hebrew text.

---

114 See GKC §68k; BDB, 2a.

115 Although it is not impossible for there to be two agents of punishment, the MT does provide a more consistent narrative.

116 Barr (1992: 219). The sudden first person form here may be compared with the intrusive first person form in Ezek 31:9. On both occasions, the majesty of a king is extolled using vivid imagery and second person forms. The invasive first person forms appear to emphasise that the majesty of the king was not due to his own merit but was the direct result of Yahweh. Scholars have often viewed the first person form in Ezek 31:9 as a later addition, added to an original hymn of praise in order to stress that Yahweh is the source of the king's splendour. Owing to the awkward syntax of the MT in Ezek 28:14 and the otherwise second person forms, it is possible that וּנְתַתִּיךָ is also an editorial addition.

Accordingly, the MT may be regarded as the *lectio difficilior* and thus may preserve a more ancient reading. The possibility that the MT is the earlier reading, over against the LXX, has important implications for our understanding of the portrayal of the king of Tyre in this pericope and the history of the Eden tradition. Barr contends: "The person addressed in the... oracle, the one who is full of wisdom and perfect in beauty, who walked among the precious stones... was a semi-divine being or a divinely placed agent, not the first man, Adam" (1992: 220).

Although the similarities between Genesis 2–3 and Ezekiel 28 are unlikely to be fortuitous, the differences between the two passages should not be harmonized in order to create better parallelism between the two, especially given scholarly uncertainty concerning the history of the Eden tradition.[117] Hence, to amend the MT picture of the king of Tyre as a cherub to conform to the Eden tradition in Genesis 2–3 is unwarranted. Indeed, Barr (1992: 222) suggests that the LXX translator of Ezekiel 28 may even have had Genesis 2–3 in mind and, consequently, he translated Ezek 28:14–16 in a way which would be consistent with the Genesis tradition.[118]

§ 1.3.2.3 A Holistic Approach

Several scholars have cautioned against the need to reconstruct a myth in order to explain the obscure images in Ezek 28:11–19. Their criticism stems from the fact that any application of hypothetical myths to a biblical passage can only ever result in speculation. Without any extant and intact myth that contains every figurative element present in Ezek 28:11–19, we will never be sure how far Ezekiel's use of imagery is the result of his own poetic creativity, on the one hand, or a purposeful adaptation of a myth, on the other.

It has been common among scholars who reconstruct a myth in order to elucidate the abstruse imagery in Ezek 28:11–19 to regard the references specifically orientated to Tyre (for example the allusions to Tyre's wealth and trade in verses 16 and 18) as secondary editorial ac-

---

117 Van Seters (1989: 333–342) presents a case for viewing Ezekiel 28 as the inspiration for Genesis 2–3.

118 This makes more sense than a movement in the alternative direction. It is difficult to provide reasons for how and why the MT text would have arisen from an original tradition that was along the lines of the LXX.

cretions.[119] However, Williams has criticised scholars who, in his view, are too quick to eliminate these direct references to Tyre. He contends, "In vv. 12–19 contemporary Tyre is described in sarcastic terms, which relate to its *present* activity of trading, as being a godlike being living in a Tyrian Eden, perfect in beauty... It is far better to understand these godlike references as being sarcastic terminology related to the self-congratulatory pride of Tyre in its economic enterprises than being derived from an ancient self-contained myth" (1976: 58). Williams compares the use of mythic images in Ezekiel 28:11–19 with the use of such images elsewhere in the book's 'Oracles against the Nations', for example the comparison of Pharaoh with a great dragon (29:3) and a majestic cedar tree (31:2b–9). He argues that the author of the poems uses such imagery as a "language of satirical hyperbole and less as a development from any mythological tradition" (Williams 1976: 59). Williams contends that references to contemporary Tyre, such as those in 28:16 and 18, should not be removed arbitrarily "in favour of a hypothesis about a first man behind Ez 28:12–19" (1976: 59), but should be retained as an integral part of the oracle. Throughout the 'Oracles against the Nations' in Ezekiel, mythic images are interwoven with contemporary references to the nation under scrutiny in order to parody the material success of that nation. Therefore, the author is not constrained by his use of a single, complete myth but rather employs popular mythic images in a creative way.

Greenberg is also keen to stress the unity and homogeneity of Ezek 28:11–19. Instead of dissecting the passage in order to reconstruct an original myth behind the text, he argues that the oracle, as it appears in the MT, makes sense as it is, and there is no need to remove references specifically directed to Tyre as editorial additions. Greenberg, like Williams, argues that the author combines mythic or traditional images with elements specific to Tyre. This technique, according to Greenberg (1997: 593), is a "signature" of Ezekiel and is used frequently by the prophet, not only in his oracles against foreign nations, but also in his domestic prophecies, such as Ezekiel 17. He asserts that this literary technique, once recognised, "finally undermines the search for a unified subtext of our oracle, because Ezekiel, 'a master of figures', drew on the full range of tradition material and tailored whatever he took of it to suit the rhetorical needs of the moment" (1997: 593).

---

119   E.g. Zimmerli (1969b: 686–687); Cooke (1936: 318) and Page (1996: 154–156)

Furthermore, Greenberg draws upon Goldberg's analysis of the structure of Ezek 28:11–19, which outlines the two sections of the lament, verses 12b^b–15 (the description of former glory) and verses 16–19 (the account of present tragedy).[120] Goldberg divides each section into two stanzas, A1 (vss. 12b–13), A2 (vss. 14–15), B1 (vss 16–17) and B2 (vs. 18). The second stanza of each pair can be seen to repeat the phrases of the first using seconding, rather than synonymous, clauses.[121] Greenberg shows how each figurative element in the first stanza is seconded in the following stanza. Thus, the seal[122] of verse 12 becomes the cherub in verse 14, the Garden of Eden in verse 13 becomes the Holy Mountain of God in verse 14, and the precious stones of verse 13 become the stones of fire in verse 14. Greenberg argues that "scarcely a word can be removed without damaging the correspondence" (1997: 589) of the pairs of stanzas. Along these lines, although we may not understand every Hebrew word, the highly organised structure of the final form of Ezekiel 28:11–19 in the MT demonstrates the reliability of the Hebrew text.

§ 1.3.2.4 Towards a New Interpretation of the Cherub

If we are correct in arguing that the MT preserves a more ancient reading than that witnessed by the LXX version of Ezek 28:11–19, there still remains the problem of what the author was trying to convey by comparing the king of Tyre to a cherub. If an Adamic myth cannot be presumed to underlie the pericope, we cannot explain the image of the cherub solely by means of references to Genesis 2–3. Instead, we should start by looking for clues within the oracle itself.

Assmann (1982: 13–61), in his study of Egyptian myth, argues that mythological stories do not necessarily underlie texts that appear to be using mythic language. He claims, instead, that complexes of ideas form "constellations", which can recur in many different texts. These constellations do not originate from one particular narrative but are

---

120 Greenberg (1997: 587–590) cites Goldberg (1989: 277–81).
121 Greenberg sets out the structure of the oracle in a useful way (1997: 587–588).
122 The MT actually reads the active participle of the verb "to seal", חתם, rather than the noun "seal, signet". Most commentators follow the versions in reading the noun. Widengren (1950: 26, n. 18), however, has argued that it is better to read with the MT and contends that the "sealer" has a similar function to the Mesopotamian gods, who sealed the tablets of destiny (see *Enuma Elish* 5, 121).

free to be used by an author without the constraints of a pre-existent framework. If we apply this theory to Genesis 2–3 and Ezek 28:11–19, we can argue that the similar motifs present in both passages are not necessarily the result of one text being derived from the other. Instead, the authors of both texts may have been drawing on the same inherited "Eden constellation".

If we look closely at the pericope of Ezek 28:11–19, we notice that there are two principal semantic clusters. The first is associated with the "Eden constellation" and relates to the sanctuary (conceived in mythic terms).[123] In this cluster, we can place, for example, גַּן־אֱלֹהִים, הַר קֹדֶשׁ אֱלֹהִים and כְּרוּב. The second cluster relates to Phoenician national identity, and particularly to Phoenician skill in craftsmanship, merchandise and trade. To this, we can assign such terms as מָלֵא חָכְמָה, חוֹתֵם תָּכְנִית and רְכֻלָּה. In the following discussion, we will argue that both these semantic clusters have been carefully and purposefully interwoven in order to express how Tyre's skill in craftsmanship and trade will be the root of her downfall.

The first image with which the king of Tyre is compared (and which is seconded by the cherub image, according to Goldberg's structural analysis) is that of the "seal" or "sealer". Most scholars tend to follow the LXX (which has ἀποσφράγισμα) and read חֹתָם, "seal", instead of the MT's active participle, חוֹתֵם, "sealer".[124] It is reasonable to argue that the image of the חוֹתֵם in Ezek 28:12b should be understood figuratively, in the same way as one would understand the epithet given to the prophet Muhammad, "The seal of the prophets" (Surah 33:40).[125] If this is the case, the comparison merely suggests that the king of Tyre is the definitive or archetypal king. However, Block has highlighted the abundance of craftsmanship vocabulary in Ezek 28:12–13, which may indicate that the image of the seal/sealer is intended to compare the king to a crafted object. Block argues that "all three descriptors" of the noun חוֹתֵם "derive from the realm of metalworking and gemstone cutting" (1998: 105).

---

123   It is this constellation that can also be perceived in Genesis 2–3.
124   Widengren (1950, 26, n. 18) argues that it is better to read with the MT.
125   See Zimmerli (1983: 91–92).

First, according to Block, the use of the term תׇכְנִית, which some have argued is not original to the text in Ezekiel 28:12,[126] may point to the intricate workmanship that was evident in the proportions of a signet. The noun is derived from the root תכן, meaning "weigh" or "measure". In Ezek 43:10, the only other occurrence of the form תׇכְנִית refers to the perfect proportions of the temple in Ezekiel's vision. Owing to this usage, Block argues that תׇכְנִית must signify here the perfect proportions of the signet.[127] Signets, in the ancient Near East, were works of art and hence the use of this term may imply that the seal displays fine craftsmanship.[128]

The second and third modifying phrases, "full of wisdom" and "perfect in beauty" have often been considered to refer directly to the king of Tyre. If this is the case, then the metaphor of the seal fades and Ezekiel refers, straightforwardly, to the referent, the king. However, the basic meaning of the root חכם has to do with "skill in craft" rather than the more generic, derived sense of "wisdom". This sense of the root is found in Exodus 25–31 and 35–40, in association with the skill needed in the design and construction of the tabernacle, its fixtures and the robes of the priests.[129] Thus, the phrase "full of wisdom" could, like תׇכְנִית, articulate proficient craftsmanship. Interestingly, the phrase "full of wisdom" is used in 1 Kgs 7:14 with reference to Hiram, the Phoenician craftsman. Likewise, the term חׇכְמָה occurs three times in the previous oracle against Tyre (in Ezek 28:4–5, 7). In Ezek 28:5, Tyre's "abundance of חׇכְמָה" is placed in apposition with her "רְכֻלָּה" ('trade/merchandise'). Tyre's great wealth (חַיִל) is attributed to her possession of these two qualities.

In the third modifying phrase, "perfect in beauty", Block finds an allusion to metalwork. He highlights a possible Akkadian cognate of

---

126   That this form only occurs here and in Ezekiel 43:10 has caused some scholars to emend תׇכְנִית to תׇבְנִית. תׇבְנִית would suit the present interpretation of the imagery as it refers to an artistic model. For example, in Ezk 8:10, the lexeme is used to refer to the design of carvings on the walls of a room in the temple. In this verse, we would have "a signet model" or "signet carving", which would harmonise well with our interpretation of the imagery (see below).

127   Also, see BDB 1067.

128   Block (1998: 104–105). Block's translation "the signet of perfection" is insufficient in expressing what Block sees to be the meaning behind the phrase. A better translation would be "a signet of perfect proportion" or "a signet of perfect design".

129   See BDB 314. This meaning of חכם (as skilful in technical work) may have been the original meaning of the word.

the Hebrew word כָּלִיל[130], *kilīlu*, which referred to gold headbands that were frequently inlaid with jewels. Given that the LXX has στέφανος (meaning "crown" or "wreath") in place of the Hebrew כָּלִיל, the text may be speaking of some kind of diadem. However, comparison with the other oracles against Tyre in the book of Ezekiel shows this expression to be something of a recurring stock phrase (see Ezek 27:3–4, 11; 28:7). In these oracles, it is the beauty created by Phoenician technical skill that is described. For example, in Ezek 27:4, the "builders" of the ship (Tyre) are said to "perfect its beauty".[131] In Ezek 28:7, the strangers are said to draw their swords עַל־יְפִי חָכְמָתֶךָ "against the beauty of your technical skill". Here, again, we read חָכְמָה as having its basic sense of "skill in craft".

In verse 13, we have the first idea belonging to the "Eden constellation". The King of Tyre is said to have been in Eden, the Garden of God (בְּעֵדֶן גַּן־אֱלֹהִים הָיִיתָ). We noted in our discussion of Genesis 2–3 (§2.3.1) that the Garden of Eden has been connected by many scholars to the temple.[132] Hence the King's position is not only privileged but sacred.

According to Block, the allusions to craftsmanship in verse 12 continue in verse 13. After the description of the king's location in the Garden of Eden, is the phrase, כָּל־אֶבֶן יְקָרָה מְסֻכָתֶךָ. The translation of the phrase depends on the meaning of מְסֻכָתֶךָ. Most scholars derive the form from the root סכך, "to cover", which is supported by the Vulgate. The idea then seems to be that the king is adorned with precious stones. Although it was not unusual for important figures to wear jewelled garments (e.g. Exodus 28:15–20 describes the pectoral worn by the high priest), it is also possible that the author has the original metaphor of the king as a signet in mind. Seals were often made of, or encrusted with, precious stones (see Block 1998: 104–105 and Platt 1992: 829).[133]

130　Block (1998:105). Black, George and Postgate (2000: 157) define the Akkadian word *kilīlu* as a "head ornament for humans, gods, of silver, gold". There is also the Aramaic cognate כְּלִילָא, "crown", and its denominative verb, "to crown", as well as cognates in Ethiopic and Arabic, cf. BDB 480.

131　The final clause of Ezek 27:4 reads בֹּנַיִךְ כָּלְלוּ יָפְיֵךְ.

132　See, for example, Wenham 1987: 86, Stordalen (2000:410–417) and Bloch-Smith (2002).

133　From Mesopotamian texts, we learn that gemstones were thought to be endowed with magical properties (see Goff 1956: 27). Collon argues that the choice of gemstone for a cylinder seal was often dictated by the magical meaning attributed to it (Collon 1993: 100). Precious stones and seals are often found in graves and were stra-

Block argues that the list of stones in Ezek 28:13 highlights the status of the king of Tyre but, at the same time, points back to the image of the king as a signet: "The King of Tyre is not only a beautifully crafted jewelled seal himself; he is adorned with a series of gemstones, many of which were exploited by ancient jewellers in the crafting of signets" (1998: 106). The author may be purposefully using ambiguous language in order to oscillate between the image, the signet, and the referent, the king.[134]

Most scholars link the list of gemstones in Ezek 28:13 to the catalogue of jewels which adorned the high priest's chestpiece of decision making, as recorded in Ex 28:17–19.[135] Yet it is not necessary for us to decide whether the list in Ezek 28:13 is immediately extracted from Ex 28:17–19 or vice versa. The list of stones may belong not only to the cluster of terminology relating to Phoenician craftsmanship and wealth, but also to the "Eden constellation" associated with the mythic sanctuary.[136] The presence of precious stones in Ezek 28:13, Gen 2:12 and Ex 28:17–19 should be attributed to the sacred significance associated with precious stones and should not be used as evidence that any one text is derived from another.

In the MT, gold is tacked onto the list of the three triads of gemstones, showing that the Masoretes viewed the gold as another precious

---

tegically placed around the body during healing rituals (see text cited in Goff 1956: 18).

134 Yet another possibility for the translation of מְסֻכָתֶךָ would be to view the word as deriving from the root נסך, meaning "to pour out". The noun מַסֵּכָה means "molten metal" or "cast image". This translation makes a good deal of sense in the context of the passage, which is full of vocabulary rooted in the semantic field of metalwork and craftsmanship.134 If this is the case, the list of stones may well apply to the king as a signet, or some form of worked figure. Indeed, if we emend תְּכוּנִית to תַּבְנִית , then מַסֵּכָה would be almost synonymous. תַּבְנִית denotes models in Deut 4:16–18; Josh 22:28 and 1 Kgs 16:10. מַסֵּכָה denotes cast idols in Exod 32:4, 8; 34:17.

135 Both lists group the jewels in triads, perhaps suggesting that they were set in rows. The catalogues begin identically and the second triad in Ezekiel is identical to the fourth triad in Exodus. However, one of the triads in the Exodus passage is entirely missing from the list in Ezekiel. This deletion could be an accidental oversight or o-riginal to the text. The LXX includes the missing triad and orders the stones in exact accordance with the Exodus passage.

136 In 2 Chr 3:6, Solomon is said to overlay the temple with אֶבֶן יְקָרָה לְתִפְאָרֶת. The 1 Kgs temple building account does not mention these precious stones. It is likely that the tradition of precious stones in the Solomonic temple had no historical basis. Never-theless, the tradition attests, once again, to a connection between the divine abode and precious stones.

stone in the catalogue. However, it is probably better to read against
the MT, and with the LXX and Syriac, in viewing וְזָהָב as connected to
the following phrase, מְלֶאכֶת תֻּפֶּיךָ וּנְקָבֶיךָ בָּךְ. This phrase is extremely
difficult to translate, as the meaning of the words and their connection
to each other is obscure. The best explanation is provided by Block. It
was common for jewels to be set in gold (or another metal) and Block
(1998: 109–110) contends that the unusual words תֻּפֶּיךָ and נְקָבֶיךָ may
refer to the perforations and mountings in which the gems were fas-
tened. נְקָבֶיךָ, from נקב, meaning "to pierce, bore" probably refers to the
punctures made in the gold, in order to set the jewels. מְלֶאכֶת is more
difficult to translate. Usually meaning "work", it may have the sense
here of "craftsmanship" as in Ex 31:3, 5 and, significantly, in 1 Kgs 7:14,
where it refers to the craftsmanship of Hiram, the Phoenician artisan
who helped construct the temple furniture. Alternatively, the graphi-
cally similar form מלאה/ת can denote the setting of a jewel, as it does in
Ex 28:17 and Ex 29:13. It may be that it is this noun that was originally
meant. תֻּפֶּיךָ is also difficult to explain. It may be derived from the root
תפף meaning "to beat, drum", hence the KJV "thy tabrets". However, it
is difficult to see what sense an allusion to drums would have here.
Block suggests following the Vg, which has *opus decoris tui*, and he
views תֻּפֶּיךָ as stemming from ופי/יפי, "to be beautiful", translating the
whole construct phrase as "the craftsmanship of your beauty".

In verse 14, a new stanza begins, according to Goldberg's poetic
analysis (see Goldberg 1989). With this new stanza, a second image is
used to refer to the king of Tyre: the cherub. The lexeme כְּרוּב can be
said to belong to the "Eden constellation", occurring as it does in both
Genesis 2–3 (in the plural) and Ezek 28:14, 16. The cherub is said to be
"anointed the guardian" (מִמְשַׁח הַסּוֹכֵךְ)[137] and is appointed by Yahweh
"on the holy mountain of God". Like Eden, the holy mountain is the
sanctuary conceived in mythic terms (see Clifford 1984). On the holy
mountain, the cherub "walks up and down" (*hithpael* of הלך) in the
midst of fiery stones. The *hithpael* of הלך is also used in Gen 3:8 (מִתְהַלֵּךְ)
to describe walking in the Garden of Eden and thus may belong to the
"Eden constellation". It is interesting that this verbal form is often used

---

137   The term הַסּוֹכֵךְ refers to the cherub as "the one who shields." The term סכך has
      cultic connotations and is used in connection with the screening of the divine pres-
      ence in Exodus 25 and 1 Kgs 8. The form מִמְשַׁח is a *hapax legomenon* but most likely
      derives from the root משח, meaning "anoint".

when referring to humans who have a close and blameless relationship with Yahweh. Enoch, Noah and Abraham are all said to "walk" with or before God (Gen 5:24; 6:9; 17:1). In Gen 17:1, Abraham is asked to "walk before God" (הִתְהַלֵּךְ) and "be blameless" (תָמִים) and Noah, in Gen 6:9, is described using the same adjective. In Ezek 28:15, the cherub is said to have been blameless (תָמִים) in his ways[138] from the day of his creation. Thus it seems that the cherub's walking has to do with his close and blameless relationship with the divine realm. It follows from this that the fiery stones may also be indicative of this elite position.[139]

Our exegetical discussion in previous sections (§§ 1.2–1.3.1) has shown that one of the primary functions of cherubim is to guard sacred space. They protect the boundary between the holy place of Yahweh and the profane environment of humanity. Cherubim thus not only signify the presence of the deity but also maintain the cosmic order by marking and preserving the boundary between sacred and profane. In this way, they are channels for the divine into the human world. Without them, humanity could not safely draw near the sanctuary of Yahweh and thereby enter into a relationship with him by offering sacrifice (see Launderville 2003: 166).

With this in mind, the comparison of the king of Tyre with a cherub is particularly appropriate. Jeppesen (1991) interprets the cherub image in relation to the previous oracle against Tyre. He sees the placement of the oracle of Ezekiel 28:11–19 after the preceding pericope as deliberate. The previous indictment against Tyre in 28:1–10 proclaims judgement on the prince[140] because of the foreign ruler's presumptuous arrogance in regarding himself as a god/El. In view of this, Jeppesen (1991: 94) argues that, in the following oracle, the author purposefully reminds

---

138 The word דֶּרֶךְ can have a physical sense of "path" rather than the more intangible "way". This fits well with the physical action of "walking" described in Ezek 28:14.

139 That the "fiery stones" of Ezek 28:14 parallel the "precious stones" of the previous stanza is also suggestive of this. Some scholars (e.g. Pope 1955: 101) have argued (on the basis of an analogy with Akkadian parallels) that the "fiery stones" are to be understood as stones that have undergone a smelting process. In this way, they are similar to the precious stones of Ezek 28:13. In the Ugaritic account of the building of Baal's dwelling-place, precious stones are fused together in fire to form the palace and burn for seven days (see *KTU* 1.4 v 32–35 and vi 23–38).

140 The view that מֶלֶךְ actually denotes Tyre's patron deity (Melkart) – as expounded by Dus (see Zimmerli 1983, 90) and Barnett (1969) – is unnecessary. The term מֶלֶךְ is not out of place, מֶלֶךְ is used to refer to Pharaoh in the oracles against Egypt for example (see Ezekiel 31 and 32).

the king of Tyre that he is not a god but merely a cherub.[141] In the oracle of Ezekiel 28:1–10, the king of Tyre boasts that he is a god, who sits
on the throne of a god in the heart of the seas (Ezekiel 28:2). In the following pericope, the poet proclaims that the king is not a god but a
cherub; he does not sit on the throne of a god but protects the throne of
God in his role as a cherub. As a cherub, the king should have preserved the boundaries between divinity and humanity but, with his
exclamation that he is a god in 28:2, the king confuses the divine and
the human.

Viewed in this light, the references to the king of Tyre "profaning
his sanctuaries" (חִלַּלְתָּ מִקְדָּשֶׁיךָ, 28:18) and Yahweh casting the king as a
profane thing (וָאֶחַלֶּלְךָ, 28:16) from the Mountain of God are thus not as
senseless as at first would seem. The king of Tyre is a cherub, whose
function was to guard the sanctuary, which could be imagined as the
Mountain of God and the Garden of Eden. His unrighteousness and
failure to fulfil his function made him corrupt and thus caused him to
pollute the sacred place in which he had been set. Consequently, it was
necessary for Yahweh to expel the cherub from his holy sanctuary.

According to the structure of Ezek 28:11–19 outlined by Goldberg
and Greenberg (1997: 587), verses 14–15 form a separate stanza from
verses 12b–13 and each stanza compares the king to a primary image:
the signet in verses 12b–13, and the cherub in verses 14–15. As Greenberg notes, the second stanza (14–15) repeats elements found in the first
(12b–13). He writes: "The repetitive overlap of second stanzas suggests
that somehow their nonrepeated elements are identical with or equivalent to their correspondents in the first stanzas" (1997: 589). If this is the
case, some kind of connection between the signet and the cherub
should be expected.

In this regard, it is important to remember that the lexeme כְּרוּב
most often refers to a cultic image. It seems reasonable to suggest, therefore, that the description of the cherub in Ezek 28:14–16 may rely (to
some extent) on the traditions concerning cherub images in the sanctuary. If the author did have such iconography in mind when choosing to
compare the king of Tyre to a cherub, this may help us to understand
the connection between the poem's first image, the signet, and the second, the cherub. In his use of both images, the author would be com-

---

141 Launderville (2003: 166); Jeppesen (1991: 94). A similar statement is made in Isaiah
     31:3 with reference to Egypt.

paring the king of Tyre to a skilfully crafted object. The image of the cherub in verse 14 (an iconographic image) then resonates with the image of the previous stanza as both stanzas compare the king of Tyre to a sculpted figure.

A further connection between the cherub and the seal concerns their function. In Gen 3:24, as well as the texts describing their images in the temple and tabernacle, cherubim have a guardian function. This is also suggested by the choice of הַסּוֹכֵךְ to modify כְּרוּב in Ezek 28:14. It is interesting therefore that signets were also thought to have apotropaic properties. Although the chief function of a seal was to be a marker of an individual's identity and authority, Pope (1977: 667) has argued that, in the Song of Songs, there is evidence of "a blending of the functions of the signet with the... phylactery." This occurs in Song 8:6, where the girl wishes to be set as a signet (חֹתָם) on the heart and arm of her lover. Pope argues that the following כִּי clause, "for love is strong as death," suggests that the signet has a guardian function, protecting him from death. He compares the imagery in this verse to that in a Cairo love song, which reads: "I wish I were the seal ring, the guardian of her..." Here, a signet is explicitly said to have a protective function. Moreover, Collon (1993: 113) maintains: "Seals, whatever their type or period, seem to have been used, first and foremost, to mark ownership and, by extension, to protect what was so marked. This protective quality gave the seal an amuletic value and the rightful owner and wearer of a seal was also protected." If seals could possess the more magical powers usually associated with amulets, then the signet in Ezek 28:12 may possess a similar apotropaic function to the cherub.[142] Both images would be particularly appropriate when applied to a king, as the monarch's foremost function was to protect the people.

---

142 Collon (1987: 62) also argues that seals were worn as amulets because of the precious nature of the gemstones used to craft them. The amuletic function of seals is also supported by the fact that seals are often found in graves and also by the fact that prayers are found inscribed on some seals (especially on Kassite cylinder seals). Cylinder seals were superseded by the stamp seal when the alphabetic script and perishable writing material, such as parchment and papyrus, became fashionable. Nevertheless, they were still treasured because of their prophylactic qualities.

§ 1.3.2.5 Summary

It appears, then, that the author of Ezek 28:14 may indeed compare the king of Tyre directly to a cherub. Not only is the Hebrew text a reliable and perhaps superior witness when compared to the LXX, but the very image of the cherub actually turns out to be an ideal figure with which to compare the king of Tyre. The syntax of the Hebrew remains difficult in places and we cannot be sure of the exact meaning of every word. Yet, by looking closely at the semantic fields used in the passage, the enigmatic images that pervade the pericope seem somewhat clearer. We do not need to reconstruct a hypothetical myth in order to explain the enigmatic imagery in this passage. Instead, we should look for answers in the vocabulary employed in the poem itself. The comparison of the king with a beautifully carved and decorated signet, a royal emblem, is an apt one. The primary image, the signet, parallels the second image, the cherub, who is not only a heavenly being but also a plastic image. Both images serve to compare the king of Tyre to a crafted object that has an apotropaic function. Just such beautifully crafted objects were crafted and traded by Phoenician artisans. The choice of the seal and cherub images is apt. The images subvert the significance of the wealth and power which Phoenician craftsmen generated for Tyre and which had become a source of pride in Phoenician national identity.

§ 1.3.3 The Song of David

A cherub, in the singular, appears in the Song of David, a poem which occurs twice in the Hebrew Bible (with orthographical and grammatical variations) in 2 Samuel 22 and Psalm 18. The cherub participates in Yahweh's theophany and is imagined as a vehicle upon which the deity descends to earth from heaven in order to rescue the speaker (2 Sam 22:11 = Ps 18:11).[143] There are several issues which relate to our interpre-

---

143 The original subject of the suffering described in verses 5–7 of Psalm 18 (2 Sam 22:5–7) is uncertain. Some scholars believe that the song does indeed date back to the Davidic period and that there is no reason to doubt that David was the one to whom it referred (see Kuntz 1983: 3). In the final verses of both versions of the song, David and "his seed" are mentioned, but, as this verse is in the third person, there is no real

tation of the cherub in this passage. First, there are textual issues that we need to address, for example the differences between the two Hebrew editions of the poem and the differences between these and the versions, many of which have the plural "cherubim" in both passages. Second, there are issues arising from the poetry. Both 2 Sam 22:11 and Ps 18:11 are scanned as bicola. Consequently, potential parallelism needs to be detected and its implications examined. Third, the fact that the cherub occurs in a theophany may be important. There are numerous theo-phanic poems and visions in the Hebrew Bible but this is the only oc-currence of a cherub playing a role in Yahweh's descent from heaven. We will need to decide what significance this may have.

§ 1.3.3.1 Textual Issues

In the particular verse in which the cherub appears in the poem, there is only one difference between the two Hebrew versions. In the second colon, 2 Sam 22:11 has וַיֵּרָא ('and he was seen') as opposed to וַיֵּדֶא ('and he soared') in Ps 18:11. It is most likely that the Samuel text has come about by means of a scribal error (mistaking *daleth* for *resh*, see Dahood 1965: 107; Cross and Freedman 1953: 24). The verb in Ps 18:11 makes more sense and parallels וַיֵּעַף in the previous colon.[144] Fokkelman (2003: 29) prefers the Samuel text for poetic reasons. He argues that verse 11 forms a strophe with verse 10, which is enhanced by the alliteration, formed from the chain of *wayyered-wayyirkab-wayyērā?*. However, it is preferable to make decisions based on semantic rather than aesthetic grounds. Otherwise, we can never be sure how far we are applying our own schema onto a text which may be less organized than we imagine. In the following verse, our poem describes how the natural elements conceal Yahweh. The notion that Yahweh is "seen" on the wings of the

---

indication that the speaker is David. Only the surrounding narrative in 2 Samuel 22 and the heading of Psalm 18 link the poem to David, although verse 43 suggests that the speaker is royalty. The heading of Psalm 18 and the introduction to the song in 2 Samuel 22 suggest that the song was associated with David's triumph over Saul. Yet, in 2 Samuel 22, the surrounding narrative links the song to the end of David's reign.

144 There is no need to read against the MT, as Stuart (1976: 184) does, and regard וַיֵּעַף as part of the second colon and a variant of וַיֵּדֶא. As Cross and Freedman (1953: 24) have observed, the use of two verbs in the first colon of a bicolon, as in MT of 2 Sam 22:11 and Ps 18:11, is prevalent in both Ugaritic and early Hebrew poetry.

wind[145] would perhaps conflict with the idea that he is hidden. Additionally, the verb דאה only occurs four times in the MT. Thus it is likely that this verb was displaced in 2 Sam 22:11 by the vastly more frequent verb ראה.

More important textual concerns for our investigation relate to the differences between the Hebrew editions of the poem and the Greek and Aramaic versions. The LXX and the Tg both have the plural (χερ ουβιν and כרובין respectively) in place of the MT singular, כְּרוּב.[146] It is important to decide which is the earlier tradition. Geller (1979: 172), following Cross and Freedman (1953:24) in their reconstruction of the original form of the Song of David, argues that the plural, כְּרֻבִים, should be restored. His only basis for this is the plural readings represented by the versions. A slightly more substantiated argument in favour of reading the plural is that propounded by Stuart (1976:184). He contends that the "plural is required by the parallelism and common usage."

Although it is true that a single cherub, appearing on its own, is very unusual in the Hebrew Bible, we can compare the cherub in the MT versions of the Song of David to that in Ezek 28:11–19. The fact that a lone cherub does occur elsewhere suggests that the plural reading in the versions is not necessarily preferable to the singular (see Dahaood 1966: 107). Elsewhere in the MT, a cherub, in the singular, is referred to twenty-five times, although in these instances two or more cherubim appear together. The fact that cherubim normally occur in pairs or groups does not altogether preclude the idea that a cherub could conceivably occur on its own. Thus Stuart's claim that we should read the plural owing to "common usage" should not be followed.

As concerns Stuart's argument on the basis of the parallelism, we need to look closer at the Hebrew text. The second colon of the verse reads, וַיֵּרָא עַל־כַּנְפֵי־רוּחַ. Stuart seems to be arguing that, because we have כַּנְפֵי instead of כָּנָף in the second colon, we should have כְּרֻבִים instead of כְּרוּב in the first colon. Such a suggestion is untenable, however, as the parallelism is actually between the cherub and רוּחַ, and not between the cherub and the wings. רוּחַ is in the singular and a cherub (as

145 Dahood's reading of kanepē rewaḥ, "wings outstretched," instead of kanepē rūaḥ, is rather forced (Dahood 1966: 107). The expression kanepē rūaḥ occurs again in Ps 104:3 and the two nouns are also connected in Hos 4:19 and Zech 5:9.

146 The Vg also has the plural in 2 Sam 22:11 but curiously not in Ps 18:11.

we know from other texts) has two wings.[147] Moreover, it is not necessary to amend a text because a bicolon presents asymmetrical grammar.
Studies of morphologic parallelism have shown that a singular noun
appearing in one colon can be purposefully contrasted with a plural
noun in the parallel colon (see Peterson and Richards 1992: 32).

Furthermore, the plural attested by the versions may not necessarily undermine the singular reading represented by the MT. There are
two reasons why the versions may have the plural here. First, it could
be that the translators took the singular form כְּרוּב to have a collective
sense. Names of creatures are sometimes used collectively and cherubim regularly appear in pairs or groups so this would be an under-
standable assumption for a translator to make. It is unlikely, however,
that כְּרוּב is being used collectively in our verse. There are no other occasions in the Hebrew Bible where the singular is used collectively and
the plural form כְּרוּבִים/כְּרֻבִים is used regularly when referring to more
than one cherub (e.g. Gen 3:24).

A second reason why the versions have the plural may be that, owing to the anthropomorphism involved in Yahweh mounting or riding
a cherub, the translators wanted to tone down the image somehow.
Certainly the Targum has a problem with Yahweh descending to earth
on a cherub. The anthropomorphic "And he rode upon a cherub and
flew" is changed in Ps 18:11 to ואתגלי בגבורתיה על כרובין קלילין, "And he
was revealed in his might upon swift cherubim." In 2 Sam 22:11, it is
the *Shekinah* and not God himself who is revealed. The change from
singular to plural could help to reduce the anthropomorphic overtones
as Yahweh is transported by his celestial host, as in Ezekiel's visions
(Ezek 1 and 10). This may have the further implication that the versions
have been influenced by an emerging *merkᵇᵇ* mysticism. In this view,
Yahweh does not ride on the back of a cherub (as a human would ride a
horse) but is transported in his chariot-throne, drawn by the cherubim.
That our text is not speaking of a cherubim chariot is evinced by the
typical usage of the verb רכב with the preposition עַל elsewhere in the
Hebrew Bible. There are thirty-five instances of this combination of
verb and preposition. Out of these, only eight do not refer to riding

---

147 This is discounting Ezekiel's vision (Ezek 10) where they are said to have four wings.
     Even so, the fact remains that a cherub has more than one wing and the parallelism
     in the verse is between the wind (with its wings mentioned explicitly in the text) and
     the cherub (with its wings implied by the very nature of the creature).

directly upon an animal (mule, horse, camel).[148] The only passage
where the verb and preposition appear with a chariot as the object is in
2 Chr 35:24. The overwhelming use of the verb רכב plus עַל to denote
riding upon a beast is evidence that, in our verse, Yahweh is riding
directly on the back of the cherub. There is no need to posit that this is a
cherubim chariot or throne as some scholars (e.g. Mowinckel 1962: 299)
suggest.

Thus we should not follow Geller, Cross, Freedman and Stuart in
viewing the singular noun כְּרוּב in the MT as a corruption of an original
plural. Indeed, it seems that the translators of the versions would have
had reason to change the singular to the plural, whereas the shift from
plural to singular in the Hebrew is both inexplicable and unlikely, considering that the singular is represented in both Hebrew versions of the
poem.

§ 1.3.3.2 Poetic Issues

Arising from the scansion of our verse as a bicolon is the issue of how
the initial colon (in which the cherub appears) relates to the second
colon. As Clines (1987) has shown, the parallelism inherent within a
Hebrew poetic couplet cannot be described in any more exact terms
than 'A is related to B'. He revises Kugel's (1981) description, which, in
Clines' view (1987: 95), placed too great a weight on repetition, seconding and emphasis.[149] Thus the relationship between the two parts of
our bicolon may be subtle, requiring careful elucidation.

Yet the vast majority of scholars have argued for rigid synonymous
parallelism in our verse, thus equating the cherub with "the wings of
the wind". This has resulted in the completely unfounded notion that
the cherub is a personification of the wind (so Greenberg 1983: 54).
Kuntz (1983: 17) is typical of scholars who place too great an emphasis
on synonymous parallelism in this verse. He argues that the equiva-
lence created by the parallelism of "cherub" and "wings of the wind"
may imply "the personification of the storm-cloud." Because, elsewhere, Yahweh manifests himself in a cloud (Ex 16:10; 40:34–38; Num

---

148 Three of these are used in poetry and refer to Yahweh riding upon clouds or "truth"
     (Ps 45:4). Of the remaining passages, 1 Chr 13:7 refers to the ark riding on a new cart,
     Lev 15:9 denotes riding upon a "saddle" and 2 Kgs 13:6 refers to drawing a bow.

149 In fact, Kugel's argument seems to be very similar to that of Clines.

17:7), in our poem this storm cloud is personified by the cherub, the wings of the wind. Such an argument does not do justice to the artistry of our poem. Indeed, we only have to look to the following verse to find storm clouds mentioned as Yahweh's booth. There is no reason to merge the images in the two verses. Yahweh does appear in a storm theophany but the cherub that he rides on is only a part of this. It is nowhere suggested that the cherub is the wind or the storm.[150]

So, if we cannot equate the cherub with the wind so precisely, how does Yahweh both "mount" and "fly" upon a cherub and yet also "soar" on the wings of the wind? To answer this question, it is helpful to look at the poetry in the following verse. However, before we can do this, we need to clear up the textual problems created by the different editions of the bicolon. The MT of Ps 18:12 reads:

יָשֶׁת חֹשֶׁךְ סִתְרוֹ סְבִיבוֹתָיו סֻכָּתוֹ חֶשְׁכַת־מַיִם עָבֵי שְׁחָקִים

This can be translated tentatively as: "He set up darkness as his hiding-place round about him his booth darkness of waters masses of clouds."[151] The Hebrew of 2 Sam 22:12, however, is rather different. It reads:

וַיָּשֶׁת חֹשֶׁךְ סְבִיבֹתָיו סֻכּוֹת חַשְׁרַת־מַיִם עָבֵי שְׁחָקִים

In this version, the noun סִתְרוֹ "his hiding-place" occurring in Ps 18:12 is not represented. In place of סֻכָּתוֹ "his booth" we have סֻכּוֹת "booths" and, instead of חֶשְׁכַת־מַיִם "darkness of waters", we have חַשְׁרַת־מַיִם, "gathering of waters". We need to clarify which is the earlier version before we can continue to analyze the poetry.

In determining whether it is 2 Sam 22:12 or Ps 18:12 that contains the earlier tradition, the LXX versions of both verses are particularly informative. The LXX of Ps 18:10 (17:12) offers: καὶ ἔθετο σκότος ἀποκρυφὴν αὐτοῦ κύκλῳ αὐτοῦ ἡ σκηνὴ αὐτοῦ σκοτεινὸν ὕδωρ ἐν νεφέλαις ἀέρων. Interestingly, for our purposes, 2 Sam 22:12 is rendered as: καὶ

---

150 Some scholars (e.g. Skinner 1910, 90) view the four "living creatures" in Ezekiel's inaugural vision (and in chapter 10) as representative of "the four winds of heaven" (cf. Ezek 39.9; Jer 49.36; Dan 8.8; 11.4; Zech 2.10; 6.5). Yet, as the creatures in Ezekiel 1 are never explicitly identified as cherubim and recognition of them as such in Ezek 10.15 may be the product of a later hand, we cannot be sure that the cherubim were originally associated with רוח beyond the notion that both appear with Yahweh in a storm theophany.

151 Punctuation has been deliberately omitted. The syntax according to the Masoretic punctuation is awkward and we will refer to this further below.

ἔθετο σκότος ἀποκρυφὴν αὐτοῦ κύκλῳ αὐτοῦ ἡ σκηνὴ αὐτοῦ σκότος ὑδάτων ἐπάχυνεν ἐν νεφέλαις ἀέρος. The differences between the two Greek versions are limited to the second half of the verse. Although the LXX of 2 Sam 22:12 becomes convoluted in the second half of the verse, it matches the Greek as well as the Hebrew of Ps 18:12 in the first half of the verse. The fact that two concealment words are present in both versions of the Greek poem (ἀποκρυφὴν and σκηνὴ) suggests that Ps 18:12 is the more reliable Hebrew version of this verse. The MT of 2 Sam 22:12 must have omitted סִתְרוֹ at a date later than it was translated for the LXX version. The reliability of Ps 18:12 over against 2 Sam 22:12 is again corroborated by the Greek translation of 2 Sam 22:12 in its inclusion of "his tent" (ἡ σκηνὴ αὐτου) in place of "booths" (MT) and "darkness of the waters"[152] in place of "gatherings of waters" (MT).

If this is the case, we can argue that there is a parallelism set up between the darkness as Yahweh's hiding-place and the clouds as his tent. The textual evidence seems to point in this direction. Although the Masoretes have punctuated the text to include the "tent" in the first colon, this may not have been the case originally. The Masoretes could have included it in the first colon because of the long list of predicates in the second colon. In which case, in the original bicolon, יָשֶׁת חֹשֶׁךְ סִתְרוֹ סְבִיבוֹתָיו could constitute part A of the bicolon, with סֻכָּתוֹ חֶשְׁכַת־מַיִם עָבֵי שְׁחָקִים as part B, thus reading against the Masoretic division of the verse. The verb יָשֶׁת would govern both parts of the bicolon. Yahweh sets up darkness as his hiding-place round about him and "dark waters, masses of clouds" as his booth.

In the old Lowthian style of interpreting parallelism, the two parts of the bicolon would have been regarded as "synonymous". In the same way as Ps 18:11 = 2 Sam 22:11, we have two different subjects, "darkness" (in part A) and "dark waters, masses of clouds" (in part B), which are both said to perform similar functions in Yahweh's theohany. Darkness forms his "hiding-place" and "dark waters, masses of clouds" his "booth". In the same way, in Ps 18:11 = 2 Sam 22:11, Yahweh "rides" and "flies" upon a cherub and yet also "soars" on the wings of the wind. The two statements in this verse are neither contradic-

---

152 The fact that the Greek represents differences in forms in the two verses is irrelevant for our purposes. Both versions witness to the notion of "darkness" and "waters". This supports the "darkness of waters" found in Ps 18:22 over against "gatherings of waters" in 2 Sam 22:12.

tory nor synonymous but complementary, just as they are in verse 12. There is no need to apply Western notions of logic to our poem. The parallelism is a method of expression, not reportage. What we have here is a volley of images, which are used to express the enigmatic and impenetrable nature of Yahweh and his salvific acts. The poem is intended to be evocative and not a piece of reportage.

§ 1.3.3.3 The Inclusion of the Cherub in a Storm Theophany

Although we have established that the cherub and the "wings of the wind" are not synonymous but are drawn together for poetic effect, it still remains somewhat surprising that the cherub occurs in a long list of natural elements (verses 7–15). The expression "the wings of the wind" may well be something of a conventional phrase. It occurs again in Ps 104:3 and variants of the expression occur in Hos 4:19 and Zech 5:9. In Ps 104:3, Yahweh is said to travel on the "wings of the wind" and he makes the clouds his chariot. In the following verse, Yahweh makes the winds his "messengers" and fire and flame his "ministers". As we noted in our discussion of Gen 3:24, these natural elements are described almost as animate beings in their role as divine agents. Thus in Ps 18:11 = 2 Sam 22:11, the union of the cherub with the "wings of the wind" may be, in part, due to their role as divine agents. Nevertheless, just because the elements are often thought of as animate to some degree, it certainly does not follow that the cherubim are natural elements or personifications of them.

The inclusion of the cherub (a specific supernatural being) in a list of natural elements, which are typical components of a storm theophany, may also have to do with the wider context of the poem. At the beginning of the theophany section of the prayer, the speaker describes how Yahweh heard his cries of distress "from his temple" (מֵהֵיכָלוֹ, verse 7). The speaker continues by describing the cataclysmic effects of Yahweh's response and descent to earth. An important feature of Yahweh's theophany is the shelter provided by the natural elements (Ps 18:12 = 2 Sam 22:12). The protection offered by the cherubim in Yahweh's temple (1 Kgs 8:6–7) is also needed when he leaves his heavenly abode. The cherub and the natural elements form a moving tabernacle by means of which Yahweh can travel to rescue the speaker, at the same time as preserving his holiness. The fact that the cherub is the only fully-fledged supernatural being other than

Yahweh to appear in our poem is testimony to the important role the
cherubim had in Hebrew tradition of safeguarding Yahweh's holiness.[153]

§ 1.3.3.4 Theophany and Divine Attendants

Although this is the only occasion in the Hebrew Bible that a cherub
features as part of a storm theophany, there are other instances where
divine attendants play an important role in Yahweh's manifestation.
Several scholars have connected the appearance of the cherub in the
Song of David with such instances. Greenberg, for example, describes
Palm 18 = 2 Samuel 22 as "the closest analogue to Ezekiel's private vision" (1983: 53). By "Ezekiel's private vision", Greenberg is referring to
the prophet's inaugural vision in Ezekiel 1. There are several interesting points of comparison to be made between the two passages: the
storm imagery, the presence of winged beings and the uttering of the
divine voice. The winged beings (חַיּוֹת) in Ezekiel 1 are named as cherubim in Ezek 10:15, 20.

Despite the points of comparison between the passages, there remain some obvious differences. In Ezekiel 1, there are four winged
beings which support the throne of Yahweh and, together with four
wheels, carry Yahweh from "the north" (verse 4) to the river Chebar,
where the prophet is situated. An important difference concerns the
spatial dimensions of the theophany. In our poem, there is a notable
vertical descent from Yahweh's heavenly temple down (√ ירד, verse 10)
to the מַיִם רַבִּים (verse 17) where the speaker is stranded. By contrast, in
Ezekiel's vision, the journey is more of a horizontal one, from one geographical location to another. The throne-chariot, equipped with
wheels, is also indicative that a different type of divine journey is imagined.

---

153 The reference to the temple in verse 7 is also significant because, according to Bloch-
Smith (2002: 84), the cultic repertoire (of which the present psalm was likely part)
may well have helped to express the symbolic significance of the temple architecture. Without it, the architecture would not have been so potent. Thus the occurrence
of the cherub in the poem may have served to communicate the significance of the
cherubim iconography in the temple.

Another fundamental difference between the theophany in the song and the theophany of Ezekiel 1 is the function that it serves. In our poem, Yahweh manifests himself in order to save the speaker from his enemies. In this way, the theophany can be characterized as a war theophany. By contrast, the reason that Yahweh manifests himself in Ezekiel 1 is so that he can pronounce judgment on the Israelites (Ezek 2:3). This is why the prophet (Ezekiel) is needed to relay the message to the people. The image of the throne is therefore fundamental to the theophany because it is from his throne that Yahweh makes his judgment. The theophanies of Isaiah 6 and 1 Kings 22 are similar in this regard: both present Yahweh on his throne, surrounded by divine attendants. The prophets Micaiah ben-Imlah and Isaiah perform a similar function to Ezekiel in that they communicate the message of judgment to the people. Consequently, the theophany in Psalm 18 = 2 Samuel 22 and the theophany of Ezekiel 1 are of a fundamentally different nature: one is a war (or salvation) theophany; the other is a throne (or judgment) theophany. Greenberg's claim that our poem is Ezekiel 1's "closest analogue" is thus an oversimplification.

The similarities between the theophanies of Psalm 18 = 2 Samuel 22 and Ezekiel 1 can be explained because the author of Ezekiel 1 has combined motifs of a storm theophany with those of a throne (judgment) theophany (see Allen 1994: 26–32). Thus it remains to be clarified whether the winged beings described in Ezekiel's vision should be identified with the cherub in the storm theophany of our poem or with the divine attendants in throne theophanies (Isaiah 6, 1 Kings 22). At first glance, it is easy to argue that the creatures should be identified with our cherub. In Ezekiel's later vision in chapter 10, the prophet identifies the creatures as cherubim (verses 15, 20). If a biblical author or editor explicitly recognizes the beings as cherubim, then this must be what they are. Yet, chapter 10 is an extremely convoluted text and there is every reason to view verses 10 and 15 as glosses (see Block 1997: 323, n. 53), designed to assimilate the enigmatic creatures of Ezekiel 1 into more familiar Hebrew tradition.

Further evidence that the creatures should not be identified with the cherub in our storm theophany is the verbal link created between them and the seraphim in Isaiah's throne theophany. In Ezek 1:11, the חַיּוֹת have two pairs of wings, one outstretched above them and the other used to cover their bodies. This statement is very similar to that of Isa 6:2, where the seraphim fly with one pair of wings and cover them-

selves with two other pairs. Elsewhere in the Hebrew Bible, the cherubim seem to have only one pair of wings (Ex 25:18–22; 37:7–9; 1
Kg 6:23–28). Furthermore, both the seraphim and the חַיּוֹת are connected
with Yahweh's throne, the seraphim above it and the חַיּוֹת under it. In
this way, they are far removed from the cherub of our storm
theophany, who provides transportation for the deity during battle. In
their transportation of Yahweh, the חַיּוֹת in Ezekiel 1 merely support the
platform upon which the throne rests. In Ps 18:11 = 2 Sam 22:11, Yahweh rides upon a cherub directly and there is no mention of a throne.

§ 1.3.3.5 Summary

Our analysis of Ps 18:11 = 2 Sam 22:11 has shown that we should not
restore a plural in place of the MT's כְּרוּב. Although the occurrence of a
lone cherub is unusual in the MT, there are several important reasons
why the singular should be retained. Scholars who attempt to change
the singular to a plural seem to be reading the text through the lens of
Ezekiel 1 in which four winged beings transport the throne of Yahweh.
Our poem (especially the theophany section) has many archaic features
(see Cross and Freedman 1953: 21) and can be quite confidently dated
to the pre-exilic period.[154] It may be that Ezekiel 1 draws on several
traditional motifs, of which the storm theophany (as occurs in our
poem) is one. Consequently, connecting the cherub in the storm
theophany of our poem with the type of transportation of the deity
found in Ezekiel 1 may well be anachronistic.

Instead, our cherub functions as part of the storm theophany, as
one of the supernatural forces of which Yahweh makes use during battle. Just as the elements (wind, thunder, clouds) become Yahweh's
weapons and shields in combat, so the cherub becomes the deity's
charger. Elsewhere in the Hebrew Bible, the apotropaic function of the
cherubim is alluded to (e.g. 1 Kgs 8:6–7; Gen 3:24). The cherub is thus a
valuable addition to Yahweh's host. The attendance of the cherub during Yahweh's theophany can be compared to the presence of cherubim
at the thresholds of the most sacred space in the temple and tabernacle

---

154 Although it is impossible to date the psalm accurately, the allusions to royalty and
the Davidic line do suggest that the psalm was composed in the pre-exilic period
(see Day 2004: 225–250).

(Ex 25:18–22; 1 Kgs 6:23–35). In both instances, the cherubim safeguard the divine presence.

§ 1.3.4 Ezekiel's Visions

The first reference to a cherub in the book of Ezekiel occurs in the middle of the prophet's vision of Yahweh abandoning his temple (Ezek 8:1–11:25) in Ezek 9:3a:

וּכְבוֹד אֱלֹהֵי יִשְׂרָאֵל נַעֲלָה מֵעַל הַכְּרוּב אֲשֶׁר הָיָה

עָלָיו אֶל מִפְתַּן הַבָּיִת

The verse can be translated provisionally as follows: "And the glory of the god of Israel went up from upon the cherub, upon which it had been, to the *miphtan*[155] of the house." The reference to the cherub seems somewhat unexpected. Given that it occurs with the definite article, it is strange that this cherub has not been mentioned previously. Since this is not the case, we would naturally assume that it is such a permanent feature of the temple that the author[156] imagined his audience would be well acquainted with the cherub to which he refers. Alternatively, some scholars (e.g. Zimmerli 1969a: 237–238) have viewed this verse as part of a literary inclusion, designed to pre-empt the similar statement made in Ezek 10:4. According to this position, 9:3a is a later addition to the text, inserted in order to create a link between the events that take place at the beginning of chapter 9 and those that unfold in chapter 10.

Already then, a preliminary glance at the first reference to כְּרוּב in the book of Ezekiel suggests the possibility of editorial activity. The

---

155 This is usually translated "threshold". Zimmerli (1969a: 233) has highlighted the use of the noun in 1 Sam 5:4. In this passage, the head and hands of the Philistine god, Dagon, are found near the מִפְתָּן. This has caused Zimmerli to argue that the מִפְתָּן must refer to an entrance in the inner part of the temple and postulates (following Koehler-Baumgartner) that the term refers to the podium for the image of the deity. However, the taboo of treading on the מִפְתָּן of Dagon in 1 Sam 5:5 (also see Zeph 1:9–10) does indicate that the מִפְתָּן was close to the ground. There is a possible parallel between the מִפְתָּן and the gate of Dagon in Zeph 1:9–10, which does suggest that the מִפְתָּן was the threshold to the sanctuary. The term has been left transliterated.

156 It is impossible to say how much input the prophet had in the writing down of the text which bears his name. Greenberg (1983) and Block (1997) would argue that Ezekiel is responsible for the original text as well as for later editorial insertions. Zimmerli (1969a), on the other hand, attributes a kernel of the text to Ezekiel and the additions to the prophet's school of disciples.

entire literary unit of 8:1–11:25 is fraught with difficulties, which most
scholars view as evidence of the text's composite nature. These difficulties intensify in the portrayal of the cherubim in chapters 9–11. The
singular כְּרוּב attested in 9:3a occurs again in 10:2, 4, 7 and 14. Yet, elsewhere, the plural occurs. This alternation causes confusion in the development of the narrative and we are left unsure as to what difference,
if any, is implied by the change in number. Furthermore, in 10:15 and
20, the text equates the cherubim in the temple vision with the חַיָּה[157] in
the prophet's inaugural vision of chapter 1. This identification creates
further tasks for the exegete. First, it obliges us to compare the description of the cherubim with the extremely problematic description of the
חַיּוֹת in chapter 1. Second, it compels us to ask why the prophet did not
immediately recognize the חַיּוֹת as cherubim in his initial vision. A yet
further problem concerns the appearance of the cherubim. In 10:14,
four wheels[158] are said to have four faces. Where in 1:10, each of the
four חַיּוֹת have four different faces, here each wheel has a different set of
four identical faces.[159] The first wheel is said to have faces of a cherub.
This seems to imply that a cherub would have a specific type of face.

---

157 It is peculiar that, in both these verses, the cherubim are equated with the singular
     חַיָּה and not the plural חַיּוֹת. Nowhere in the literary unit 8:1–11:25 is the term חַיּוֹת
     used. In the vision of chapter 1, the singular is used once to refer to the plural crea-
     tures in a bizarre expression, עַל־רָאשֵׁי הַחַיָּה (Ezek 1:22). The singular חַיָּה has proba-
     bly crept into the text under the influence of the expression רוּחַ הַחַיָּה, "wind/spirit of
     life", which occurs in the previous two verses (cf. Block 1997: 100, n. 71). This is con-
     trary to the opinion of some scholars (e.g. Zimmerli 1969a: 7; Greenberg 1983: 48)
     who take the singular in 1:20–22 as a collective, or a reference to the whole phe-
     nomenon as a חַיָּה. Certainly this is how the author/editor of chapter 10 has under-
     stood it. The LXX and the Vg both corroborate the interpretation "wind/spirit of life"
     in 1:20–21. Our interpretation of the verse could be viewed as evidence that the au-
     thor /editor of chapter 10 is not the same as the author of chapter 1.
158 The incongruous description of wheels with faces and other body parts (10:12) has
     been explained by the surreal nature of the visionary experience. Yet it may be that
     the text is in disarray and that the anatomical features were originally applied to the
     cherubim (Block 1997: 324). Another explanation, propounded by Halperin (1988:
     45–47), views the entire section of 10:9–17 as a midrashic insertion designed to turn
     the "wheels" into angels. In 10:10, the four wheels are said to be alike in appearance,
     which seems to contradict the idea that they had different sets of faces (10:14).
159 This is the basic sense of verse 14. However, Dijkstra (1986: 74) argues that the nu-
     merals refer to the faces and not the wheels. If this is the case, the description is simi-
     lar to that in 1:10 and each wheel has four different faces. The order of the faces is
     different, however, and cherubic faces (whatever they may be) feature instead of bo-
     vine.

Yet, if the cherubim = חַיּוֹת equation is taken literally, then we would expect four faces (human, lion, bull, eagle – 1:10) to be a feature of cherubim. Thus one of the wheels would have four faces, each one being made up of a further four faces. The description is hard to visualize. Additionally, the physical attributes of the cherubim in this passage contrast with how they are depicted elsewhere in the Hebrew Bible. Each cherub is said to have four faces and four wings with hands (or a hand) underneath (Ezek 10:8, 21). This seems to conflict with the portrayal of cherubim in the Song of David, 1 Kings and Exodus, where they appear to be quadrupeds with one face and one set of wings (Ps 18:11 = 2 Sam 22:11; Ex 25:18–22; 37:7–9; 1 Kgs 6:23–28). There have been various attempts to make sense of the depiction of the cherubim in this passage and it is helpful to review some of the most prominent expositions before embarking upon our own exegesis of the text.

§ 1.3.4.1 Earlier Exegesis

At first glance, the apparent orderliness of the book of Ezekiel, with its clearly delineated and dated oracles, together with its first person narrative, would suggest that the final form of the text should be attributed entirely to the hand of the prophet. However, in the early twentieth century, the onset of rigorous redaction criticism resulted in the prophet being denied authorship of a large proportion of the book that bears his name (cf. Hölscher 1924; Irwin 1943). The three principal commentators on Ezekiel of the last fifty years (Zimmerli 1969a; Greenberg 1983; Block 1997) have taken a stance somewhere in between these two extremes. Their interpretation of the cherubim in chapters 9–11 depends to a large extent on the degree of editorial activity they see underlying the text and the value they ascribe the final form.

Zimmerli draws upon literary evidence in order to argue that the equation of the cherubim with the חַיּוֹת in 10:15, 20 was not part of the original text. He maintains that "die Nachdrücklichkeit der Unterstreichung läßt vermuten, daß hier Dinge nachträglich zusammengebracht sind, die zunächst je ihr eigenes Leben hatten" (Zimmerli 1969a: 203). For Zimmerli, literary peculiarities (such as repetition, emphasis and disorderly arrangement) are evidence that the vision of Ezek 8:1–11:25 is the work of a long editorial process, carried out predominantly by Ezekiel's disciples.[160] The input of the disciples is nowhere more obvious than in chapter 10, the passage in which the cherubim play the most significant role. According to Zimmerli, Ezekiel 10 is predominantly the result of a large scribal insertion, in accordance with chapter 1. This insertion was not lifted word for word, but restructured and modified in order to suit its current placement and smooth out some of the grammatical and hermeneutical problems of the original vision.

Zimmerli retains only fragments of 10:2, 3, 4, 7, 18 and 19 as part of the original base text. His textual surgery means that there is very little information about the cherubim left for us to draw upon. Yet a cherub subtext does remain. He argues: "Die Analyse hatte ergeben, daß in ihr Aussagen, die von einem einzelnen Keruben reden, nachträglich von der breiten Füller der Aussagen, die von einer Mehrheit von Keruben in der Art der Lebewesen von Ez 1 reden, überlagert sind" (Zimmerli 1969a: 231). Thus the subtext originally spoke of only one cherub (10:2, 4, 7), and the subsequent cherubim layer, inspired by Ezekiel 1, has been superimposed on top of this base text.

The original cherub, for Zimmerli (1969a: 231), was one of the two golden statues placed at either end of the ark (Ex 25:18–22). He argues that 1 Kgs 8:8 indicates that the ark was placed lengthways in the Holy of Holies with the narrow end opposite the exit. This would mean that someone entering the Holy of Holies would, at first, face only one cherub, and the pair would not be immediately in view. Thus, just as in Ezek 9:2 the "upper door" and the "bronze altar" refer to real architectural features within the temple, so too the cherub in 10:2 denotes the actual statue within the Holy of Holies, and not the חַיּוֹת inspired cherubim of 10:14–16. Yet this cherub was not regarded by the prophet merely as the work of an artisan, rather it was understood as a living reality, able to hand coal to the man in linen in verse 7.

Zimmerli accounts for the identification of the cherubim as the חַיָּה by appealing to the overarching theology of the book of Ezekiel, which

160   Ezekiel is mentioned several times as sitting in his house, with the elders and others 'sitting before' him in order to hear the word of Yahweh (Ezek 8:1; 14:1; 20:1; 33:30–33). Zimmerli (2003: 77) views these meetings as a feature of pre-literary prophecy. Elisha, for example, is described in strikingly similar terms in 2 Kgs 4:38; 6:1; 32. Consequently, he argues, Ezekiel had the same type of 'prophetic school' as did Elisha and it was members of this prophetic school who compiled and organized his prophetic teaching, which we now have in the form of the book of Ezekiel. The prophetic activity of Ezekiel bears many similarities to pre-literary prophetic activity (cf. Zimmerli 2003: 77–78).

the prophet's disciples wished to emphasize. He argues that the disciples found it illogical that Yahweh had appeared to Ezekiel by the river Chebar in chapter 1, when he does not leave the Jerusalem temple until chapter 11 (Zimmerli 1969a: 237). Accordingly, the disciples wanted to harmonize the vision of Ezek 8:1–11:25 with the prophet's inaugural vision in chapter 1. In editing the vision of 8:1–11:25 to bring it into line with chapter 1, the apparent disorder in the course of the narrative is smoothed over. Yahweh appears to the prophet in Babylon and then travels back to the temple in Jerusalem in order to command the destruction of the city and formally abandon it. The cherub in the original text is then incorporated into the new narrative arrangement by interpreting it as one of the חַיּוֹת who transported the throne of Yahweh in Ezekiel's initial vision. This would then have the further purpose of clarifying exactly what the חַיּוֹת were, by assimilating them into more familiar Hebrew tradition. Since both cherubim and חַיּוֹת are hybrid supernatural beings, with a close connection to Yahweh, it was easy for Ezekiel's disciples to make this connection.

The type of methodological approach employed by Zimmerli is strongly criticized by Greenberg in his commentary and elsewhere (1983: 18–27; 1986: 123–135). He argues that the literary features, which Zimmerli viewed as evidence of editorial elaboration, are actually part of the prophet's rhetorical style. The notion that repetition, thematic inconsistency and structural disorder are indications of inauthentic material is the upshot of modern critical prejudices (Greenberg 1983: 20). Thus Greenberg reverts to a more conservative view of the text and takes a more 'holistic' stance. Yet he (Greenberg 1983: 196, 199) does admit to observing signs of editorial work, especially in our passage (Ezek 8:1–11:25).

In dealing with the identification of the cherubim as the חַיָּה in 10:15, 20, Greenberg fluctuates in his methodology. Concerning verse 20, Greenberg employs his holistic approach. However, in his treatment of verse 15, Greenberg utilizes a similar method to that which he criticizes in the introduction to his commentary. He argues that verse 15 is an "awkward anticipation" of verse 20 and is thus a fragment copied in at the wrong place (Greenberg 1983: 183). Thus he, like Zimmerli, finds something wrong with the repeated identification of the cherubim as the חַיָּה. But where Zimmerli sees this unnecessary emphasis as evidence that the whole cherubim = חַיּוֹת equation is a later addition to the text, Greenberg merely sees verse 15 as a later addition. As verse 20 is original to the text, he argues, the identification of the cherubim as the חַיָּה in verse 20 must be understood in the light of Ezekiel 1. Thus he sees the later vision as a genuine continuation from the initial one.

The fact that the prophet does not recognize the חַיּוֹת immediately is of no surprise to Greenberg. He appeals to the biblical record as a whole, which nowhere documents a prophetic vision of a cherub. If no one had ever seen a cherub, then we cannot expect Ezekiel to know what one would look like. According to Greenberg, the people of the ancient Near East were conscious that their pictorial representations of gods were inadequate expressions of the supernatural reality. He compares Ezekiel's failure to recognize the חַיּוֹת to the Sumerian Gudea's ignorance of the god Ningirsu, who appears to him in a dream. Ningirsu must have been depicted in iconography and yet it is left up to a goddess to inform Gudea of the apparition's identity (Greenberg 1983: 184). For Greenberg, this comparison shows that we should not view the identification of the cherubim in verse 20 as a later addition because we should not expect Ezekiel immediately to recognize a cherub.

Concerning the strange alternation from singular to plural in Ezekiel 9–11, Greenberg again fluctuates in his methodology. In his treatment of 10:2a, Greenberg (1983:181) appeals to text critical methods. Since the subsequent references to the event described in 10:2 refer to the cherubim in the plural (2b, 3a, 6, 7), he views the singular in 10:2a as an error by haplography, where the final *ym* has been omitted owing to the similarity of the first two letters of the next word *wml*? He corroborates this by appealing to the versions, which have the plural. However, in his handling of the singular in 9:3, 10:4 and 7, Greenberg again takes a more holistic stance. In these verses,[161] the LXX again has the plural.[162] Yet Greenberg ignores the versions in his analysis of these verses. Instead, he understands the singulars in 9:3 and 10:4 to be referring to the two golden cherubim of the Holy of Holies (1 Kgs 8:7–11). The use of the singular is because the two statues form a pair, whereas

---

161 In verse 7, the LXX does not name the subject at all. Nowhere in the LXX of Ezekiel 9–11 is the singular כְּרוּב of the MT represented as χερουβ. Greenberg does not deal with the differences between the MT and LXX renderings of verse 7.

162 One could also argue that 10:18, 19; 11:22 are subsequent references to the events described in 9:3, 10:4 and these verses have the plural.

the plural (elsewhere in the passage) refers to "two pair" (Greenberg 1983:199), i.e. the חַיּוֹת cherubim under the mobile throne.[163]

Thus, for Greenberg, there are two types of cherubim in Ezekiel 9–11, the real and the artificial. The real cherubim are equated with the חַיָּה and are referred to using the plural כְּרוּבִים. The artificial cherubim are denoted by means of the singular. According to this interpretation, the sequence of the narrative emerges as follows: the כְּבוֹד־יְהֹוָה descends from the cherubim statues in 9:3, 10:4[164] and ascends onto the throne above the real cherubim in order to leave the temple (10:18, 19; 11:22).

In the most recent major commentary on Ezekiel, Block (1997) makes use of a similar type of methodology to that advanced by Greenberg. He criticises scholars such as Zimmerli who pay, in his view, "inordinate attention… to isolating… layers, at the expense of interpreting each statement in the light of its current context" (Block 1997: 314). The textual difficulties that Zimmerli views as evidence of editorial work are viewed by Block as an important feature of the genre of prophetic vision (1988: 432). He follows Greenberg (1983: 200) in viewing the repetitive and confused imagery as evidence of the awe which was felt by the prophet at the time of writing the passage. The prophet was so overwhelmed by the experience that lucidity in conveying the incident was impossible.

With respect to the confusion over singular and plural, Block does not provide a wholly persuasive solution. Concerning 9:3a, he argues that the singular הַכְּרוּב "need not be considered erroneous" (Block 1997: 305). He cites the singular suffix on עָלָיו (9:3) and the singular forms in chapter 10 to corroborate this. In his textual notes to 9:3a, he argues that the singular should be viewed as a collective as also in 10:4 (Block 1997: 300, n. 5). Like Greenberg, he sees the use of the singular as a way for the author to distinguish this figure from the cherubim in chapter 10 (1997: 305). However, in his textual notes to 10:2 (1997: 317:

---

163 To accept Greenberg's argument, we must understand Ezekiel to have a heightened sense of perception, whereby he can see into the Holy of Holies and out into the court from his position in the inner court (8:16). Yet this seems to conflict with the way in which Ezekiel is led around the temple by Yahweh in order to see each individual abomination.

164 The repetition remains odd and Greenberg does not fully explain why it is necessary. Slightly different vocabulary is employed, which may suggest two different authors, though Greenberg (1983: 199) views this as deliberate variation.

n. 21), he suggests reading the plural in this verse and in 10:4, following the versions. Thus Block's argument seems to be quite inconsistent. In his discussion of chapter 9, he hints at a difference implied by the use of the singular as opposed to the plural, and yet in his discussion of chapter 10 he merely changes the singulars in 10:2 and 4 to plurals, in order to smooth out the tensions in the narrative.

Concerning the cherubim = חַיָּה identification in 10:15, 20, Block again follows Greenberg in viewing 10:15 as a later addition to the text, but verse 20 as original. Yet he maintains (contrary to Greenberg 1983: 183) that the wording is too different from that of verse 20 to view it as a copyist's error. Instead, he suggests that 10:15 is the result of a marginal gloss which was intentionally inserted into the text. As the gloss is in the first person, the editor may have been the prophet Ezekiel himself (Block 1997: 323, n. 53).[165] Since the cherubim = חַיָּה equation in 10:20 was part of the original text, and not a later explanatory gloss, Block then has the task of explaining why the prophet did not recognize the creatures as cherubim in his initial vision. He views the location of the prophet as integral to the reason why the connection was not made earlier. Descended from a priestly line (Ezek 1:3), Ezekiel would have been familiar with cherubim as temple adornments. He would not have expected to have a vision of cherubim far away in Babylon. Thus he fails to make the connection until he is transported back to the Jerusalem temple in his later vision (8:1–11:25) where he sees them a second time. The difference between the cherubim in Ezekiel's visions and those described elsewhere in the Hebrew Bible also contributed to the prophet's failure to comprehend the exact nature of the חַיּוֹת.[166]

§ 1.3.4.2 Critique

The attempts by Zimmerli, Greenberg and Block to make sense of the portrayal of the cherubim in Ezekiel 9–11 stem from two paradigmatic approaches to reading the text. Whereas Zimmerli reads the text diachronically (attempting to engage with the text's historical develop-

---

165 However, it is not impossible for an editor to include statements in the first person.

166 Block does not give an explicit reason for the difference between the cherubim in Ezekiel 10 and those depicted elsewhere in the Hebrew Bible. He does imply that there was some difference between the real heavenly cherubim and the temple statuary (1997: 139). Thus his position may be similar to Greenberg's.

ment), Greenberg and Block read it synchronically (attempting to make sense of the text as it stands in its current arrangement). Although Greenberg and Block criticize the type of method employed by Zimmerli, neither a synchronic nor a diachronic approach should be regarded as inadequate from the outset (see Tuell 2004: 241).[167] Nevertheless, the arguments of the three commentators require some critique.

Block criticizes Zimmerli's handling of chapter 10 (1997: 314, n. 3) for devoting disproportionate space to the "authentic" Ezekiel material (four columns) which, according to his treatment, only comprises of fragments. His handling of the later material only takes up three columns and yet deals with eighteen verses. Thus it seems that Zimmerli attributes much greater value to the original material than to the editorial. This is certainly a flaw within Zimmerli's commentary. Although he attempts to find reasons for the editorial and does not arbitrarily remove material merely because it is problematic, he does tend to view the later additions in a negative light. He argues that the editors could not grasp the tension between Yahweh appearing to the prophet in Babylon and yet at the same time dwelling in the Jerusalem temple (Zimmerli 1969a: 237). Ezekiel's disciples are thus portrayed in a somewhat pejorative light, unable to comprehend the true complexity of the prophet's message.

Despite Zimmerli's partiality towards the original material, he does at least attempt to explain the composite nature of chapter 10. Both Greenberg and Block admit that the text is in disarray (Greenberg 1983: 196, 199; Block 1997: 314), yet neither one is particularly willing to account for its inherent problems. They seem satisfied just to admit that there are signs of editorial activity without wishing to explain how and why this has occurred.

Block's reasoning that some of the textual difficulties stem from the genre of the passage as a prophetic vision is extremely tenuous. Although such an explanation may be given for the grammatical problems and the analogical vocabulary in chapter 1 (see Block 1988: 428–431), chapter 10 irons out these irregularities and drops the analogical language used in the initial vision. Moreover, that such confusion as we

---

167 Frolov (2004: 27–36), in his study of 1 Samuel 1–8, provides an excellent summary of the diachronic versus synchronic debate. He argues (2004: 29), "Diachronic and synchronic frames of reference are thus perfectly valid; there is no theoretical warrant whatsoever to eschew one of them or assign it an inferior status vis-à-vis the alternative approach."

find in chapter 10 should be regarded as a generic characteristic of divine visions is nowhere supported elsewhere in the Hebrew Bible. In Isaiah 6, the text is entirely problem free. So too, Micaiah's account of his vision of the divine council in 1 Kings 22 displays no such disarray. Although the Revelation of John does exhibit signs of disorder (Block 1988: 437), the text is heavily dependent on Ezekiel 1. Thus the idea that textual difficulties are a generic feature of a divine vision is untenable. Certainly, in chapter 10, the type of confusion (structural rather than grammatical) cannot be linked to the prophet's emotion at the time of writing. We must find alternative reasons to account for these problems and not just explain them away as a consequence of Ezekiel's psychological state.

Greenberg's interpretation, which is largely followed by Block, ties the difficulties in Ezekiel 10 to the tension in the narrative between the heavenly cherubim and the cherubim statues. Thus Ezekiel only recognizes the cherubim as the חַיָּה in 10:20 and not earlier because the creatures did not look like the temple statues. Yet, if we are to accept this, it still remains surprising that it is not until verse 20 that the connection is made. The prophet has spent nineteen verses describing the cherubim before realizing that they were the חַיָּה.

Furthermore, if we are to accept Greenberg's analysis we must, to some degree, believe that the text of Ezekiel accurately describes visions of Yahweh that the prophet really experienced. Indeed, in his analysis of 10:13, Greenberg (1983: 182) argues that the prophet must have actually heard a voice that renamed the wheels as the גַּלְגַּל because he would have had no reason to change the terms himself. Thus Greenberg tends to view the text of Ezekiel as a verbatim record of the prophet's words, designed to report accurately his visionary experience. In which case, any theological message within the text must be attributed to Yahweh and not to Ezekiel (or the writer) as an author. Thus the author's theological agenda would not be found within the text. Such a view does not do justice to Ezekiel (or the writer) as an author, particularly considering the political climate within which he was active.

§ 1.3.4.3 The Cherubim in Ezekiel 9–11

A closer look at the text is now required in order to highlight the key problems concerning the interpretation of the cherubim in this passage. The text will be read from *both* a diachronic *and* a synchronic perspective in order that the cherubim may be understood in terms of the text's possible historical development as well as in terms of its current arrangement.[168] Our exegesis will follow a four step procedure. First, we will attempt a close reading of the Hebrew. This will mean that inconsistencies and contradictions within the extant Hebrew text will be underscored. Following this close reading, we will attempt to engage with diachronic issues. We will investigate the inconsistencies, highlighted by our close reading, with regard to possible evidence of editorial activity. Possible expansions and the reasons for them will be proposed. The third stage of the exegesis will attempt to postulate a base narrative and interpret the cherubim according to this. Finally, a synchronic reading will attempt to make sense of the cherubim in their current literary context.

Before we begin, it is important to note that a definitive solution to the problems surrounding the interpretation of the cherubim in Ezekiel 9–11 may be unobtainable. In an article on Ezekiel's inaugural vision, Wilson (1984: 123) notes: "To date no single reconstruction has proven to be totally convincing." The same is true of Ezek 8:1–11:25. If so many exegetes have tried and failed to explain the inconsistencies within the passage, then we may have to accept that the current state of the text is such that we will never be completely confident of its exact sense (whether this be its original meaning or that of its final form). Certainly, we will never be sure as to precisely which elements of the current passage constituted the "Urtext" of Ezek 8:1–11:25, even though there are clues within the text which give grounds for speculation. Nevertheless, a close reading of the text and a thorough contemplation of its inconsistencies will assist our interpretation of the cherubim in this passage.

---

168 This is in accordance with Barr's statement concerning the text of Gen 2–3 that "an approach through the 'final text' does not negate, but positively demands and benefits from, an attention to the previous stages out of which the final text has been derived" (Barr 1992: 59).

§ 1.3.4.3.1 A Close Reading

As stated at the beginning of our discussion on this passage, the first reference to "the cherub" in 9:3a is somewhat surprising as it has not been mentioned previously. Indeed, the whole of 9:3a and its reference to the movement of the כָּבוֹד seems to interrupt the natural progression of the surrounding narrative, which is centred on the six men and Yahweh's instructions to them. Nevertheless, that we should find a cherub in the Jerusalem temple is unremarkable, given the descriptions of cherubim iconography elsewhere (1 Kings 6–8; 1 Chr 28:18; 2 Chronicles 3–5; Ezek 41:18–25). At this point in the narrative, Ezekiel is standing in the inner court of the temple, at the entrance to the הֵיכָל, observing the twenty-five apostates pray to the sun. Presumably, the כָּבוֹד[169] enters this area with the prophet, as he brings (8:16) him into the precinct and speaks to him regarding the activities there (8:17–18). In 9:2, the prophet describes the entrance of six men from the upper gate, which faces north. They enter (וַיָּבֹאוּ) and stand beside the bronze altar. There is a degree of difficulty concerning the scope of the prophet's vision. The fact that Ezekiel, from his standpoint in the inner court, can see the men entering from the direction of the upper gate, facing north, suggests that the prophet has a heightened sense of perception. This may be due to the nature of his visionary experience whereby he has an overview of the entire temple complex. Yet this seems to be contrary to the way in which the כָּבוֹד leads him through the temple in order to show him the different abominations taking place therein.

The six men stand by the bronze altar, which was presumably in the inner court (1 Kgs 8:64; 2 Chr 4:1; 7:7).[170] If the כָּבוֹד is present with

---

169 The fiery human figure, who seems to be identified as the כְּבוֹד־יְהוָה in Ezek 1:28 and who appears to the prophet and takes him to Jerusalem in 8:2–3, is somewhat disassociated from the כְּבוֹד אֱלֹהֵי יִשְׂרָאֵל in 8:4. This verse states that the כָּבוֹד appeared again, just as it had in the valley (Ezek 3:23). Yet, if it is to be equated with the fiery human (as Ezek 1:28 implies), then it has appeared to Ezekiel more recently, in Babylon (8:2–3), and (if the כָּבוֹד is responsible for Ezekiel's movement as 8:3 may suggest) would have been with him from the beginning of the journey. Thus 8:4 would be slightly unnecessary. Certainly, there seems to be some confusion in Ezekiel 1–11 as to whether the כָּבוֹד is the fiery human figure (Ezek 1:26–27, 8:2–3) or something more intangible.

170 This would be in keeping with Haran's principle of material gradation (1978: 158–159), whereby any cultic object for use within the הֵיכָל would be made of gold,

Ezekiel and the six men in the inner court, then we would not expect the cherub referred to in 9:3 to be one of the cherubim statues in the *debhir* (1 Kgs 6:23–28). These would have been out of view of the human attendants.[171] However, 1 Kgs 8:8 suggests that the ends of the poles of the ark could be seen from the הֵיכָל. As Ezekiel is standing at the entrance of the הֵיכָל, it may be that one of the cherubim figures on the end of the ark is meant (Ex 25:18–20).[172] Alternatively, the text may be referring to a cherub decorating the inner court. 1 Kgs 6:34–35 states that there were cherubim carved on the doors of the הֵיכָל. The ten stands (embellished with cherubim) were probably also in the inner court (1 Kgs 7:27–39). Thus it is possible that the כָּבוֹד is supposed to be resting on one of these cherub adornments.

It is the כָּבוֹד אֱלֹהֵי יִשְׂרָאֵל and not the כְּבוֹד־יהוה that is mentioned in 9:3a. This is the second time that this epithet is used.[173] Earlier in the book, it is the latter that is employed. There is no apparent distinction implied by the different phrases and both refer to the glory of the divine presence, which appears to the prophet. The כָּבוֹד is said to go up from upon the cherub to the מִפְתָּן of the house. מֵעַל is usually taken to be partitive rather than having the meaning 'above' (e.g. Ps 50:4). The idea is then that the כָּבוֹד leaves the cherub upon which it had been (עָלָיו אֲשֶׁר הָיָה). The 3ms pronoun on עָלָיו is thus usually regarded as resumptive.

The exact location of the מִפְתַּן הַבַּיִת is difficult to ascertain. It could be either the threshold of the entrance to the הֵיכָל or the threshold of the entrance to the inner court. That the הֵיכָל could be denoted by הַבַּיִת is perhaps suggested by 9:6, where the elders (who are initially described as being in the inner court in 8:16) are said to be in front of the house (לִפְנֵי הַבַּיִת). Given the current context, the entrance to the הֵיכָל is probably supposed. The other occurrences of the term מִפְתָּן in the Hebrew Bible suggest that it had an important cultic significance, perhaps in association with the manifestation of the deity. Indeed, the parody of

---

whereas any for use within the court would have been made of the less valuable material, bronze or copper.

171 Again, it is possible to argue that Ezekiel has somewhat supernatural powers of observation, owing to his visionary experience. In which case, the כָּבוֹד may be resting on a cherub in the Holy of Holies.

172 Such an interpretation would mean that the description of the Exodus tabernacle (with its cherubim statues) *either* reflects accurately what the ark actually looked like *or* that the Exodus tradition was already known to Ezekiel.

173 The first reference is in Ezek 8:4. We noted earlier (note 13) that this verse creates confusion as to the identity of the fiery figure in 8:2.

the god Dagon and the taboo of walking on his מִפְתָּן (1 Sam 5:4–5; Zeph 1:9–10) may be subverting a common idea that this is where the deity appears. In Ezek 46:2, the prince is said to bow down to/upon the מִפְתָּן and, in Ezek 47:1, the מִפְתָּן is the source of the life-giving waters.

After this somewhat intrusive reference to the movement of the כָּבוֹד, a cherub is not mentioned again for the rest of the chapter. Although the movement of the כָּבוֹד is pivotal for understanding the theology expressed in the wider narrative, it is difficult to see what function 9:3a serves. The arrival of the כָּבוֹד is noted in 8:4 and it seems to travel around the temple complex with Ezekiel (as is implied by the hiphil וַיָּבֵא in 8:7, 14, 16). The gradual abandoning of the temple is an important theological motif in 8:1–11:25, yet it is difficult to isolate when this movement from inside to outside begins. Ezekiel's movements are in the opposite direction as he is gradually brought further and further into the temple complex (until 11:1). It may be that, in 9:3a, we have the first stage of the departure of the כָּבוֹד. Yet the intrusive nature of the statement in the surrounding narrative, together with the very similar movement described in 10:4, complicates the development of this important theme.

The remainder of chapter 9 describes Yahweh's command to the six men, its completion and Ezekiel's response. The chapter ends with the man in linen reporting to Yahweh that his command has been carried out (9:11). Yahweh's next instruction to the man (10:2) is interrupted by the second reference to cherubim in the book of Ezekiel (this time plural, not singular) in 10:1. The verse reads:

וָאֶרְאֶה וְהִנֵּה אֶל־הָרָקִיעַ אֲשֶׁר עַל־רֹאשׁ הַכְּרֻבִים

כְּאֶבֶן סַפִּיר כְּמַרְאֵה דְּמוּת כִּסֵּא נִרְאָה עֲלֵיהֶם

A tentative translation is as follows: "And I looked and behold: above the platform, that was over the head of the cherubim, as a stone of sapphire, as the appearance of the likeness of a throne appeared above them." As in 9:3a, there is a problem concerning substantives occurring with the definite article, which have not been mentioned previously: הָרָקִיעַ and הַכְּרֻבִים. Notably, cherubim (this time in the plural) seem to encroach into the surrounding narrative for a second time. The רָקִיעַ ('platform') is said to be over the head (singular) of the cherubim. The setting of the narrative at this point is the same as that of 9:3a and thus we may still attribute the occurrence of cherubim to the temple location. However, a רָקִיעַ is nowhere listed as a feature of temple furniture and we are left confused as to its form and function. The only רָקִיעַ to

have been mentioned previously in the book of Ezekiel is that occurring
in Ezek 1:22–26, but we have heard nothing of it since chapter 1. As we
continue reading the verse, however, we begin to detect a noticeable
difference in style concerning the reportage of the prophet. Where, in
chapters 8–9, the prophet's vision is concerned predominantly with
earthly matters,[174] in chapter 10, the prophet seems to be witnessing a
more celestial apparition. Analogical vocabulary (כְּאֶבֶן סַפִּיר כְּמַרְאֵה דְּמוּת)
is suggestive of the otherworldliness of the vision as the prophet cannot
describe precisely what he sees. As he looks, a throne appears on the
platform above the head of the cherubim. Again, that כְּרֻבִים occurs with
the definite article is odd. There is no reference to these cherubim earlier
in the narrative and, as this verse seems to be describing more celestial
realities, we cannot so readily attribute them to the temple iconography.

10:2 resumes the narrative of chapter 9. Yahweh again commands
the man in linen. In this verse, the confusion of number concerning the
cherubim is particularly problematic. Yahweh instructs the man to
enter between the גַּלְגַּל, to beneath the cherub, in order to fill his hands
with coals of fire from between the cherubim and scatter them over the
city. Again, we have a problem with the definite article on לַגַּלְגַּל. Although this may be purely a feature of the vocalized text, we have the
same determination used with ל three times in the MT of this verse.
What is meant by גַּלְגַּל in this context is difficult to determine. There are
nine occurrences of the noun in the Hebrew Bible, three of which refer
to a whirlwind or sandstorm (Ps 77:19; 83:14; Isa 17:13). The idea of a
sandstorm may be connected partially to the term גַּל, which is used to
refer to a heap of stones. The verb גָּלַל has the sense of 'rolling'. The
other six occurrences of גַּלְגַּל refer to a wheel (as part of war chariot in
Isa 5:28; 28:28; Jer 47:3; Ezek 23:24; 26:10 or a well's mechanism Eccl
12:6). The term only occurs once in the singular with the definite article
in Eccl 12:6. In this instance, the use of the definite article is likely because of the proverbial nature of the wisdom teaching. The term גַּלְגָּל
appears frequently in the Hebrew Bible with the definite article to refer
to a place, Gilgal. As five different places are called Gilgal in the Hebrew Bible, it may be that the term originally denoted any sanctuary
which contained a sacred stone circle or heap.

---

174 Although it is true that the six men (and the man in linen) who carry out Yahweh's
slaughter are, to some degree, enigmatic, there is no implication that they are divine.

An educated guess at the meaning of לַגַּלְגַּל then depends to some extent on whether we see the celestial tone of the previous verse as persisting in 10:2. Because of the narrative link with 9:11, we may presume that the command refers to an earthly object and thus view the גַּלְגַּל as a cultic object of some sort, perhaps a heap of sacred stones or coals (given that these are what the man is asked to obtain). Alternatively, we may understand the term in relation to the celestial vision of 10:1. רָקִיעַ, in the previous verse, is often used to allude to the sky (e.g. in Genesis 1; Ps 19:2). If then the celestial imagery is sustained in verse 2, the גַּלְגַּל may refer to a whirlwind (connected with a storm theophany of Yahweh in Ps 77:19). The form of the preposition בֵּינוֹת (for בֵּין), here occurring with אֶל, is used exclusively in Ezekiel. The sense seems to be that the man is to enter into the space between the גַּלְגַּל. Following this reading, the גַּלְגַּל should probably be taken as a collective.

The place that the man is commanded to enter is further substantiated by the phrase אֶל־תַּחַת לַכְּרוּב. The singular כְּרוּב with the definite article may imply that this is the same cherub that Yahweh moved from in 9:3a rather than one of the cherubim below the platform in 10:1. There is no evidence that it should be taken as a collective. The plural כְּרֻבִים/כְּרוּבִים is used frequently elsewhere in the Hebrew Bible (e.g. Gen 3:24) as it is in the present passage. If 10:2a refers to the cherub mentioned in 9:3a, then it too could be a part of the cult furniture. The preposition אֶל־תַּחַת may have the sense of "at the foot of" rather than "underneath". So, the man is to enter between the גַּלְגַּל, at the foot of the cherub, and fill his hands with coals of fire (נַחֲלֵי־אֵשׁ). Coals of fire are an important part of Yahweh's concealment during his theophany (2 Sam 22:12–13 = Ps 18:12–13). Lev 16:12–13 shows that this idea was transferred into the cult. Here, Aaron takes coals of fire from the altar in a censer, together with incense in his hands[175], and enters into the Holy of Holies. Once there, he adds the incense to the fire in order to create a cloud of smoke which conceals the כַּפֹּרֶת. If he does this, he will not die whilst in the presence of the divinity. Thus the significance of the coals of fire in our passage might have to do with the concealment of Yah-

---

175 Interestingly, the Leviticus passage contains similar wording to that of 10:2. In both Lev 16:12 and Ezek 10:2, Aaron/the man in linen is told to fill (מלא) his hands (חפן). In Lev 16:4, Aaron is instructed to dress (לבש) in linen (בַּד), the apparel of the man in our passage.

weh, during his departure from the temple. The incense altar (as opposed to the bronze altar) was probably in the הֵיכָל (1 Kgs 6:22). Thus Yahweh's command might stipulate that the man is to enter into the הֵיכָל in order to take the coals. If so, the cherub may have been one of the cherubim statues in the Holy of Holies that could possibly be seen from the הֵיכָל.

The coals of fire are said to be between the cherubim (מִבֵּינוֹת לַכְּרֻבִים). The statement is confusing. The man had entered between the גַּלְגַּל and beneath (or to the foot of) the cherub and now fills his hands with coals of fire from between the cherubim. Again, problems in interpretation concern whether we link these cherubim to those in 10:1, which seem to form part of a celestial apparition, or to the singular cherub in 9:3a (and earlier in 10:2), which may form part of the temple furnishings.

In 10:3, the cherubim are standing to the south of the house. If these are the same cherubim as those mentioned in 10:1, then the man does not enter into the הֵיכָל as verse 2 seems to imply, but enters between the cherubim under the platform. "The cloud" (הֶעָנָן) in the second half of the verse has not been mentioned previously. Although a cloud is a common feature of divine theophany, the כָּבוֹד has been present from the beginning of the pericope and, if this is the reason for the cloud's appearance, it is odd that it is only mentioned at this point. However, in this verse, the cloud seems to be associated with the movement of the man in linen, and not with the movement of the כָּבוֹד. We compared the coals of fire to those taken by Aaron in Lev 16:12–13. Interestingly, the result of Aaron's action is a cloud (עָנָן), which conceals the כַּפֹּרֶת. Consequently, if the action of the man in linen can be compared in some way to that of Aaron's incense offering, we might argue that the cloud is the result of him taking the coals of fire from the altar.

10:4 reverts to the movement of the כָּבוֹד. The first half of the verse is strikingly similar to 9:3a, as the כָּבוֹד rises up from upon (or above) the cherub to (or upon) the מִפְתָּן of the house. Nothing has been said concerning the position of the כָּבוֹד since 9:3a, thus the movement described here is unnecessary, if not illogical, as (according to 9:3a) the כָּבוֹד is already at the מִפְתָּן. It is surprising that the movement is repeated. Interestingly, the same movement is described using different vocabulary and word order. In 10:4a, the usual verb-subject-object word order is employed, whereas in 9:3a the subject precedes the verb. In 10:4, it is the כְּבוֹד־יְהוָה and not the כְּבוֹד אֱלֹהֵי יִשְׂרָאֵל of 9:3a that is the subject, and the verb רום is used instead of עלה. The change in preposition (עַל instead of אֶל) is also noteworthy. Zimmerli (1969a: 6) observes that the usage of these two prepositions often overlaps in the book of Ezekiel, which may be due to the influence of Aramaic. The explanatory phrase אֲשֶׁר הָיָה עָלָיו (of 9:3a) does not occur in 10:4.

In the second half of verse 4, the cloud is mentioned again, together with the brightness (נֹגַהּ) of the כָּבוֹד. This time, however, it is associated with the movement of the כָּבוֹד, and not with the action of the man in linen. It seems that the movement of the כָּבוֹד somehow occasions these phenomena. No such repercussions of its movement are reported after 9:3a. The repeated description of the cloud filling the inner court (10:3, 4) is also confusing and somewhat unnecessary.

Verse 5 shifts the focus back to the plural cherubim. Whether the cherub in the previous verse is one of these cherubim is difficult to say. Because the מִפְתָּן is an architectural feature of the temple, it seems likely that the cherub in 10:4 is, like that of 9:3a, one of the statues or friezes of the temple iconography. Yet the placement of 10:4 between 10:3 and 5 seems to indicate that this cherub is one of the cherubim under the platform described initially in 10:1. Here, the wings of the cherubim are mentioned for the first time and the noise created by them indicates that they are in motion. Thus we can be sure that what we have here is a vision of real heavenly cherubim, and not inert temple statues. The noise can be heard as far as the outer court and is compared to the voice of El Shadday speaking, which emphasizes the otherworldliness of the scene.[176]

Again, in 10:6, we have another sudden switch in subject matter, back to the man in linen, about whom no reference has been made since verse 3. The first half of the verse seems to serve as a reminder to the reader of what was happening before the interruption (vv 4–5). The syntax of the verse indicates that what is described happened simultaneously to the events depicted in verses 4–5. The command to the man is thus repeated but notably with slight variations. Some of these variations seem to be the result of the author's desire to abbreviate. This is a recap and there is perhaps no need to fully restate what was initially commanded. For example, the man is instructed to take fire, rather than 'coals of fire'. Likewise, this time, there is no reference to the cherub

---

176 Block (1997: 321, n. 34) notes that the reference to El Shadday speaking may reflect Shadday's function as head of the divine council (as portrayed in the Balaam text).

(beneath which/at the foot of which the man was supposed to go/enter). Instead, the command only includes the instruction to take fire from between the גַּלְגַּל, between the cherubim. Interestingly, in 10:2 (when the order is first given) the man is told to enter between, and not to take fire from between, the גַּלְגַּל. In 10:2, the fire is only said to be located between the cherubim, not between the גַּלְגַּל. The sense of 10:6 may be equivalent to the implied sense of 10:2. Nevertheless, the variation causes some confusion.

According to 10:6, when the man was commanded to take fire, he entered and stood by "the wheel". Once more, we have a substantive with the definite article that has not been mentioned previously. What is this wheel? We noted that one of the meanings of גַּלְגַּל is "wheel" (linked to the meaning of the verb גלל, "roll"). Such a usage occurs in Isa 5:28; Jer 47:3; Ezek 23:24 and 26:10. The reader may now connect the גַּלְגַּל, between which the man was commanded to enter (10:2) and between which the fire is said to be (10:6a), with the wheel (הָאוֹפָן) beside which the man stands. Consequently, the definite article can be explained. Its presence indicates that the אוֹפָן is to be identified with the גַּלְגַּל (which has been mentioned previously and is also definite). Yet we still have not solved the problem. אוֹפָן is never used collectively in biblical Hebrew. Therefore, if we want to view the גַּלְגַּל as a collective, we must postulate that the author meant אוֹפָן to be understood collectively in this verse, under the influence of גַּלְגַּל, despite the fact that the term is never usually employed in this way. If this is the case, the man is said to enter (we are now confused as to precisely where) and stand beside the wheels. However with this interpretation a yet further problem emerges concerning the initial command in verse 2. The man is instructed to enter between the גַּלְגַּל. Yet, in verse 6, the man has already entered when he stands beside the אוֹפָן. Thus a simple equation between הָאוֹפָן and the גַּלְגַּל (as is stressed later in 10:13) does not resolve the tensions within the text.

What these wheels are is again open to interpretation. Wheels and cherubim are mentioned together as features of the bronze stands positioned in the inner court of the temple (1 Kgs 7:27–39; 2 Chr 4:14). Yet there is no reason for there to be fire between the wheels and the cherubim. These stands supported basins, which were probably used as part of sacrificial ritual, perhaps for washing (see § 1.1.1.3). The wheels may have functioned to move the sacrifice from one place to another. However, there is no indication that the stands were used for burning the sacrifice. Another possibility is that the wheel is to be associated with one of the wheels by the חַיּוֹת in Ezekiel 1. These are the only wheels (אוֹפַנִּים) mentioned previously in the book of Ezekiel, but we have heard nothing of them since chapter 1.

The action of the man in linen retains the focus in verse 7. Yet, again, there is confusion generated by the reference to cherubim in both singular and plural. "The cherub" is said to stretch out its hand from between the cherubim to the fire, which was between the cherubim, and give to the hands of the man in linen. Once more, we have an enigmatic use of the definite article. Which cherub is being referred to? Even if we argue that this is one of the heavenly cherubim mentioned earlier, it is still odd that the substantive occurs with the definite article. The cherub reaches out from between the cherubim to the fire that was between the cherubim. These repeated references to cherubim add to the obscurity of the verse. The second half of the verse is laconic and somewhat staccato. The cherub lifts up and gives to the hands of the man in linen who takes and goes out. The abruptness of the ending of this narrative thread is intriguing. Given the repetitive preamble to the action (10:2, 6), it is strange that the action itself, and indeed the completion of the command, do not warrant further consideration by the author.[177] Verse 7 contains the final reference to the man in linen in this pericope (8:1–11:25). There is no reference to him scattering the coals over the city or to the implications this action would have. Thus the reader is left somewhat frustrated as to the conclusion of this element of the plot. Indeed, if we compare this command and its execution to the previous one (to which the entire of chapter 9 is devoted), there are significantly fewer verses apportioned to it (10:2, 6–7). Thus it seems strange that what we would view as a significant strand in the development of the narrative (the second command to the man in linen) is given so little attention.

10:8 is an explanatory statement, designed to clarify verse 7. It is an interesting extension to the previous verse. Hands are never mentioned elsewhere in the Hebrew Bible as an attribute of cherubim. Indeed, 2 Sam 22:11 = Ps 18:11 suggests that a cherub has the physique of a quadruped animal and thus Ezekiel's description of the hand in 10:7 is

---

177 If we connect the scattering of the coals of fire with Aaron's incense offering (and therefore the concealment of Yahweh) then the action has the effect of sparing the righteous remnant in Jerusalem when the כָּבוֹד goes up from the midst of the city (11:23). The coals produce smoke which saves the righteous from the consequences of seeing Yahweh (just as they spare Aaron in Leviticus 16).

rather surprising. The inclusion of the further explanatory statement of 10:8 may well suggest that the attribution of hands to a cherub would have been unusual even to the original Hebrew audience.

A new section is begun in 10:9 with the formula וָאֶרְאֶה וְהִנֵּה, "And I looked, and behold!". Four wheels are situated beside the cherubim, one beside each cherub. Thus, in this verse, the אוֹפַן and the cherubim mentioned in verse 6 are further elucidated. It seems that there are four cherubim and four wheels which the man had entered between. The number of wheels is reminiscent of the wheels in Ezekiel's inaugural vision. The reader begins to realize that some form of vehicle is being alluded to.

Verses 10–14 provide us with an intricate description of the wheels. They are described in similar terms to the wheels in Ezekiel 1. All four look alike and their appearance is as a wheel within a wheel (Ezek 1:16; 10:10). Their movement is such that they do not need to turn (Ezek 1:17; 10:11).[178] Verse 12, although containing somewhat similar information to 1:18, is rather bewildering. The wheels are said to possess physical attributes (flesh, backs, hands and wings). Perhaps, then, these are no ordinary wheels, but are some kind of heavenly creature.[179] All four anatomical parts mentioned occur with third person masculine plural suffixes. As they are mentioned immediately after the description of the wheels in 10:11, we assume that these physical attributes belong to the wheels. Yet, if this is the case, the following וְהָאוֹפַנִּים, which is tacked on to the list of body parts, seems odd. It is possible to take the following וְהָאוֹפַנִּים as referring solely to the wheel structure, with the anatomical parts being somewhat supplementary features to this. Yet we are left with the impression that these body parts may refer to the cherubim, even though the structure of the narrative does not suggest this.

As in 1:18, "eyes" feature in relation to the wheels. In that verse, however, the "eyes" feature solely on the rim/back (גַּב) of each wheel. This has caused most scholars to interpret the "eyes" as studs, designed to hold the wheel together. However, in 10:12, the "eyes" can no longer

---

178 In Ezek 10:11, we are given more information than 1:17. The wheels are said to follow the chief (רֹאשׁ) wheel.

179 Anatomical features are sometimes used to describe architectural and geographical features in biblical Hebrew. 1 Kgs 7:22 describes wheels with "hands" (probably axles) and "backs" (probably rims). However, the wings and flesh in Ezek 10:12 remain peculiar.

be interpreted in this way. It is unlikely that the backs (again, גַּב) should be interpreted as rims, as the term is listed with anatomical features. Hence it seems that the wheels (together with the anatomical appendages) are covered in real eyes. What significance this has can only be conjectured. Certainly, it adds to the monstrous description of the wheels.

In verse 13, we are finally given confirmation that the אוֹפַנִּים should be equated with the גַּלְגַּל of verses 2 and 7. The prophet has heard them called such. It is odd, however, that this equation has not been made sooner. Prior to this statement, we have been unsure as to the identity of the גַּלְגַּל. The appearance of the wheels goes entirely unheralded in the narrative and their presence seems rather incompatible with the temple setting. If we are to view the wheels as forming a vehicle (as they do in chapter 1), it is still curious that the arrival of this vehicle on the scene is not announced with greater fanfare (as it is in Ezek 1:4–5).

Additional anatomical features, in the form of four faces, are attributed to the wheels in verse 14. The basic sense of the Hebrew seems to imply that each wheel has a different set of four identical faces. The first has faces of *the* cherub; the second, those of a man; the third, those of a lion; and the fourth, those of an eagle. The description of the wheels is becoming more and more abstruse. Not only do they have flesh, backs, hands and wings, all covered in eyes, but they also have four faces of various creatures. Again, we might think that such anatomical features would be better ascribed to the cherubim rather than the wheels. Yet the description becomes even more puzzling when the first wheel is said to have faces of *the* cherub. Which cherub? We have learnt that there are four cherubim on the scene (although there would have been more, if we count the artificial cherubim of the temple iconography). Thus the use of the definite article here is extremely peculiar and it is not employed with reference to the other types of faces. Dijkstra (1986: 74) argues that the numerals refer to the faces and not the wheels. If this is the case, the description is similar to that of the חַיּוֹת in 1:10 and each wheel has four different faces. The order of the faces is different, however, and cherubic faces (whatever they may be) feature instead of bovine.

With verse 15, our attention is diverted back to the cherubim. They are said to be lifted up (presumably by the wind). The noise of the wings described in 10:5 had suggested that the cherubim were moving, but now we are given details as to their movement. In the second half of the verse, the prophet has a surprising realization. He recognizes the cherubim to be the חַיָּה that he has seen by the river Chebar, during his inaugural vision. The reference to the חַיָּה in the singular is somewhat strange, given that there are four cherubim. The reader must infer that the prophet is connecting the cherubim with the four חַיּוֹת described in Ezekiel 1. The writer seems to be using the term as a collective, which is odd, considering the term is only used in this way once in Ezekiel 1 (in verse 22).

The reader is finally in no doubt as to the exact identity of the cherubim and the wheels. The cherubim are real heavenly creatures who, together with the wheels, formed the vehicle which transported the כָּבוֹד to Ezekiel in Babylon. We are reminded of the throne mentioned in 10:1 which can now be linked to that described in 1:26. There, the throne had the כָּבוֹד of Yahweh seated on it, but now the throne appears to be empty. The previous references to a singular cherub (9:3a; 10:2, 4, 7, 14) can then be retrospectively interpreted as alluding to one of the four cherubim. Yet, following the cherubim = חַיּוֹת equation, the reader is left even more perplexed as to the description of the faces of the wheels. If one of the wheels has four cherubic faces, and a cherub (as described in 1:10; 10:21) has four faces, then this particular wheel would have sixteen faces. Four of these would be those of a man; four, a lion; four, a bull; and four, an eagle. The picture is bizarre. If we read the numerals as relating to the wheels, then each wheel has similar faces to those of the חַיּוֹת, the only difference being the substitution of a cherubic face for a bovine one. This does not refine the picture, as now each wheel should have seven faces: two human, two leonine, two aquiline and one bovine. The peculiar picture may be attributed to the nature of a prophetic vision. Perhaps we should not attempt to apply logic to a visionary experience. Yet the development of the narrative and its theological significance are, to some extent, eclipsed (or at least confused) by the baffling imagery.

Despite the surprising (and somewhat intrusive) statement of verse 15b, verses 16–17 continue the theme of 15a in their description of the movement of the cherubim. The verses recall Ezek 1:19–21 and the wording is strikingly similar in places. The wheels and the cherubim move in unison. They do not turn but are buoyed by the wind.

The movement of the כָּבוֹד has not been mentioned since 10:4, which stated that it had gone up from the cherub to the מִפְתָּן of the house. Verse 18 resumes this narrative thread, describing how the כָּבוֹד

"went out" from upon the מִפְתָּן of the house and stood above the cherubim. The statement generates further confusion concerning the progression of the כָּבוֹד thus far. In 9:3a, we learnt that it had moved from the cherub to the מִפְתָּן, an action which was strangely repeated in 10:4. It seems that the כָּבוֹד has moved from being above one of the cherubim to the מִפְתָּן (9:3a, 10:4) and then back over the cherubim (10:18). If this is the case, the reader is bemused as to the reason for this movement. What possible purpose could it serve within the narrative? We could conjecture that the כָּבוֹד left the throne over the cherubim in order that the man in linen could enter between the wheels. In which case, the reason for the movement may have something to do with maintaining distance between the כָּבוֹד and the man. Yet this seems contrary to how the כָּבוֹד (if we can equate this with the fiery human in Ezek 1:26–27; 8:2–3) interacts with the prophet in 8:2–3. The exit of the כָּבוֹד from the temple is a significant theme in subsequent verses (10:19; 11:22–23) and is anticipated in 8:6. Yet this movement from the cherub to the מִפְתָּן and then to the cherubim does not seem to add to this plot development. Once again, we begin to wonder whether the singular cherub (9:3a, 10:4) may be different to the cherubim of 10:18.

Yahweh's departure from the temple (prefigured in 8:6 and possibly begun in 9:3a; 10:4) occasions a fuller description in 10:19. The vehicle is powered by the wings of the cherubim. The use of the verb יצא confirms the direction of the movement: the vehicle is leaving the inner court. It stops at the entrance gate to the house of Yahweh (presumably the main entrance of the temple, to the east). Thus the exit of the vehicle is a gradual one, perhaps suggesting that the movements described in 9:3a and 10:4 should be regarded as the first stages of the departure. The final statement of verse 19 reminds us that the כָּבוֹד is above the vehicle. However, unlike the previous verse, the term used is כְּבוֹד אֱלֹהֵי יִשְׂרָאֵל and not כְּבוֹד־יְהוָה.

The final verses of the chapter are somewhat summative in character. Verse 20 restates the cherubim = חַיּוֹת equation of verse 15. Again, the singular חַיָּה is used as a collective. Here, the location of the חַיָּה is further qualified by the phrase תַּחַת אֱלֹהֵי־יִשְׂרָאֵל, 'under the god of Israel', and there is further emphasis on the identification in the statement, וָאֵדַע כִּי כְרוּבִים הֵמָּה. Verses 21–22 confirm that the cherubim had the same four faces as the חַיּוֹת and (like them) four wings, with human hands underneath. The movement described in the final statement of verse 22 remains enigmatic. Each one is said to move in the direction of its faces. For this to make sense, we must assume that the faces all point in the same direction. Yet this seems to run counter to the description of the faces in 1:10.

In Ezek 11:1, the narrative is resumed and Ezekiel is brought by the רוּחַ to the east gate of the house of Yahweh. Hence the prophet is transported to the location where the כָּבוֹד and the cherubim vehicle are resting in order for him to observe the twenty-five apostates and hear the word of Yahweh concerning them. There is a degree of difficulty concerning the appearance of these twenty-five men at this point in the narrative. In 9:11, the man in linen has reported that all apostates in the city have been killed. Thus it is strange that twenty-five are still alive. There is also some tension between these twenty-five men and those appearing in 8:16, who are also possibly alluded to in 9:6. The sequence of the narrative seems muddled.

The final reference to the movement of the כָּבוֹד occurs in 11:22–23. Verse 22 recalls the movement made in 10:19. The cherubim lift up their wings, with the wheels next to them and the כָּבוֹד אֱלֹהֵי יִשְׂרָאֵל above them. By contrast, the wording of verse 23 recalls 9:3a; 10:4. The יְהוָה־כְּבוֹד goes up (עלה) from upon (מֵעַל) the midst of the city to the mountain to the east of the city. In this verse, the כָּבוֹד moves directly and there is no mention of the cherubim vehicle. With this statement, the theme of the departure of Yahweh from his temple ends and, in the following verse, the prophet is transported back to exile in Babylon.

§ 1.3.4.3.2 A Diachronic Approach

Greenberg's major critique of diachronic readings of Ezekiel is that the criteria used for detecting redactional layers within a text are arbitrary (Greenberg 1986: 123–135). In relation to our text, Block (1997: 314) agrees, arguing: "Chapter 10 is obviously composite, but the criteria used to identify the layers of tradition are frequently subjective." The results of redaction criticism of our passage have been extremely varied, thus casting doubt on the methodology of those attempting to reconstruct a base text. Yet, just because it is extremely difficult to uncover the original text beneath the editorial strata, it does not follow that we should abandon the enterprise altogether. The synchronic readings of Greenberg and Block are extremely important in establishing the meaning of the final form of the text and both scholars are, in many respects, right to criticise the methodology of some redaction critics. Yet it does not follow that we should stop attempting to read the text diachronically. A purely synchronic reading of Ezek 8:1–11:25 may well overlook clues within the text which could have a significant bearing on our understanding of the cherubim in this passage.

Both Greenberg and Block (critics of diachronic readings of Ezekiel) admit that the text of Ezekiel 10 shows signs of editing (Greenberg 1983: 196, 199; Block 1997: 314). Consequently, it seems that there are some tensions within the text that are difficult to account for by means of a purely synchronic reading. Thus we need to establish what can be used as appropriate evidence of additions to the text before we can begin to decide what might be later insertions and what significance this has.

There are three major sources of evidence from which we can draw in order to determine editorial activity in Ezek 8:1–11:25. First, there are the internal problems within the text, such as repetition, structural disorder and thematic inconsistencies. The use of this type of evidence has been much criticised by Greenberg (1986). He argues that modern critics, who attempt to excise material which interferes with the coherence of the narrative, are not doing justice to the peculiarities of ancient texts. Digression and repetition, for example, are often found in many ancient Near Eastern texts and may be used for rhetorical reasons. Nevertheless, in our text, we are not just dealing with a simple digression or repetition. The narrative chops and changes to the extent that we are sometimes left entirely unsure of what is being described. Reading the text as it stands, we are faced with a puzzle of contradictions. Thus although we should be careful in our use of these internal problems to determine later additions, we can be sure that all these difficulties are not the result of rhetorical strategy.

The second source of evidence for later additions to Ezek 8:1–11:25 is its relationship to Ezekiel 1. The description of the cherubim and wheels in Ezekiel 10 is very similar to that of the חַיּוֹת and wheels in Ezekiel's initial vision. The similarities and differences between the two texts may give us some indication of how the texts are related. If so, a comparison may also yield evidence of editorial activity within the texts. We might be able to detect explanatory glosses, harmonization or attempts to smooth over hermeneutical and grammatical problems.

The third source of evidence for determining later material in Ezek 8:1–11:25 is the LXX version of the text. The Greek translation displays several divergences from the MT and offers a shorter text. Although it is difficult to argue that either the Hebrew or the Greek preserves a text closer to the original, a comparison between the two versions may expose areas of the text where editing is more likely to have occurred.

Thus we have three sources of evidence for editorial elaborations in Ezekiel 10. We might think, therefore, that we can suggest additions with some conviction. Yet this is not the case. The evidence is simply not sound enough for us to make any claims of certainty about the development of the text. The confidence with which scholars such as Zimmerli separated original from later material has been undermined by the criticisms of Greenberg and Block. Instead of ascribing each verse or half verse to a definite redactional layer, we can only look in a more general way for patterns of editorial activity.

Our first source of evidence, the internal inconsistencies within the text, can be further divided into three different types: grammatical/syntactical, stylistic and thematic. We will thus begin our diachronic investigation by looking at grammatical and syntactical problems as possible evidence of editorial activity. Arguably one of the most frequent syntactical problems within our text is the use of the definite article with substantives that have not been mentioned previously in the narrative (9:3a, 10:1, 2, 3, 4, 6, 7, 14). We have seen how this use of the definite article creates problems even from the first reference to a cherub within the narrative (9:3a). Moreover, this peculiar use of the definite article occurs only with reference to the cherubim, the platform and the wheels and does not occur elsewhere in the pericope. It is possible to argue that many of these examples stem from the retrospective identification of the cherubim with the חַיּוֹת. Although not expressly stated, the cherubim/חַיּוֹת vehicle arrived on the scene with the כָּבוֹד and hence "*the* cherub(im)" (in 9:3a, 10:1, 2, 4, 6–7, 14) is accounted for. Yet although this is what the final form must imply, the first time reader would have difficulty in grasping that this is what has occurred (at least until 10:15). It seems more likely that a later editor, wishing to include the vehicle of chapter 1 in the narrative of Yahweh's departure from the temple, has purposefully added some of the substantives with the definite article in order to point the reader back to Ezekiel 1. This seems to be the case particularly with הָרָקִיעַ and therefore הַכְּרוּבִים in 10:1.

Yet the difficulties associated with the peculiar use of the definite article are exacerbated by the constant alternation between כְּרוּב and

כְּרוּבִים. This oscillation between singular and plural is another gram-
matical/syntactical problem within the text which may be suggestive of
editorial activity. הַכְּרוּב in 9:3a and 10:4a cannot refer to one of the
cherubim under the throne because the throne is above all four cherubim. It seems unlikely that the כָּבוֹד could have been situated over one
in particular. This is supported by the fact that, in 10:18, the כָּבוֹד stands
above "the cherubim", not above "the cherub", when it boards the
cherubim vehicle. Thus to understand the use of the definite article in
9:3a and 10:4a we must view the cherub as an important feature of the
temple iconography, upon which the כָּבוֹד had been resting.

Greenberg (1983: 181) and Block (1997: 317: n. 21) suggest either
amending the singular forms of כְּרוּב to the plural or viewing them as
collective. The LXX represents the plural in every instance and never
refers to a cherub in the singular in this pericope. Nevertheless, the fact
that the MT alludes to a cherub five times in the singular suggests that
there was originally a "cherub" subtext. The LXX, if loyal to its Vorlage,
may well witness to a process of harmonization which masked the earlier distinction between singular and plural. The idea that the singulars
in the MT should be taken as a collective is untenable. Scholars who
argue for taking them as such are exploiting a convenient solution for
the difficulties rendered by the alternation from singular to plural. If
the singulars are collectives, then why is the collective not used elsewhere in the passage? The plural is used sixteen times in Ezek 8:1–11:25
and is used regularly elsewhere in the Hebrew Bible. It would be very
strange for an author to use a singular as a collective five times to refer
to plural creatures, which are mentioned in the grammatically correct
form on sixteen further occasions in the same text. Thus it is possible
that the confusing alternation of singular and plural forms of כְּרוּב is
evidence of editorial activity. The editor, wishing to include the vehicle
in chapter 1 in the current pericope, may have used the "cherub" subtext as a suitable peg on which to hang his "cherubim" veneer.

The most common stylistic problems within the text are repetition
and emphasis (9:3a//10:4, 10:2//10:6, 10:8//10:21b, 10:15//10:20). Although such stylistic features can be used by an author for rhetorical
reasons, in some instances no rhetorical purpose for the repetition can
be given. For example, the repeated movement of the כָּבוֹד from the
cherub to the מִפְתָּן of the house (9:3a and 10:4a) is odd. We can offer no
explanation for this repetition other than that one of the references is
the result of editorial activity. Indeed, the important theme of Yahweh's

departure from the temple is convoluted by the repetition. As the subject of Yahweh's movement fits the narrative of chapter 10 better than chapter 9, we may infer that 10:4a is the original statement. We have already noted that 9:3a interrupts the flow of the narrative concerning the six men and Yahweh's instructions to them. There are thus several reasons to view this half of the verse as an editorial insertion. The motives for this insertion may be multiple. First, the crucial theme of Yahweh abandoning his temple, which is so prominent in the following chapters (10:18–19; 11:22–23), would be prefigured by the addition of 9:3a. The insertion would explicitly connect Yahweh's departure from the temple with his punishment of the apostates, in accordance with 8:6. In addition, the reference to the cherub at this stage in the narrative would help to introduce the idea of the cherubim vehicle, which rather suddenly becomes the focus in the following chapter.

The rather excessive emphasis on the identification of the cherubim as חַיּוֹת (in 10:15, 20 and 22) may also be a clue to the editorial history of chapter 10. Why is it so necessary to place such great stress on the connection? The repetition would make more sense if we attribute one or all of these verses to an editor who knew that his readers would find the equation difficult. A somewhat similar emphasis occurs concerning the "hands" of the cherubim. 10:8, the purpose of which seems to be to explain 10:7, is recapitulated in 10:21. With the exception of the reference to the hands in 10:8, nothing is said of the physical features of the cherubim until the final two verses of the chapter.[180] Thus it seems very strange that the hands are singled out in this way. This emphasis may be evidence that a later editor wanted to reiterate the fact that the cherubim had hands, possibly because hands were not usually considered characteristics of cherubim.[181]

The third type of internal problem which may be suggestive of editorial activity is thematic and structural inconsistency. As we have already observed in our close reading of the cherubim references in Ezek 8:1–11:25, the narrative oscillates sharply between topics. Chapters 8 and 9 are, in the main, well structured, and the central themes of the

---

180 This is providing we attribute the anatomical features in 10:12 to the wheels, as the text implies.
181 This would accord with the portrayal of a cherub as a quadruped in 2 Sam 22:11 = Ps 18:11 (see §2.3.3).

narrative are thus effectively communicated. By contrast, in chapter 10, the narrative seems inchoate. Indeed, there appear to be three inter-weaving themes within the narrative: the cherubim with the wheels, the man in linen, and the departure of the כָּבוֹד. Deciding which is the principal theme of chapter 10 is complicated. In terms of the number of verses devoted to each subject, the cherubim and the wheels predomi-nate. Yet, if we are to view the subject matter of chapter 10 as a genuine continuation from that in chapter 9, then the command to the man in linen seems a more suitable contender. It is my view that the action of the man in linen is inextricably linked to the theme of Yahweh depart-ing from the temple.[182] If this is the case, we should not view the latter as a separate theme. Thus, arguably, the action of the man in linen and the departure of the כָּבוֹד form the principal theme of chapter 10.

Yet, unlike the previous two chapters, this principal theme is un-derdeveloped and even neglected. Instead, attention is lavished on the cherubim and the wheels. Yet despite the inordinate interest in these phenomena, both the cherubim and the wheels go entirely unheralded in the text. Unlike chapter 1, where the dramatic entrance of the vehicle is carefully described (1:4–5), in chapter 10 the arrival of the vehicle goes unannounced. This seems odd, particularly when we consider the amount of words devoted to describing the physical appearance of the phenomena, particularly the wheels. Again, the inchoateness of the principal theme and the abrupt appearance of the cherubim vehicle are best explained as evidence that the two narrative threads have been intertwined by a later editor, rather than by the original author. It is likely that the cherubim vehicle was added to the narrative because of a desire by the editor to include it in Yahweh's departure from the tem-ple.

Hence, viewing the internal problems as evidence of editorial activ-ity has highlighted the possibility that the cherubim may well have been part of a later redactional insertion in agreement with Ezekiel 1. If this is the case, then a closer look at the similarities and differences between the cherubim vehicle in this pericope and the חַיּוֹת and the

---

182 This is based on my premise that the scattering of the coals of fire on the city is designed to protect the righteous remnant from the sight of Yahweh as he departs from the temple (cf. Lev 16:12–13).

wheels of Ezekiel's initial vision may help to reinforce this supposition and possibly clarify the nature of the insertion.

When we compare the description of the cherubim in chapter 10 to that of the חַיּוֹת in Ezekiel 1, we notice that precise details concerning the physical features and position of the חַיּוֹת in Ezekiel 1 are not so explicitly depicted in Ezekiel 10. This is in striking contrast to the description of the wheels in Ezek 10:9–17, which follows the parallel text in Ezek 1:15–21 very closely (see Block 1988: 440–442).[183] Thus, in Ezekiel 10, details concerning the appearance and movement of the wheels are elaborated upon (just as they are in Ezekiel 1). By contrast, the physical features of the cherubim are not depicted in the same detail as those of the חַיּוֹת in Ezekiel 1. For example, in Ezek 1:10–11, 23, the faces of the חַיּוֹת and the position of their wings are described in great detail. However, the wings and faces of the cherubim are mentioned only fleetingly in Ezek 10:21–22. Several details of the physical appearance of the חַיּוֹת described in Ezekiel 1 are altogether lacking in the description of the cherubim in Ezekiel 10. For example, the חַיּוֹת are said to have the form of a human being (Ezek 1:5) and straight legs with bronze calves' feet (1:7). Such physical features are not attributed to the cherubim in Ezekiel 10. These differences may be the result of the author's unwillingness to repeat what the reader already knows. Yet, when we compare the description of the cherubim to that of the wheels in Ezekiel 10, it is surprising that the text does not go into more detail. In my view, these omissions are purposeful, designed to underplay the physical traits of the חַיּוֹת that would not be consistent with those usually ascribed to cherubim.

There is one exception to the lack of detail concerning the physical description of the cherubim in Ezekiel 10 and that is the repeated emphasis on the hands (10:8, 21). We have noted already that this emphasis might be designed to reiterate the fact that hands, usually not considered characteristics of cherubim, were indeed a feature of them. Why then is this attribute of the חַיּוֹת underscored, when other attributes (such as the bronze feet) are omitted altogether? I would argue that this emphasis is included because the "hand" of a cherub plays a key role in the development of the narrative. In 10:7, the cherub stretches out its hand and gives fire to the man in linen. Thus one attribute of the חַיּוֹת, the hands, became integral to the story in Ezekiel 10. Consequently, they could not be omitted. Nevertheless, hands would

---

183 This is with the exception of Ezek 10:12 which elaborates on the physical appearance of the wheels.

still have been considered strange features of cherubim, hence the repeated references to them (10:7, 8, 21).[184]

If these speculations have some merit, we may make the further
surmise that the bodily parts mentioned in 10:12 (most of which are
attributed to the חַיּוֹת in Ezekiel 1) have been ascribed to the wheels
rather than the cherubim for the same purpose: to play down the
physical connection between the חַיּוֹת and the cherubim. The editor
wants to draw the reader's attention away from the physical appearance of the cherubim because the physical traits of the חַיּוֹת would not
have been typical of cherubim and thus highlighting these features
would have weakened the cherubim = חַיּוֹת equation.[185] Thus a comparison between Ezekiel 1 and 10 suggests that the חַיּוֹת may not have
been cherubim, even though the cherubim are subsequently interpreted
as the חַיּוֹת.

One feature of the cherubim vehicle that is present in both Ezekiel 1
and 10 is the coals of fire. We have already noted a possible connection
between the coals of fire in Ezek 10:7 and those taken by Aaron as part
of his incense offering (Lev 16:12). However, the identification of the
cherubim as חַיּוֹת may indicate that we are supposed to compare the
coals of fire to those appearing in Ezek 1:13–14. The MT of 1:13 reads:

וּדְמוּת הַחַיּוֹת מַרְאֵיהֶם כְּגַחֲלֵי־אֵשׁ בֹּעֲרוֹת כְּמַרְאֵה

הַלַּפִּדִים הִיא מִתְהַלֶּכֶת בֵּין הַחַיּוֹת וְנֹגַהּ לָאֵשׁ

וּמִן־הָאֵשׁ יוֹצֵא בָרָק

"And as for the likeness of the חַיּוֹת: their appearance was like burning
coals of fire, as the appearance of the torches that went up and down
between the חַיּוֹת. And the fire was bright. And from the fire came forth
lightning." Hence the MT compares the appearance of the creatures to
coals of fire. In the Hebrew Bible, divine attendants are often described
as fiery in nature (Ps 104:4; Gen 3:24 and possibly Isaiah 6). Hence it
warrants no surprise that the חַיּוֹת are described in this way. Yet, in the
LXX version of this verse, the creatures are not compared to the coals of

---

184 If this is the case, the question then arises of how the cherub in verse 7 stretches out
     its hand, when hands were not features of cherubim. We will see, in our discussion
     of the LXX evidence below, that the cherub may not have been the original subject in
     this verse.

185 Halperin's idea (1988: 46–47) that the editor wanted to portray the wheels as a sec-
     ond class of angels is not inconsistent with my interpretation.

fire. Instead, the coals are said to be in the middle (ἐν μέσῳ) of the creatures. Thus the LXX of Ezek 1:13 bears a greater resemblance to Ezek 10:2 than it does to the MT of Ezek 1:13.

Usually, scholars view the LXX as representative of a more original text in 1:13. Likewise, they deem the absence of 1:14 in the LXX to be evidence of elaboration in the MT. Yet the Qumran fragments follow the MT and not the LXX Vorlage (see DJD 15: 216–217). Whichever witnesses to the earlier tradition, there remains the possibility that, originally, Ezekiel 1 never alluded to coals between the creatures. Instead, the appearance of the creatures is like coals of fire, an idea that persists in 1:14 where the creatures dart about like flashes of lightning. If the MT preserves the earlier tradition, then we may not be justified in comparing the coals of fire in 10:2 to those in 1:13. Indeed, the variation in tradition between the LXX and MT of Ezek 1:13 may be evidence in favor of seeing the position of the coals "between the cherubim" in 10:2, 6 and 7 as later insertions by an editor who wished to harmonize Ezekiel 1 and 10.

The LXX offers another interesting variation in 10:7. As we discussed earlier, the Greek text never refers to a singular cherub and has the plural χερουβιν in 9:3a, 10:2 and 10:4a.[186] Interestingly, in 10:7, when "the cherub" stretches out its hand in the MT, the LXX does not represent a subject for the verb ἐξέτεινεν, "he stretched out". As the action seems to continue from 10:6, the Greek seems to imply that it is the man in linen who stretched out his hand. Yet, later in the verse, the LXX states that "he gave it to the man in linen". The man cannot give the fire to himself. Thus the subject of ἐξέτεινεν in the LXX is questionable.

There are several possible reasons for the differences between the LXX and the MT in 10:7. First, if the LXX witnesses to a process of harmonization which masked an earlier distinction between singular and plural (as observed in the MT), then the omission of "the cherub" as the subject of ἐξέτεινεν may be in keeping with this. The LXX author (or the author of its Vorlage) may have purposefully left out the reference to the cherub in order to smooth out the problems created by the singular cherub in the earlier tradition (witnessed by the MT). In which case, the LXX of 10:7 further substantiates our surmise that the references to the singular cherub in MT 9:3a, 10:2, 10:4, 7 and 14 point to a "cherub" subtext which was concealed by a "cherubim" layer at a later date. On the

---

186 The LXX omits 10:14 completely.

other hand, the LXX of 10:7 may be indicative of a tradition in which the cherub was not the original subject of שׁלח. If this is the case, the problems associated with the application of a hand to a cherub (which are suggested by the repetition in 10:8 and 21) disappear. Originally, the man in linen did as he was commanded in 10:2 and took the fire on his own accord. It was then only later that an editor, wishing to integrate the חַיּוֹת vehicle into the narrative of the man in linen, gave the cherub a more significant role to play.

§ 1.3.4.3.3 The Cherub Subtext

Attempting to read the text diachronically, we can make some suggestions as to the general pattern of editorial activity in Ezek 8:1–11:25. It seems likely that the text of Ezekiel 8–9 and 11 is in relatively good order. There are few inherent problems concerning the narrative flow and theological intent of these passages. By contrast, Ezekiel 10 displays many internal problems which can only be reasonably accounted for by appealing to editorial activity. The evidence from Ezekiel 1 and the LXX corroborates this. Editorial work thus seems to centre on the cherubim vehicle.

If we are right to assume that all the references to the cherubim vehicle are later insertions, then we need to attempt to determine the subtext of Ezekiel 10 in order to clarify what place, if any, the cherub/cherubim had in the original text. The central themes of the pericope of 8:1–11:25 are, arguably, the killing of the apostates and the abandonment of the temple. Thus, any cherub(im) subtext needs to have some connection to these themes.

We have argued already that the references to the singular cherub in the MT of 9:3a, 10:2, 4, 7 and 14, as the *lectio difficilior*, may witness to an original "cherub" subtext. Thus the references to "cherubim" may be later additions designed to link the narrative about Yahweh's departure from the temple with the vehicle that transports the deity to Babylon in chapter 1. The LXX seems to represent a Vorlage which has gone one step further than the MT and has attempted to remove any traces of the original "cherub" narrative from its text. The first reference to a cherub in the singular is in 9:3a. We have argued, however, that this reference is a rehashed version of 10:4a that has been inserted into chapter 9 in order to anticipate the sudden reference to the cherubim vehicle in 10:1. Consequently, we must argue that the first reference to a singular cherub in the original text was in 10:2. This cherub is mentioned in the instructions given to the man in linen, a central figure in the narrative.

According to our analysis, the action of the man in linen is the central theme of the subtext of chapter 10 and the references to the cherub vehicle (with which this theme has been interwoven) may be regarded as later insertions. If we are correct in our interpretation of the symbolism of the action of the man in linen (in accordance with Lev 16:12–13), then the man is preparing the city for the departure of the כָּבוֹד. In the original text of Ezekiel 10, as in Lev 16:12–13, the priestly figure is to enter the most sacred place in the sanctuary in order to collect the coals of fire from the incense altar. In which case, the cherub in 10:2 is part of the architectural features of the temple and not one of the cherubim under the throne in 10:1. Where exactly this cherub was situated cannot be said with any certainty. It could have been carved on the lintel above the door to the הֵיכָל (1 Kgs 6:34–35), in which case the man in linen is to enter beneath (אֶל־תַּחַת) the cherub. Alternatively, אֶל־תַּחַת may have the meaning "at the foot of". If this is the case, one of the cherubim statues inside the הֵיכָל could be supposed. This could have been a cherub frieze on the wall, a cherub statue visible at the end of the ark (see Zimmerli 1969a: 231)[187] or one of the large cherub statues described in 1 Kgs 6:23. It is not possible to say with any certainty.

The reference to the cherubim (in the plural) in 10:2 could be original or a later insertion. If the former, it may refer again to architectural appurtenances within the temple. However, if the latter, it should probably be regarded as an addition designed to integrate the חַיּוֹת vehicle into the original text. In which case, the editor wished to stress that the place where the man entered was between the cherubim and wheels of the vehicle, not the הֵיכָל. This would mean that the symbolism of the scattering of the coal is, to some extent, obscured. Scholars have often debated as to the purpose of the scattering (some viewing it as an act of purification, e.g. Joyce 1989: 61–66, some as one of punishment, e.g. Zimmerli 1969a: 232). That this is not an act of punishment is obvious from the narrative. The apostates within the city have already been punished in chapter 9. Only righteous inhabitants remain.[188]

---

187 This would mean that the author of Ezek 10:2 knew of the Exodus ark traditions.

188 This is perhaps with the exception of the twenty-five officials referred to in chapter 11.

Therefore, to burn the city would be nonsensical, particularly in view of the restoration of the city to the exiles as is promised in chapter 11. This action is inextricably linked to the departure of the כָּבוֹד from the temple. The instruction to the man in linen is to scatter the coals over the city (הָעִיר). In 11:22, the כָּבוֹד goes up from the midst of the city (הָעִיר מֵעַל תּוֹךְ). If the action of the man in linen can be compared to the incense offering of Aaron, designed to protect him from the sight of Yahweh, then the symbolism of the action is concerned with protecting the righteous remnant in the city from the sight of Yahweh's departure. If the man was to enter between the cherubim to the south of the temple (10:3) and not the הֵיכָל, as the current arrangement of the narrative implies, the connection between his action and the incense offering is eclipsed.

The next reference to the cherub occurs in 10:4. The כָּבוֹד rises up from upon the cherub to the מִפְתָּן of the house. This would have been the first reference to the movement of the כָּבוֹד in the original text. If we are right to presume that the action of the man in linen initially took place in the הֵיכָל, then it is likely that this is where the כָּבוֹד moves from. We noted earlier that the מִפְתָּן was probably situated at the entrance to the הֵיכָל. Thus the כָּבוֹד moves from the interior of the הֵיכָל to its threshold. If this is the case, then the cherub may be the same as that mentioned in 10:2. This would be a logical progression for Yahweh's departure from the temple. The abandonment occurs gradually, with the כָּבוֹד moving from the cherub to the מִפְתָּן (10:4) to the entrance gate (10:19) to the mountain east of the city (11:23). The movement begins from the most holy space within the temple (the הֵיכָל), where the כָּבוֹד usually resides (1 Kg 8:10–11).

10:5 is likely the product of editorial activity in accordance with 1:24. Verse 6, however, may preserve some remnant of the original text. Here, the topic of the man in linen is resumed and the command recapitulated. Yet the text states that the man was told to take fire from between the גַּלְגַּל, which is not a precise restatement of 10:2. Indeed, if we are excising 10:3 and 5 from the original text, then the recapitulation is perhaps unnecessary. Thus, it may be that this verse has been added in order to return the focus of the narrative to the action of the man in linen in 10:7. The second half of verse 6 contains the surprise reference to the אוֹפַן. We may think, therefore, that this should be attributed to the hand of an editor, who wished to identify the גַּלְגַּל with the אוֹפַנִּים. Yet the definite article on אוֹפַן is odd, considering it occurs in the singu-

lar. Dijkstra (1986: 67, n. 58) argues that the strange use of the singular
here should be attributed to a scribe who, conscious of the tradition
that the גַּלְגַּל and the אוֹפָן should be equated, substituted an original
הַגַּלְגַּל for the less ambiguous הָאוֹפָן. This is a possibility which may allow us to view verse 6 (particularly in the second half) as containing
some vestiges of the *Urtext*.

Verse 7 continues the narrative concerning the man in linen and
thus should retain original material. As we have seen, the LXX version
of this verse could witness to a process of harmonization, the aim of
which was to remove references to the original lone cherub. If this is
the case, and the MT version reflects an earlier tradition, then we must
argue that the cherub in the הֵיכָל has come alive. This is not impossible.
The cherub can be compared to the seraph in Isa 6:6, who takes a רִצְפָּה
(piece of coal?) from the altar in tongs that were "in its hand" (בְּיָדוֹ).
Alternatively, the variation between the LXX and the MT may suggest
that, in the earlier tradition, the man took the fire of his own accord (as
he was commanded in 10:2). Accordingly, the cherub has been added
into the MT of 10:7 in order to indicate that the cherub of 10:2 and 4
was no static piece of artwork, but was one of the living cherubim under the throne (10:1).

The repeated references to the location of the fire and the cherub in
10:7 are unnecessary and should perhaps be regarded as later editorial
elaborations, designed to emphasize that the fire was between the living cherubim and not in the הֵיכָל. The reference to the cherub stretching
"from between the cherubim" is missing in the LXX. Indeed, the original text of 10:6–7 may not have had any reference to a cherub at all, but
merely stated that the man entered, took the fire and went out. If this is
the case, וַיִּתֵּן אֶל־חָפְנֵי לְבֻשׁ הַבַּדִּים, in the second half of verse 7, may also
be attributed to the hand of an editor.

After verse 7, the description of the cherubim vehicle engulfs the
original narrative and we do not return to it until 10:18. Here, the
theme of the departure of the כָּבוֹד continues from verse 4 and it leaves
the מִפְתָּן where it had been resting. The reference to the cherubim vehicle in 10:18 cannot be original to the text, according to our analysis.
Instead, it seems more likely that, in the earlier tradition, after the כָּבוֹד
had gone out from the מִפְתָּן (10:18), it went directly to stand at the entrance gate of the house of Yahweh (וַיַּעֲמֹד פֶּתַח שַׁעַר בֵּית־יְהוָה הַקַּדְמוֹנִי,

10:19). This is supported by the fact that the verb וַיַּעֲמֹד in verse 19 is
masculine singular, as it is in 10:18, despite the fact that the natural
antecedent is the cherubim (masculine plural).[189] The scribal insertion
could have been based on the וַיַּעֲמֹד of 10:19 and thus the elaboration
begins with the same verb in 10:18 (וַיַּעֲמֹד עַל־הַכְּרוּבִים). The כָּבוֹד no
longer moves by itself but ascends onto the cherubim vehicle in order
to be transported away from the temple. Thus 10:18–19 may have
originally read:

$$\text{וַיֵּצֵא כְּבוֹד יְהוָה מֵעַל מִפְתַּן הַבָּיִת וַיַּעֲמֹד פֶּתַח שַׁעַר}$$

$$\text{בֵּית־יְהוָה הַקַּדְמוֹנִי}$$

The כְּבוֹד in 10:18 is the כְּבוֹד יְהוָה and not the כְּבוֹד אֱלֹהֵי־יִשְׂרָאֵל of 10:19.
Zimmerli (1969a: 237) argues that the variation between the two epi-
thets is evidence of editorial elaboration. This may indeed be the case.
The only two prior references to the כְּבוֹד אֱלֹהֵי־יִשְׂרָאֵל in 8:4 and 9:3 occur in verses which should most likely be attributed to a later hand.
Thus its inclusion in the second half of verse 19 supports our view that
there has been editorial activity at this point, incorporating the cherubim vehicle into the original narrative concerning the departure of the
כָּבוֹד from the temple.

The final reference to the departure of the כָּבוֹד occurs in 11:22–23.
Again, a later hand has included the cherubim vehicle in the original
text. This time, however, the addition is more obvious. Verse 22, with
its reference to the כְּבוֹד אֱלֹהֵי־יִשְׂרָאֵל and the cherubim, is the insertion.
Verse 23, however, with its use of the term כְּבוֹד יְהוָה and the absence of
the cherubim vehicle is original. The references to the city also occur in
verse 23. These references are integral to our understanding of the scattering of coal. The coal is to be scattered over the city (10:2) because the
כָּבוֹד is about to move from the enclosed holy space where it usually
resides and go up over the city to the mountain to the east (10:23). Thus
the righteous remnant are to be spared the awesome sight of the כָּבוֹד
by means of the ritual of the man in linen.

From our reconstruction, we can see that the vast majority of the
references to cherubim are to be attributed to a later hand. Indeed, the
entire section of 10:8–17 is probably the result of a large scribal insertion. Nevertheless, a cherub still features in the original text. This
cherub is probably part of the temple furniture. The כָּבוֹד begins its
departure from this cherub and, considering there would be plenty of

---

189   The preceding verb וַיֵּרוֹמוּ (10:19) is in the plural.

cherubim iconography in the הֵיכָל, and this is where the כָּבוֹד usually resides, there is every reason to view the cherub as part of this. That said, there remains the possibility that this cherub comes alive (as verse 7 of the MT suggests) in order to hand the coal to the man in linen. All references to the cherubim and wheels under the throne must be viewed as later insertions designed to integrate the vehicle of Ezekiel 1 into the original narrative concerning Yahweh abandoning his temple.

§ 1.3.4.3.4 Implications of our Cherub Subtext

There are further implications of our reconstruction of the possible cherub subtext in Ezekiel 10. First, we are faced with the question: what were the חַיּוֹת? If the cherubim = חַיּוֹת equation was not original to the text, then perhaps the חַיּוֹת were not originally cherubim. Second, if the two types of creature were originally distinct, then why have they been connected by a later editor? We will attempt to provide tentative answers to both these questions.

Concerning the identity of the חַיּוֹת, we already noted in our discussion of the Song of David (§1.3.3.4) that scholars are wrong to connect the cherub upon which Yahweh descends to heaven (Ps 18:11 = 2 Sam 22:11) with the חַיּוֹת vehicle in Ezekiel 1. We noted that the חַיּוֹת occur in a throne theophany. The vision authenticates the commissioning of the prophet and validates his message of judgement to the people. By contrast, the cherub participates in a storm theophany, whereby Yahweh descends from heaven in order to save the speaker. The חַיּוֹת are thus much more similar to the seraphim in Isaiah 6 (again a prophetic commissioning text) than they are to the cherubim depicted in Gen 3:24 and the Song of David.

The symbolism of the חַיּוֹת has been well expounded (see e.g. Block 1997: 93–98). They are four in number with four wings and four faces. Their wings stretch out upwards, perhaps supporting the firmament (1:23). Their movement, combined with the wheels, is such that they can move in every direction without needing to turn (1:17, 19). The creatures thus embody the universality of Yahweh. Traditionally, throne theophanies, similar to that depicted in Ezekiel 1, were linked to the divine council (to which the prophets had access). Such visions were thus more likely to have occurred in temples or palaces (which reflected the seat of judgement in heaven on earth). For Ezekiel and the exiles in Babylon, their location meant that the decisions of the divine council would have been unavailable to them. What Ezekiel's vision does, therefore, is to allow the prophet to receive his commissioning (in the same way as Isaiah) but in a foreign land. Yahweh is no longer restricted to his temple in Jerusalem but is transported to the bank of the river Chebar in order that Ezekiel can have access to the divine word.

If this interpretation is correct, then the חַיּוֹת are more similar to the seraphim than the cherubim. Indeed, the verbal link between Ezek 1:11, 23 and Isa 6:2 (concerning the wings of the creatures) supports this. The חַיּוֹת have four wings (rather than the six of the seraphim) because the symbolism of the number four is fundamental to this passage. Moreover, the name of the seraphim (from the root שׂרף "to burn") may also mean that we can compare them to the חַיּוֹת in MT of 1:13–14. These are enigmatic fiery creatures, who serve Yahweh in his throne theophany.

Interestingly, the locomotive function of the חַיּוֹת is not explicit in Ezekiel 1. It is the wheels and the wind that are necessary for the vehicle to move and the wings of the creatures function only to support the platform and cover their bodies (1:23). This is in stark contrast to the wings of the cherubim in Ezekiel 10, which help power the vehicle (10:16). Hence, as the locomotive function of the חַיּוֹת may not even be evident in Ezekiel 1 (see Block 1997: 97), there is even less reason to connect the חַיּוֹת with the cherub of the Song of David.

Consequently, disregarding Ezekiel 9–11, there is really no indication whatsoever that the חַיּוֹת should be interpreted as cherubim. We have already noted that their appearance is different from the cherubim described elsewhere in the Hebrew Bible. The term חַיּוֹת is usually translated as "living creatures". I would argue that this choice of gloss enervates the חַיּוֹת. Translations of Daniel 7, in which four similar creatures occur, render the Aramaic term חֵיוָא (which is cognate with Hebrew חַיָּה) as "beast" (e.g. RSV, NIV). The main reason why a distinction between the two terms has been maintained in translations of Daniel 7 and Ezekiel 1 is because of the identification of the cherubim as חַיּוֹת in Ezekiel 10. If this identification is to be regarded as secondary, then perhaps we are better to gloss חַיּוֹת as "beasts", when referring to them outside of their canonical context.[190] The חַיּוֹת are monstrous animals that epitomize the universality of Yahweh. They are not cherubim.

So, why are the cherubim linked to the חַיּוֹת by a later editor when they are actually quite different from each other? There are several probable reasons for the identification. First, the חַיּוֹת are enigmatic beings, which do not occur in biblical texts earlier than Ezekiel.[191] Hence the first readers of Ezekiel 1 may have been somewhat perplexed as to their identity. The cherubim = חַיּוֹת equation thus assimilates these enigmatic creatures into more familiar Hebrew tradition. The cherubim and the חַיּוֹת are supernatural winged beings with a close connection to Yahweh. Hence the equation was not wholly illogical. Second, as Zimmerli (1969a: 237) suggests, the important theme of the departure of the כָּבוֹד from the temple in Ezekiel 10–11 does not sit comfortably with the idea that the כָּבוֹד has already appeared to the prophet in Ezekiel 1. Originally, the prophet's vision of the temple in Ezek 8:1–11:25 was probably independent from his inaugural vision. Thus, when the two visions were brought together into a collection, the movement of the כָּבוֹד in Ezekiel 9–11 needed to be linked to the type of transportation described in Ezekiel 1. The vision of the חַיּוֹת and throne formed a natural introduction to the collection because, without it, the prophet's commissioning (Ezekiel 2) would not have been validated in the traditional way. The identification of the cherubim as חַיּוֹת, in this regard, does not stem from the inability of Ezekiel's disciples to understand the prophet's true message (as Zimmerli 1969a: 273 suggests), but from a desire to organize originally independent visions into a unified collection.

§ 1.3.4.3.5 A Synchronic Approach

If we can argue that the final text of Ezek 8:1–11:25 (and especially Ezekiel 10) is the result of a lengthy editorial process, which transformed its original meaning, then we must also admit that it was, in the main, standardized at a date earlier than its translation into Greek and the

---

190 The term ζῷα used in Revelation 4, a text undoubtedly inspired by Ezekiel 1 and Daniel 7, is only used elsewhere in the NT to refer to beasts (in a pejorative light). This supports our interpretation of the חַיּוֹת as beasts.

191 The beasts in Daniel 7 were probably inspired, to some extent, by Ezekiel 1.

copying of the Ezekiel scrolls at Qumran.[192] Thus a synchronic reading is important in order to do justice to the cherubim in their current context.

From a canonical perspective, the description of the cherubim in Ezekiel 1; 9–11 is arguably one of the most informative in the entire Hebrew Bible. This is the most thorough depiction of their physical appearance, especially in the form of real heavenly creatures rather than inanimate statues. As opposed to the lifeless statues described elsewhere in the Hebrew Bible (Ex 25:18–22; 1 Kgs 6:23–29; 2 Chr 3:10–13), the cherubim in Ezekiel's visions are monstrous and enigmatic. The differences between Ezekiel's cherubim and the cherubim iconography are striking. It may be that Ezekiel, or the writer, knew that the cherubim statues could never do justice to their heavenly counterparts and thus portrayed the cherubim in a way which would add potency to the theology he wished to express. Yet the quadruped cherub in the Song of David is a heavenly creature and not an inert statue. The cherubim in Ezekiel's visions are probably not quadrupeds (Ezek 1:5–7). If not, then we have conflicting descriptions of the physical form of animate cherubim in the Hebrew Bible. A synchronic reading of the cherubim in Ezekiel 1; 9–11, when compared to the cherub in the Song of David, may thus suggest that "cherubim" could be a label for different types of supernatural creatures and not one definite category. Alternatively, a synchronic reading may imply that cherubim were enigmatic creatures, whose physical appearance could be transmogrified.[193]

As for their function, we have noted in our discussion of other texts that the cherubim had both an apotropaic and a locomotive function. Their position within the temple and at the entrance to the Garden of Eden suggests that the cherubim guarded sacred space. Their appear-

---

192 The fragments of Ezekiel found at Qumran largely follow the MT (DJD 15:211–219 and DJD 23 – see Washburn 2002:134–136 for further references). Thus the significance attributed to the shorter LXX text must be kept in check. Nevertheless, it does not follow that the LXX stems from a desire to rid a longer and more complex text of its problems. It may be that there were two different traditions (one shorter, one longer) circulating at a very early stage.

193 Both interpretations show how a canonical reading of the cherubim biblical texts renders the physical form of the cherubim elusive. The ambiguous depictions of the cherubim in the Hebrew Bible may help to explain the varying and vague traditions concerning the physical appearance of the cherubim in early Jewish tradition. It may also explain Josephus' claim: "No one can tell, or even conjecture, what was the shape of these Cherubim" (*Ant* 8:73).

ance in the storm theophany in the Song of David also points in this direction. Their locomotive function is suggested by the description of Yahweh riding upon a cherub in Ps 18:11 = 2 Sam 22:11. In Ezekiel's visions, the guardian role of the cherubim is less perceptible. Instead, it is their ability to transport the deity that it underscored. Yet, where in the Song of David the deity rides on the back of a cherub, in Ezekiel's visions four cherubim unite in order that they can carry the deity in any direction. Consequently, they become Yahweh's throne carriers, an idea not made explicit in other biblical texts.

Furthermore, in Ezekiel's visions, the cherubim are transformed into creatures that symbolize the universality and omnipotence of Yahweh. The quaternity of heads (human, leonine, bovine, and aquiline) represents the four main domains of Yahweh's rule: those of man, wild and domestic animals, and birds. To some extent, the cherubim also become cosmic creatures, holding up the sky with their wings (1:23). They are thus deeply symbolic beings, epitomising divine supremacy. Their transformation suits well the theology of the final form of Ezekiel 1; 9–11. These passages are pivotal in understanding the overarching message of Ezekiel 1–11. Yahweh appears to the exiles in Babylon because it is with them that hope lies. The divine presence is no longer tied to the temple as the older theology suggested (1 Kgs 8:8) but can become a "sanctuary" for those in exile (Ezek 11:16). Thus the sanctuary provided by the temple and its cherubim is now available to the exiles by means of this new cherubim vehicle.

Moreover, in Ezekiel's vision, there is the first hint that the cherubim are part of an angelic order. Links are created between the cherubim and the seraphim. Both occur in prophetic commissioning texts and may be fiery creatures able to take part in rituals (Isa 6:6; Ezek 1:13–14, 10:7). Both have multiple pairs of wings, one of which covers their bodies (Ezek 1:11, 23 and Isa 6:2). In Ezek 3:12, the prophet hears the voice of the cherubim crying: "Blessed is the glory of the Lord from his place".[194] Their doxology can be likened to that of the seraphim in Isa 6:3 (see Halperin 1988: 44–45). Hence, in this verse, the cherubim are transformed into agents of praise. In a similar way, the wheels of the cherubim vehicle are transformed from inanimate mechanisms into angelic beings in Ezek 10:12–14 (see Halperin 1988:45–47), equipped

---

194 The doxology does not make much sense and, reading the text diachronically, *barukh* was probably originally *berum*, which makes a good deal more sense.

with heads, wings and eyes. Thus the manner in which the cherubim
and the wheels are described in Ezekiel 1–11 paves the way for the
angelic hierarchies that are more explicitly developed in later texts such
as 1 Enoch, *The Songs of the Sabbath Sacrifice*, and the Revelation of John.

§ 1.3.4.4 Summary

Our exegesis of Ezek 8:1–11:25 has shown that, if we are to do justice to
the significance of this text in relation to its portrayal of the cherubim,
then we must read the text from *both* a diachronic *and* a synchronic
perspective. This pericope is pivotal for recognizing how ideas about
the cherubim changed over time. They are transformed in this passage
from apotropaic beings, guarding the divine locale, into a category of
angelic beings. They become creatures that are symbolic of divine omnipotence and universality, who carry the throne of Yahweh to the
exiles. This transformation did not occur in the first edition of the text.
Originally, only one cherub featured in the narrative. This cherub was
part of the iconography of the הֵיכָל, the most holy area of the temple
where the divine presence resided. This cherub thus conformed to the
traditional conception of the creatures. It was a guardian of the divine
abode. Only later, when someone incorporated this vision into a collection (together with Ezekiel 1), was the lone cherub transformed into a
cherubim vehicle.

§ 1.4 Conclusions Emerging from Biblical Exegesis

Having examined all the biblical texts in which the כְּרֻבִים appear, we can now summarize our findings. Our evaluation of the semantics and syntax of the divine epithet, יֹשֵׁב הַכְּרֻבִים, has shown that it may not mean "Enthroned upon the Cherubim" as most scholars (e.g. Mettinger 1982b, 1999; Haran 1976: 246–259 and Block 1997: 306) argue. Indeed, this interpretation places far too great a weight on archaeological evidence, in the form of two Late Bronze images from Megiddo. Linguistic and literary evidence suggests that יֹשֵׁב is more likely to have the sense of "dweller" or "ruler". The former is preferred and may be interpreted as referring to Yahweh's residence in the temple, in accordance with traditions represented in 1 Kings 6–8.

Mettinger's theories concerning the historical place of a cherubim throne in the cults of Shiloh and Jerusalem (1982a, 1982b, 1999) can be dismissed as unsustainable. In particular, the occurrence of the cherubim formula in the Samuel ark narratives cannot be used to argue for the presence of a cherubim throne in the cult of Shiloh. It is used, in these Samuel passages, for literary rather than historical reasons. Moreover, any claims concerning the historical architecture of the temple/tabernacle can only ever be tentative. Frequently, the biblical evidence cannot be used as a witness to a historical reality but only as a witness to traditions that arose concerning sanctuary and cult.

In our discussion of the כְּרֻבִים as cultic images in § 1.2, we observed that they always occur within the most sacred areas of the sanctuary. Their appearance on walls, doors and curtains may be indicative of their apotropaic function. The sacred vegetation, with which the cherubim occur, may be symbolic of the divine threshold and thus also point to the tutelary function of the cherubim. The cherubim on the wheeled lavers (1 Kgs 7:27–39) function to set apart the space upon which offerings were made. The two cherubim statues in the Holy of Holies may also have a guardian role, screening the space above the ark and protecting the divine presence.

It has also been argued that the description of the cherubim images in the books of Chronicles and Ezekiel (texts which, on the whole, contain later traditions to those described in 1 Kings) display a shift in thinking concerning the cherubim. We suggested that Ezek 41:18–25

shows that the physical form of the cherubim had become associated
with the appearance of the cherubim in Ezekiel's visions (Ezekiel 8–11).
Similarly, the description of the cherubim in 1–2 Chronicles shows
signs of dependence on the Ezekiel traditions and perhaps an emerging
merkābāh theology.

The passages describing the כְּרֻבִים as real heavenly beings do not
give us precise details concerning the rank and role of the cherubim in
relation to other heavenly beings. Gen 3:24 does suggest, however, that
cherubim were associated with menacing apotropaic beings. This is
also implicit in the Song of David (2 Sam 22:11 = Ps 18:11), where the
cherubim occur with natural elements that become the weapons and
shields of Yahweh. The fact that the cherub is the only fully-fledged
supernatural being other than Yahweh to appear in the poem is testimony to the important role the cherubim had in Hebrew tradition of
safeguarding the divine presence.

The elevated status of the cherubim, their unique position in the
sanctuary and their apotropaic function are stressed in the poem of
Ezek 28:11–19. Here, the King of Tyre is granted an elite position as a
cherub on the holy mountain/the Garden of Eden (the divine abode).
Instead of respecting his position, the king profanes his sanctuaries and
is hence thrown down from the mountain.

The locomotive function of the cherubim is underscored in the Song
of David (2 Sam 22:11 = Ps 18:11). Here, a cherub becomes Yahweh's
charger, as he descends from heaven to earth. This function is also suggested in the final form of Ezekiel 8–11. This time, however, four cherubim hold up the platform upon which Yahweh's throne is situated.

Our discussion of the cherubim in Ezekiel 8–11 (§ 1.3.4) is critical to
how we understand biblical traditions concerning the cherubim to de-
velop over time. In the final form, the cherubim are identified as the
חַיּוֹת of Ezekiel 1 and thus, to some extent, acquire their characteristics.
Originally, a cherub was conceived as a quadruped (1 Sam 22:11 =
Ps 18:11) with one face and one set of wings (Ex 25:18–22; 37:7–9;
1Kgs 6:23–28). Following their identification with the חַיּוֹת in Ezekiel 10,
the cherubim become enigmatic beasts with fours faces and four wings.
Moreover, in the final text, a connection between the cherubim and the
seraphim is suggested in the description of their wings (1:11) and in the
doxology of the חַיּוֹת in Ezek 3:12. This connection was not original to
the text but occurs in an early but extensively revised edition of Ezekiel 8–11. It is the portrayal of the cherubim in Ezekiel which inspired
post-biblical cherubim traditions, such as those expounded in *The Songs
of the Sabbath Sacrifice* and the Enochic texts.

Part II
The Root *k-r-b* and Comparative Semitic Material

The word כְּרוּב looks like a typical form of Hebrew noun. From a tri-
literal root, it appears to belong to the same group of nouns as גְּבוּל,
'border', and רְכוּשׁ, 'goods'. However, the stem כרב is otherwise un-
attested in biblical Hebrew. Consequently, if we only had the Hebrew
Bible to help us, the meaning of the word כְּרוּב would have to be
decided from the context of the passages in which it appears. Yet
several scholars[195] have attempted to illuminate the meaning of כְּרוּב by
tracing its etymology. By examining instances of the root *k-r-b* in other
Semitic languages, scholars hope to determine the 'original' root meaning of כְּרוּב. This 'original' meaning is then thought to shed some light
on the biblical use of the word.

It is important to remember, however, that the meaning of any
given word cannot be established simply by exploring its origins. Barr,
in *The Semantics of Biblical Language* (1961: 107–160), exposed a popular
tendency to place too great an emphasis on the etymology of a word.
He argues that "etymology is not, and does not profess to be, a guide to
the semantic value of words in their current usage, and such value has
to be determined from the current usage and not from the derivation"
(1961: 107). Yet, according to Barr (1961: 107), there is a propensity
among some people to "feel that in some sense the 'original', the 'etymological meaning', should be a guide to the usage of words" and that
"when a word becomes in some way difficult... an appeal to the
etymology will lead to a 'proper meaning'."

In the case of the word כְּרוּב, it is perhaps all the more necessary to
ensure that etymology gives way to synchronic evidence when
attempting to establish the meaning of the word. This is because,
although scholars have argued that etyma of כְּרוּב exist in several other

---

195 E.g. Cooke (1936: 112), De Vaux (1960: 99), Dhorme (1926), Pfeiffer (1922) and
Vincent (1926)

Semitic languages, the absence of another Hebrew word with the base כרב means that we have to resort to more remote languages, both geographically and temporally, in order to uncover the possible etymology of the word. The semantic theorist, Lyons (1977: I, 244), argues that, "all too often in the past, grammarians and lexicographers have taken texts from widely separated periods and treated them as samples of the same language." According to Lyons (1977: I, 244), this is an example of the "etymological fallacy", "the failure to respect the distinction between diachronic and synchronic in semantics." Thus in order to evaluate the etymological data pertaining to כְּרוּב, we must acknowledge the fact that the meaning of the Hebrew word could have evolved beyond all recognition from its antecedents.

Having recognized the limitations of etymology, it may still remain helpful to survey the stem *k-r-b* in the other Semitic languages. Although the basic meaning of the word כְּרוּב is best sought in the synchronic, biblical evidence, the comparative Semitic data may still augment our understanding of the word כְּרוּב with additional nuances. Indeed, Barr (1961: 158) himself admits that "etymological recognition may be used in conjunction with the context of the Hebrew word to give a good semantic indication for its occurrence."

As we have seen in chapter 2, the word כְּרוּב refers to a type of winged, supernatural being, or representation of such a being. The seraphim in Isaiah 6 are often viewed as the closest biblical parallel to the cherubim. They too are winged creatures with a close connection to Yahweh. It is generally accepted that *their* name, from the root שׂרף, meaning "burn", points to the "fiery" or serpent-like quality of these beings. In the same way, it is possible that the cherubim received their name because the root *k-r-b*, at some point in its history, connoted a particular attribute or function of the creatures. Consequently, it is useful to examine the stem in other Semitic languages in order to decide whether or not the biblical use of the word כְּרוּב was influenced by a wider usage of the root.

At the beginning of the Twentieth Century, several Akkadian texts were published that generated new discussion concerning the origin of the Hebrew word כְּרוּב. In 1923, Langdon (1923: 190, n. 3), in his work on the Babylonian creation epic, declared that the Akkadian *kāribu* and *kurību* (which he argued have the sense of 'interceding statue') are "clearly identical with the Hebrew kĕrûb, cherub." Kāribu is the present participle of the verb karābu and has the meaning "one who prays" or "intercessor". Kurību is a diminutive form from the same root. Langdon was followed by Cooke (1936: 112) who, in his commentary on Ezekiel, argued that, by comparison with the Akkadian kāribu, "the source and meaning of the Hebr. kᵉrûb, kᵉrûbhîm, may now be considered fairly well ascertained." He contends, "the Hebrews... borrowed the name, and to some extent the functions, of the kᵉrûbhîm from Babylon" (1936: 112–113). It is Dhorme's article on the name of the cherubim, published in 1926, which remains the most thorough examination to date on the etymology of כְּרוּב. He states that "le kâribu et le kerûb appartenaient à la meme racine et, par conséquent, présentaient une signification analogue" (1926: 338).[196] Dhorme suggests that inherent within the Akkadian words kāribu and kurību, as well as the biblical כְּרוּב, was the meaning "to pray for", or "intercede". He claims that not only was the Hebrew word כְּרוּב borrowed directly from Akkadian, but that the significance and function of the cherubim were, to some extent, influenced by the meaning of the Akkadian cognates. He thus concludes that the cherubim had, like the Akkadian kāribu and kurību, an intercessory function, to pray to Yahweh on behalf of the king and his people. It is the purpose of this chapter to reassess the etymology of the Hebrew word כְּרוּב and to challenge Dhorme's view that the Akkadian data is sufficient evidence for the intercessory role of the biblical cherubim.

Before engaging with Dhorme's article in more detail, it is helpful to review the comparative Semitic material, not least because, since the publication of Dhorme's article, there have been several new texts discovered which contain the root k-r-b. Although the stem is not otherwise known in Biblical Hebrew, it is found frequently in East Semitic (in Akkadian) and in South Semitic (in Old South Arabic and Ethiopic). In North-West Semitic, the root occurs in Aramaic and Syriac (Freedman and O'Connor 1995: 310) and some scholars have argued for its existence in Phoenician and Ugaritic. As the South Semitic data tends to agree with the East Semitic material, we will not examine the

---

196 De Vaux also sees a connection between the Akkadian and Hebrew words but argues that the Hebrew writers did not borrow כְּרוּב directly from Akkadian, but rather that the word entered Hebrew via a West-Semitic language (De Vaux 1967, 237-238).

respective texts in detail but will refer to them if necessary. As
Phoenician and Ugaritic are deemed to be of the same branch of Semitic
as biblical Hebrew, it is suitable to begin with the possible attestations
of the root *k-r-b* in the extant Ugaritic and Phoenician texts, before
moving on to the Aramaic and Akkadian material.

In *A Dictionary of the Ugaritic Language* (2003: 454), del Olmo Lete
and Sanmartín include two entries for the stem *k-r-b*. The first entry is
marked as a very uncertain reading in *KTU* 1.19 i 2 and is listed as
being cognate with the Arabic *karaba*, Ethiopic *karabā* and Syriac *ʾetkreb*,
which have the meaning "twist" or "plait". This uncertain instance of
the root *k-r-b* occurs at the beginning of a notoriously difficult passage
of the Aqhat myth and the exact reading and meaning of the section
has been widely debated by scholars. Some scholars tentatively read
tkrb followed by a word-divider.[197] Huehnergard (1987: 140) suggests
that the reading *tkrb* could be a verb from the root *k-r-b* meaning "to
twist, curl, bend" with the goddess Anat as its subject. He views the
verb as parallel to *tql* in line 3, meaning "she falls, stoops". A better
interpretation of the passage is that given by Wyatt (2000: 288), who
maintains that the reading *tkrb* is very uncertain here. He follows
Driver, who reads *trd*, "came down", which makes for a much better
parallel to *tql*. He also follows other scholars in seeing Aqhat's bow,
and not Anat, as the subject of both verbs. This seems more likely, as
the bow is certainly the subject of the verbs in lines 4 and 5. Owing to
the fact that this is a dubious instance of the root *k-r-b* in Ugaritic, it
seems fruitless to try to argue for the existence of an etymon of the
Hebrew כְּרוּב here.

Huehnergard (1987: 140) has suggested that another occurrence of
the root *k-r-b* (with a meaning cognate to *k-r-b* "plait, twist" in Syriac,
Ethiopic and Arabic) exists in adjectival form in the syllabic transcription of *PRU* 6 121:4, modifying the noun "sheep". He presumes that the
term denotes a specific attribute of the sheep or, more plausibly, their
wool (being matted or curly). He also lists the Hebrew root *k-b-r*[II] as a
possible cognate to this word, the *b* and *r* switching by metathesis.
Although this root does not exist in verbal form in biblical Hebrew, the
nouns כְּבָרָה "sieve", מַכְבֵּר "netted cloth" and מִכְבָּר "grate" show that

---

the root probably had a similar meaning to *k-r-b* "twist, plait" found in other Semitic languages. If, as Huehnergard contends, the Ugaritic *k-r-b* is cognate with the Hebrew root *k-b-r*[II], then we have to infer that metathesis has occurred in one or other of the forms at some point in its history. It cannot be said with any certainty whether or not these forms are etymologically related to Hebrew כְּרוּב. Unquestionably, however, there is a difficulty in perceiving a connection between the biblical portrayal of the cherubim and the meaning "to twist, plait". A lack of correspondence between the diachronic and the synchronic evidence here makes it difficult to argue for the existence of an etymological relationship between the words, even if there originally was one.

The second entry included by del Olmo Lete and Sanmartín refers to the appearance of the stem in the Ugaritic onomasticon.[198] The etymology of the root in these proper names is uncertain, though it is possible that it entered Ugaritic via Akkadian. These names are of limited value to our inquiry into the etymology of כְּרוּב because names are not necessarily accurate representations of the language spoken in the society where they occur. They can, for example, preserve archaic or foreign qualities.[199]

Freedman and O'Connor (1995: 310) mention two other possible occurrences of the root *k-r-b* in the Ugaritic texts. However, they regard both readings as unreliable. The first appears in *KTU* 1.16 i, 2. Here, *k·krb·b* has been read by some scholars, although what this phrase means is not clear. The reading *kklb·bbtk*, "Like a dog at your house/tomb,"[200] accepted by the majority of scholars, makes much better sense. Here, *klb*, 'dog', is paralleled with *ʾinr*, 'whelp', a pairing which is also found at *KTU* 1.114:12–13. The fact that 'dog' and 'whelp' occur together elsewhere in the Ugaritic texts is enough to argue that the reading *krb* in *KTU* 1.16 i, 2 is likely a scribal error. As the Ugaritic letters 'l' and 'r' cannot easily be mistaken it is likely that this error was an auditory one.

The second alleged occurrence of *krb* mentioned by Freedman and O'Conner is at *KTU* 1.3 i, 12. Here, the text reads, *bkrb·ẓm·r'idn*.

---

198 See Grøndahl (1967: 151), Watson (1995: 223; 1996: 100)

199 For more on this, see Huehnergard (1987: 9)

200 See Wyatt (2002: 219, n. 195)

However, Herdner (1963: 14) argues, "peut-être convient-il de séparer à la suite de Cassuto, Gaster et Ginsberg: *bk rb ʾ ẓm rʾidn*." The Ugaritic *bk*, cognate with Aramaic *bq* and Greek *bĩkos*, refers to a 'beaker' or 'large cup'[201] and occurs again at *KTU* 1.45:10. The amended division of the line thus makes a good deal more sense, given the context of Baal's feast, and should be translated, "A large cup, mighty to behold."[202]

From our survey of the relevant data, it appears that there is no extant Ugaritic cognate which could help shed light on the meaning of the Hebrew כְּרוּב. Although it is conceivable that Ugaritic *krb* meaning "to plait" or "twist" is related to Hebrew כְּרוּב, it is difficult to see how this can enrich our understanding of the biblical cherubim.

The Phoenician evidence for the stem *k-r-b* is, unfortunately, even less helpful. Only one attestation of *k-r-b* in Phoenician has ever even been argued for.[203] Grelot (1957: 273–279) claimed that the root features in an inscription on the Al-Biqʿah arrow-head, dated to the 11th–10th Century B.C.E. The arrow-head was first published by Milik (1956: 3–6), who read the inscription as *ḥ ṣzkrb/bnbn ʿn* and divided the text thus: *ḥ ṣ zkr {b} / bn Bn ʿn*. The final 'b' of the first line is regarded by Milik as a dittography, a common scribal error when passing from one line to the next. Hence he translates the inscription, "Arrow of Zakkur, son of Binʿan(a?)".

Grelot (1957: 276), on the other hand, proposes to divide the text differently (*ḥ ṣ z krb/bn Bn ʿn*) and translates, "Arrow that Bn Bnʿn offered". He thus regards *krb* as a verb, meaning 'to offer', and views the inscription as evidence that the arrow was part of a cultic offering or dedication. As the only other use of the stem *k-r-b* in North-West Semitic with a cultic sense is found in the Hebrew כְּרוּב, Grelot (1957: 273) justifies his translation of *krb* by means of an etymology based on Akkadian and South Arabic. As stated previously, the root *k-r-b* occurs frequently in South and Eastern Semitic. In both, it can have the meaning "to bless, pray". Grelot refers to certain occasions in South

---

201 See del Olmo Lete and Sanmartín (2003: 219)

202 See Wyatt (2002: 70, n. 4)

203 There is also a Punic inscription from Sainte-Monique which reads *w t krbm ʿl*, 'and the cherubim above' (see Donner and Röllig 2002, 96, 2). However, this text dates to a period too late to argue for Phoenician influence on the biblical use of כְּרוּב.

Arabic where the stem *k-r-b* receives a cultic significance, which surpasses the idea of prayer and concerns, instead, "une certaine catégorie d'oblations votives," similar to that of the dedication of the Phoenician arrow-head. As for the Akkadian evidence, Grelot appeals to the meaning of *ikribu/ekrebu*, a derivative of the root *karābu* ('to pray, bless'), identified by Landsberger (1928: 303). According to Landsberger, *ikribu/ekrebu* has the sense of "devote" or "present a votive offering" (see Grelot 1957: 275). Grelot argues that the Akkadian usage of the root is similar to that of the South Arabic and that both these uses of the root support his hypothesis that the Phoenician arrow-head inscription not only contains the verb *krb*, but that this verb means "offered".

Yeivin (1958) contests Grelot's translation and criticises his reliance on etymological data that goes beyond the bounds of North-West Semitic. In addition, he highlights a further problem with Grelot's division of the text: the absence of a personal name in the inscription. According to Grelot, the designation of the offerer solely by his patronym can be compared to the names in the list of Solomon's functionaries in 1 Kings 4:7–19a. He argues that this way of naming men is not unexpected because these particular individuals are distinguished by their hereditary social position, handed down by means of their family name. However, according to Yeivin (1958: 586), the double patronym, בן בן־ען, "serait assez étrange." The Al-Biqʿah arrow-head is one of several similar arrow-head inscriptions found in Lebanon and Palestine. According to Gibson (1982: 1), "all the texts have the word חץ followed by a personal name with or without a patronymic or qualifying adjective." Thus it seems very unlikely that the Al-Biqʿah inscription would have a different formula from all the other Phoenician arrow-head inscriptions of the same period, having instead: חץ, followed by the relative pronoun, a finite verb and, finally, the personal name in the form of a double patronym. Gibson (1982: 8) follows Yeivin (1957: 586–588) in arguing that the tip of the Al-Biqʿah arrow-head has worn away and that the line *ḥṣ zkrb* would originally have read *ḥṣ zkrbʿl*, "Arrow-head of *Zkrbʿl*."[204] Thus it seems extremely unlikely that we

---

204 *Zkrbʿl* is a personal name made up of the verb *zkr*, 'remember', and *bʿl*, 'lord'/'Baal'. This name is attested elsewhere in Phoenician in the Wen-Amon report (*ANET*, 26) where it designates the 11th century king of Byblos.

have here a verbal form of the root *k-r-b* with which we can compare the biblical noun כְּרוּב.

In Aramaic, the use of the stem *k-r-b* agrees with that in the Hebrew Bible. However, in all the late East Aramaic dialects there exists the verb כרב meaning 'plough'. This sense of the root *k-r-b* is also found in Arabic and Akkadian, for example in the Akkadian word *nukaribbu*, meaning 'gardener' or 'date grower' as well as the denominative form *nukaribbūtu(m)*, 'gardener's work, gardening'. Unlike the Ugaritic data which we discussed earlier, there may be a correspondence here between the diachronic and the synchronic, i.e. between the Aramaic meaning of the stem *k-r-b* and the biblical portrayal of the cherubim.

First, the Hebrew Bible associates the cherubim with vegetation. The best known passage in this regard is Gen 3:24, where Yahweh places the cherubim to the east of the Garden of Eden in order to guard the way to the Tree of Life. In Ezek 28:14 and 16, a cherub is also situated in the Garden of Eden. In Ezek 41:18–19 and 1 Kings 6–7, cherubim are depicted on the walls and doors of the temple, alternating with palm trees and open flowers. Hence there may be a correspondence between the meaning "to plough" or "garden" and the function of the cherubim.

Yet, there is no evidence that the cherubim ever actually tended the plants. They are never described as ploughing or tilling the soil. In Gen 3:24, they are given a clear task: to guard the way to the Tree of Life. The iconography described in Ezek 41:17–19 also points in this direction, with a cherub either side of a central tree. Hence the function of the cherubim seems to be to guard the sacred plants, not to tend to them and thus the Aramaic meaning of *k-r-b* does not illuminate the function of the biblical cherubim.

On the other hand, other scholars have suggested that the connection between the cherubim and the meaning "to plough" lies in their physical appearance and not in their purpose or function (see Dhorme 1926: 330). They argue that the cherubim could have been associated with the oxen that pulled the plough. Evidence for this connection is found in Ezekiel's vision of the cherubim in chapter 10. Where, in Ezekiel's vision in chapter 1, the four faces attributed to each beast are said to be that of a man, a lion, an ox and an eagle, in the second vision the four faces are said to be that of a man, a lion, a *cherub* and an eagle (10:14). This has caused some scholars to claim that the prophet saw a certain resemblance between the cherub, on the one hand, and the ox, on the other.

However, the assertion that the prophet changed the face of the ox to that of a cherub merely because he saw a correspondence between the two is not sufficient. There is a more plausible explanation for the removal of the bovine features of the face. This is given by Halperin in his important work, *The Faces of the Chariot* (1988), where he argues that the author of Ezekiel 10:14 purposefully deleted the ox's face of 1:10 and substituted it instead with the rather uninformative "cherub's face". The reason for this replacement is, according to Halperin, that the ox's face was a reminder of the golden calf episode at Sinai and hence represented Israel's apostasy. Such an interpretation of this substitution is made explicit in rabbinic tradition.[205] Hence, there is no need to argue for the equation of cherubic and bovine features and thus the Aramaic etymology of *k-r-b* does not tell us anything about the physical appearance of the biblical cherubim.

It is to East Semitic that we have to turn in order to find the root *k-r-b* used with any measure of frequency. As stated earlier, it is the study by Dhorme which remains the most comprehensive examination to date of the etymology of Hebrew כְּרוּב. It will be useful to summarize briefly his argument before proceeding to evaluate its reasoning. First, Dhorme asserts that the Akkadian *karābu*, "to pray or bless", can be related etymologically to the Hebrew verb בָּרַך, "to bless". Not only are the semantic ranges of both words remarkably similar,[206] but Dhorme argues that one word is clearly a derivative of the other, 'b' switching with 'k' by means of metathesis (1926: 331). The present participle of the verb *karābu* is *kāribu* and, Dhorme argues, has the meaning "one who prays" or "intercessor". It refers in many texts to the devout and faithful person, who comes to pray in the temple (see Dhorme 1926: 334), however, it can also refer to a god or goddess, who intercedes on behalf of humanity. According to Dhorme, the *šedu* and *lamassu*, which he describes as winged bulls, are such intercessory gods. Their

---

205   E.g. Tanh. Buber ʾEmor #23 (ed. 49a-b [222]), cited in Halperin (1988: 163)
206   The semantic fields of both words include the blessing of god by man as well as the blessing of man by god.

intercessory function is described in the code of Hammurapi. They are said to intercede on behalf of the king in the presence of the god Marduk and the goddess ,arpanit at the entrance of the temple in Babylon (see Dhorme 1926: 335–336).

According to Dhorme, the *šedu* and *lamassu* effectively play the part of the "dieux *kāribu*," "the gods who intercede," a phrase also found in a Babylonian religious chronicle (see King 1910: 84). This chronicle dates to the time of *Nabū-mukīn-apli*, around 990–995 B.C.E. The text recounts several miracles or supernatural events that were interpreted as either good or bad omens. Dhorme (1926: 335–336) translates the text as follows: "Dans l'année 24 du roi *Nabû-mukîn-apli*, le dieu *karîbu* qui [se trouve] à droite de la porte du naos, on vit qu'il marchait." He argues that this "dieu *kāribu*" was an intercessory god, who stood by the entrance to the sanctuary. The fact that the text speaks specifically of the "dieu *kāribu*" to the right of the door, implies, in Dhorme's view, that the god is one of a pair. This, he argues, would be similar to the pair of cherubim made for the Holy of Holies of Solomon's temple in 1 Kings 6.

For Dhorme, the *kāribu* is, like the *šedu* and *lamassu*, one of a pair of intercessory gods, who guard the way into the sanctuary. The gods were deliberately placed in their positions in the temple in order to intercede on behalf of the king, or of ordinary worshippers, with the principal deity of the sanctuary (Dhorme 1926: 338). However, the difference between the *kāribu*, on the one hand, and the *šedu* and *lamassu*, on the other, is that the *kāribu* is situated at the entrance to the Holy of Holies (*papaḫu*) and not merely at the door of the sanctuary. The *kāribu* is closer to the principal deity and is thus the "orant par excellence" and, as such, "évoque singulièrement celui de keroub" (Dhorme 1926: 336).

Another text, which Dhorme contends supports the connection between the Akkadian *kāribu* and the Hebrew כְּרוּב, is a building inscription from the reign of the Assyrian king, Esarhaddon. In this text, the king describes his restoration of the temple of Assur (see Borger 1956: 87). Dhorme (1926: 338) translates the text as follows: "Les portes en bois de cyprès, dont l'odeur est bonne, d'une incrustation d'or je revêtis et j'en consolidai les battants. La demeure d'Assur, mon seigneur, je recouvris d'or. Des dieux *laḫ-me*, des dieux *ku-ri-bi* en vermeil, de part et d'autre je dressai. A l'intérieur du naos (*pa-paḫ*) d'Assur, mon seigneur, des statues d'or... à droite et à gauche, je dressai." It is clear in this text that the *kāribu* (or in this case *kurību*) gods are statues of deities, which are placed in the Holy of Holies. The position of these statues in the sanctuary is remarkably similar to the position of the cherubim in 1 Kings 6 and, as their names both appear to derive from a root *k-r-b*, Dhorme claims that the Akkadian *kāribu* and *kurību* are the prototypes of the Hebrew cherub.

According to Dhorme, just as Hebrew ברך is cognate with Akkadian *karābu*, so כְּרוּב is related to Akkadian *kāribu*. Thus he concludes that the Israelites borrowed the cherubim from the Mesopotamian concept. Consequently, he contends that the cherubim are "les êtres dont le nom était le symbole de la prière perpétuelle et de l'adoration ininterrompue" (1926: 339). They constantly interceded with Yahweh on behalf of humanity. Dhorme suggests, then, that the Hebrew understanding of the cherubim was influenced by the etymology of the noun כְּרוּב, which, derived from the Akkadian *kāribu* or *kurību*, had, innate within it, the meaning of the Akkadian stem *k-r-b*, "to pray, bless, intercede".

A closer scrutiny of Dhorme's argument, however, reveals several flaws, which may prevent us from placing too great an emphasis on the link between כְּרוּב and *kāribu*. First, his initial premise, that the Hebrew verb ברך can be connected etymologically to the Akkadian verb *karābu* by means of metathesis, has since been refuted. Mitchell, in his study on the meaning of ברך in the Old Testament, argues that "in spite of the close similarity in meaning to NW Semitic *brk* "to bless," it is unlikely that the two are related; metathesis of the first and third radicals of a root is extremely rare" (1987: 11). He maintains that Akkadian *karābu* is related instead to the South Arabic *krb*, "to consecrate, sacrifice". Thus, even if כְּרוּב does derive from the Akkadian use of *krb*, it seems questionable whether the Hebrew authors and their audience would have necessarily made a connection between the cherubim and the meaning "to pray, bless". Moreover, in none of the biblical passages is an intercessory function of the cherubim made apparent. The cherubim are said to guard the way to the Tree of Life in the Garden of Eden (Gen. 3:24), adorn cultic furniture (e.g. Ex 26:1) and transport Yahweh from heaven to earth (2 Sam 22:11 = Ps 18:10). They are never described as praying or interceding with Yahweh on behalf of humankind.[207]

A second major flaw in Dhorme's argument is his failure to recognize the difference between the present participle *kāribu* and the diminutive *kurību*. Towards the end of his article, Dhorme states, "Nul doute que le *kuribu* ne corresponde au *kâribu* d'antan" (1926: 338). Later, he adds, "Quel que fût le nom adopté, *kâribu* "orant", *kuribu* "petit orant"... il s'agit toujours du même être qui se trouve à l'entrée du sanctuaire" (1926: 339). In the *Chicago Assyrian Dictionary*, however, an important difference between the two forms is noted. *Kāribu* is recorded as an adjective (CAD VIII, 216), whereas *kurību* is said to be a substantive (CAD VIII, 259). If this is the case, *kāribu* may be nothing more than a descriptive word, modifying a god (or a statue of a god), and not a noun designating a type of divine being. Indeed, the data suggests that *kāribu* is used in a generic way, to refer to any statue which was fashioned in a position of prayer. If this is the case, then Dhorme's translation of the Babylonian chronicle is somewhat misleading as it implies that the term *kāribu* is the name of a divine being. Consequently, instead of Dhorme's rendering, "the god *kāribu*", it would be better to translate, "the god who is in a position of prayer". The Akkadian *kāribu* can thus be used to denote any deity in a position of prayer and not a specific type of deity who was the "orant par excellence."

Furthermore, Dhorme contends that the *šedu* and *lamassu* were "dieux *kāribu*", interceding deities. He describes these deities as winged bulls, which, if correct, takes us one step further towards the biblical

---

207 We must be careful, in this regard, not to be misled by the apparent function of the seraphim in Isaiah 6. Scholars often link the seraphim to the cherubim, as both are winged supernatural beings associated with Yahweh's throne. Consequently, it may be tempting to see a shared function between these two types of divine beings. As they appear in Isa 6, the main function of the seraphim seems to be to praise Yahweh. Yet a further role of these beings may be to intercede between Yahweh and humanity. This is perhaps evident in Isa 6:6-7, where it is not until a seraph purifies Isaiah's lips with a burning coal that the prophet is able to communicate with Yahweh and receive his mission. Divine Council settings such as that of Isaiah 6 often appear when God needs to make a decision about the future of humanity. Hence the need for an intercessor, to plead the case of mankind, seems all the more appropriate. Nevertheless, ultimately it is Isaiah who fulfils that task and not the seraph and thus the intercessory function of the seraphim remains questionable.

cherubim which may also be winged quadrupeds (see § 1.3.3 and Part III). Yet, Black and Green in their dictionary, *Gods, Demons and Symbols of Ancient Mesopotamia*, firmly state that these deities were of human form, the *lamassu* being a female protective deity and the *šedu* being her male counterpart. Although we cannot be entirely sure of the physical appearance of the *šedu*, Black and Green (1992: 115) argue that the *lamassu* is "usually depicted in quite consistent form, usually introducing worshippers into the presence of important deities, and wearing a long, often flounced skirt, with one or both hands raised in supplication to the major god." Described in this way, the *lamassu* seems to be a far cry from the biblical cherubim both with respect to her gender and physical form and with respect to her ideological function within the temple.

Turning to the diminutive form *kurību*, we *can* argue that the word refers to a statue of a specific type of divine being. In the Esarhaddon text, cited by Dhorme, the *kurību* statues appear together with *laḫmu* figures. The *laḫmu*, whose name means "hairy", was of human form and, like the *šedu* and *lamassu*, was a beneficent and protective supernatural being. *Laḫmu* figures have been found in the foundations of buildings dating to the Neo-Assyrian period, which suggests that their function was to ward off malevolent demons and thus protect the edifice. In another building text from the reign of Esarhaddon, figurines of *kurību* appear again, but this time in connection with a series of other statues of animals and monsters (see Borger 1956: 33:10). The *Chicago Assyrian Dictionary* (VIII, 559) translates the passage as follows: "I had fashioned (for the entrance of the Ištar temple in Arbela) lion (representations), *anzû* (represented as) shouting, *laḫmu*-monsters, *ᵈku-ri-bi* (of silver and copper)." The lion, the *anzû* and the *laḫmu* are all examples of apotropaic or guardian beings. They are situated at the entrance of the Arbela temple in this passage, just as the *laḫmu* are placed at the entrance to the cella of Assur in the previous Esarhadddon text, to protect the building from evil. The *kurību* is connected with these apotropaic figures. Thus Dhorme's argument that the *kāribu* or *kurību* figure was an "orant par excellence", situated in the Holy of Holies, not merely at the entrance to the sanctuary, is inaccurate. The Esarhaddon texts show that the *kurību* could be found both adjacent to the Holy of Holies and on the outer gates of a temple.

The physical form of the *kurību* is unknown, yet one text, describing an Assyrian prince's vision of the underworld, suggests that it was not human. In his vision, the prince sees a succession of fifteen monsters, the first of which is said to have the head of a *kurību* but human hands and feet (see Von Soden 1936: 16; *ANET*, 109). This text is unique in two ways. First, it is the only text that does not refer to the *kurību* as a figurine or statue and, second, it implies that the *kurību* had, like some of the other guardian figures in the Esarhaddon texts, bestial or supernatural physical features. Thus the *kurību* has more in common with the theriomorphic, or therianthropic, *anzu* and *laḫmu*, than with the anthropomorphic *šedu* and *lamassu*.

Having focused on the Akkadian terms *kāribu* and *kurību* in more detail, it appears that *kāribu* is used to describe gods in a position of prayer, whereas *kurību* is used in connection with apotropaic beings. In none of the texts that allude to the *kurību* is an intercessory role made apparent. Consequently, Dhorme's view that "Nul doute que le *kuribu* ne corresponde au *kâribu* d'antan" cannot be sustained. What this difference may show, in regard to the biblical cherubim, is that the Hebrew word כְּרוּב has more in common with the Akkadian *kurību* than *kāribu*. This suggests that, if כְּרוּב was borrowed from the Akkadian use of the root *k-r-b*, as Dhorme and others argue, the original root meaning, "to pray for, intercede", has not necessarily filtered into the Hebrew understanding of the word כְּרוּב. The word *kurību* seems to refer, first and foremost, to an apotropaic figure and not to an interceding god or statue of a god, as Dhorme suggests. Hence the Hebrew word כְּרוּב, if borrowed from the Akkadian *kurību*, may only have within it this sense of the word, and not the meaning "to pray for" or "intercede". If this is the case, Dhorme's argument that the cherubim were beings whose name was the symbol of perpetual prayer and uninterrupted adoration, cannot be upheld.

Dhorme demonstrates in his article that it is the Akkadian usage of the root *k-r-b* which undoubtedly presents the best parallel to Hebrew כְּרוּב. However, it is the meaning of the substantive *kurību* and not the adjective *kāribu* which evokes the biblical cherubim. In the *Chicago Assyrian Dictionary* (VIII, 559), a *kurību* is said to be a "representation of a protective genius with specific non-human features." This certainly accords with the biblical description of the cherubim. Thus, if the

Hebrew כְּרוּב is related etymologically to the Akkadian *kurību*, it is an apotropaic or guardian role of the cherubim, and not an intercessory one, which should be stressed.

In conclusion, it appears, from our survey of *k-r-b* in Semitic, that there are three roots. First, the Ugaritic data yielded *k-r-b* meaning "twist" or "plait", which also occurs in Aramaic and South Semitic. Second, in late Aramaic, Arabic and Akkadian, *k-r-b* occurs with the sense of "plough" or "garden". Finally, in Akkadian and South Arabic, a root *k-r-b* means "pray" or "intercede". Alternatively, all three may be derivations of a single original root, perhaps with the basic meaning "to bring together". All three roots could be etymologically related to the Hebrew כְּרוּב, yet there is (as is so often the case when studying ancient languages) no firm evidence on which to prove an etymological connection. Nevertheless, where there is a correspondence in meaning between the synchronic and the diachronic data, i.e. between the biblical and the comparative Semitic evidence, there is firmer ground on which to argue for a link between the two. Consequently, shades of meaning that are attributed to the cherubim in the biblical texts can be further accentuated by means of a comparison with the corresponding Semitic data. It is the form *kurību*, derived from the Akkadian word *karābu* "to pray", which provides us with the closest lexical parallel to the biblical כְּרוּב. If the two words are etymologically related, then the Akkadian evidence highlights the apotropaic qualities of the cherubim. Subsequently, the use of the verb שׁמר in relation to the cherubim in Gen 3:24 and סכך in Exodus, Kings, Chronicles and Ezekiel, may acquire greater significance in the light of the Akkadian evidence. The cherubim are placed at the boundary between the sacred and the profane, to protect the holy from contamination.

Part III
The Archaeological Evidence

In fifty-six out of the ninety-one occurrences of the lexeme, כְּרוּב denotes cultic objects or decoration rather than abstract heavenly beings. Thus, although the כְּרֻבִים exist solely as a textual phenomenon, it is inevitable that they have been compared to figures depicted in cultic iconography in the extant ancient Near Eastern archaeological record. How far we can be justified in comparing the biblical cherubim to archaeological data is a contentious issue. There are seldom labels attached to ancient iconography and there is such a plethora of weird and wonderful creatures depicted in ancient Near Eastern art that we may only be able to guess at which of these a cherub might be (see Freedman and O'Connor 1995: 316–318). Moreover, depictions of 'cherub-like' beings are often thought either to represent an avatar of a particular deity (or sometimes king) or to function as an attribute creature of that deity.[208] Thus it is difficult to determine which image may denote a cherub in its own right, and which may signify another supernatural being altogether. Nevertheless, in the three most important encyclopaedia entries for כְּרוּב, archaeological evidence is always drawn upon. Mettinger (1999) and Meyers (1992) view the iconographic evidence as integral to our understanding of the biblical cherubim, as opposed to Freedman and

---

208 This problem comes to the fore if we try to compare the cherubim of the Solomonic temple with the hybrid creatures decorating the temple at ʿAin Dara (see Abu Assaf 1990: 25-31). The hybrids occur with lions, on gateways and around walls, as do the cherubim in the biblical descriptions of the temple and its furnishings. Thus some (e.g. Bloch-Smith 2002: 90) have argued that we can legitimately compare these hybrids to the cherubim. Yet, the temple (which is very similar to the Solomonic temple in architectural design and proportion) is dedicated to the goddess Ishtar, who is often identified with the lion and hybrid creatures (indeed, the hybrids decorating the temple have notably feminine characteristics). Thus, it may be inappropriate to associate the biblical cherubim with the ʿAin Dara hybrids, given that their occurrence may be inextricably linked to the goddess Ishtar and not to their ideological role vis-à-vis the sanctuary.

O'Connor (1995), who remain skeptical concerning its value. It is worth discussing further the issues involved when incorporating archaeological evidence into a study of a biblical concept.

Meyers (1976: 3), in her study of the tabernacle menorah, coins the phrase "biblical artifacts" to denote cultic appurtenances described in biblical texts and for which we have no certain archaeological parallels. She argues that because the design of a cultic object often outweighs its function, the object may be classified a work of art. In this way, it belongs to the world of forms rather than ideas. She cites Focillon, who argues: "In order to exist at all, a work of art must be tangible. It must renounce thought, must become dimensional, must both measure and qualify space. It is in this very turning outward that its inmost principle resides" (Meyers 1976: 3). Thus the cherubim statues and decoration described in the Hebrew Bible belong to a visual world, which evokes emotion, not intellect. They constitute "biblical artifacts" and, as such, Meyers argues that we must interpret them in the same way as real material remains (Meyers 1976: 3). She states: "The problems that beset an archaeologist when he unearths a cultic device are of the same order as the problems that must be dealt with in the examination of the textual description of a cultic device. The description of some appurtenance in the tabernacle texts must be considered as belonging to the same order of evidence as the published plate of some such object in an excavation report. We should not be concerned if the verbal description found in the biblical account does not always provide us with an accurate mental image or an exactly reproduceable object; for the possession of such an image or object in itself would tell us no more than does the possession of an actual artifact" (Meyers 1976: 2). Thus Meyers argues that "biblical artifacts" must be handled within the iconographic sphere if their true cultic meaning is to be understood.

Although there is much of value in Meyers' argument, there is one important difference between a "biblical artifact" and a real material artifact. While we can be sure that real archaeological remains were an actual physical reality in the lives of ancient people, this is not so with "textual artifacts". There is no reason why a "biblical artifact" could not be a literary creation and thus never actually have functioned in the cult of Israel or Judah at all. For example, although we can be sure that the cult stand found at Taanach[209] actually existed as a cultic object (and was probably utilized in the worship of Astarte or Asherah), we can never be sure (in fact, we are highly doubtful) that the cherubim affixed to the כַּפֹּרֶת of the Exodus tabernacle ever existed, or functioned, as real cultic objects in the way they are described. Nevertheless, what Meyers' argument does show is that we are likely to find comparative material for the biblical cherubim in the archaeological remains of the ancient Near East because of the status of the cherubim as cultic objects and decoration.[210] Even if the cherubim of the כַּפֹּרֶת never existed, their literary creator did not imagine them *ex nihilo* but must have been influenced by common cultural acceptances concerning the design of cultic appurtenances.

Yet we must be careful as regards the questions we can reasonably expect the archaeological evidence to answer. As is often said (e.g. Miller 1991: 96–97), material artifacts are somewhat "mute" as they do not often tell us who designed them and where they originated.[211] Precious objects, such as amulets and seals, could travel long distances.[212] Skilled artisans, famous for their expertise, were employed by foreign dignitaries, who desired the opulent fashions of the day (see e.g. 2 Sam 5:11; 1 Kgs 5; 7:13–45). Small kingdoms and tribal confederacies were frequently overthrown by the dominant empire of the time and subjected to vassalage and the cultural influences of their masters. It is certain, therefore, that the population of Israel and Judah (particularly the affluent elite) would have come into regular contact with foreign symbols and iconography. It does not follow, however, that such symbols and iconography would have

---

209 See Gadon 1989: 174, fig. 97. The stand dates to the 10th Century B.C.E. and was found at Taanach, Northern Israel. It was probably used in the worship of Astarte or Asherah. For discussion of the stand's iconography, see Hadley 2000: 169-176 and Keel 1998: 157–160.

210 This is in contrast to other heavenly beings described in the Hebrew Bible. For example, the seraphim in Isaiah 6 are never described as material artefacts and it is thus more difficult to find, and less appropriate to look for, iconographic parallels to them.

211 This pejorative view of iconographic evidence is, in fact, unnecessary. Textual material (especially that written in an ancient and foreign language) also needs to be interpreted in its own way and does not speak for itself. We have come across many ambiguities in our exegesis of the cherubim texts (notably of Ezekiel 10 and 28). Both artifacts and texts present their own unique hermeneutical problems. For a discussion of these issues see Cornelius 2004: 13–19.

212 See Curtis 1988: 21. He observes that the period of 1000–538 B.C.E. was characterized by "extensive trading between various parts of the Near East, and also large scale movement of objects through other means such as the seizure of booty or the paying of tribute, so the findspot of an object is not necessarily an indication of its origin."

connoted the same thing to the mind of an Israelite or Judahite as they would to the mind of someone from the symbol's indigenous culture. Although the symbol patterns persisted, what they could potentially connote was changeable. Thus foreign symbols may have become associated with more traditional Israelite and Judahite concepts.[213]

We must, therefore, be cautious not to read too much into the archaeological evidence. Instead of attempting to answer larger questions concerning, for example, the origin of the cherubim, we are better to focus on narrower issues, such as the possible physical appearance and cultic contexts of the cherub image. We may be able to restrict questions raised by our exegesis of the biblical texts concerning the physical appearance of the cherubim by looking at the depiction of comparable figures in the extant iconography. We can also examine the possible functions of the cherub image in the cult. For example, the idea of a 'cherubim throne' (evidence for which is often found by scholars, e.g. Mettinger 1982a, in the biblical texts) may be more appropriately discussed within an iconographic context, where the design of royal/divine thrones can be more easily evaluated.[214]

A final problem we encounter when comparing the biblical cherubim to the extant iconography concerns how we delimit the evidence. As stated previously, the abundance of winged supernatural beings depicted on ancient Near Eastern seals, plaques and figurines, together with the absence of any label reading "This is a cherub", means that we are overwhelmed with comparative material. The כְּרֻבִים exist solely as a textual phenomenon and so our study should, rightly, be constrained by the biblical evidence. Thus we will need to establish a typological profile of the biblical כְּרֻבִים in order to help us determine what is appropriate comparative archaeological material.[215]

---

213 How far we can speak of direct foreign influence on, or input into, the iconography
    of Israel and Judah is difficult to say. It may be better to speak more generally in
    terms of a relationship between the Israelite and Judahite iconography and that of
    their neighbours. The Samarian Ivories, for example, may have been imported into
    Israel (see Sukenik 1938: 7). However, Keel and Uehlinger (1998: 80) note that there
    appear to have been workshops at this time in the Northern Kingdom of Israel in
    which ivory and seal carving took place. Thus some of the ivories may have been
    locally produced (see Winter 1981).

214 We have found no evidence for a cherubim throne concept in the biblical texts. See
    § 1.1.1-§ 1.1.3.

215 Iconographic evidence is not subsidiary to textual evidence in any way. Yet, because we
    are investigating what is essentially solely a textual phenomenon, which exists
    exclusively in the biblical texts and not in epigraphy, we are rightly constrained by the
    biblical evidence in our analysis of the material remains.

In a similar way, we will need to set spatial and temporal parameters within which we can discuss the evidence. Inevitably, these will be somewhat artificial as the ease with which certain objects could be transported means that artefacts can be dug up in completely different temporal and geographical contexts to those in which they were first produced. Nevertheless, we will need to decide the best possible parameters within which our archaeological study can proceed.

§ 3.1 Delimiting the Evidence 1:
A Typological Profile

We need to establish a visual profile of the כְּרֻבִים, in accordance with the texts, in order that we can identify appropriate comparative archaeological evidence. This profile will consist of two main kinds of information: first, the typical physical characteristics of the cherubim and, second, the typical cultic contexts in which they are said to appear. We will need to be aware, however, that the biblical texts often give us contradictory evidence, especially concerning the physical appearance of the cherubim.

In terms of the typical physical characteristics of the כְּרֻבִים, the biblical texts actually tell us very little. Indeed, the only thing we can be sure of is that they are winged supernatural beings[216] with heads, feet and possibly hands (Ezek 1:8; 10:7, 21 and see §§ 1.3.4.3.1–2). Whether they are bipedal or quadrupedal is a matter for discussion. The description in Ps 18:11 = 2 Sam 22:11 suggests quadrupedal, whereas that of Ezek 1:7 suggests that they are bipedal. As we discussed in our exegetical sections, the Ezekiel descriptions of the physical characteristics of the cherubim are extremely convoluted. We argued that the inconsistencies inherent in the description probably witness to editorial activity, whereby an originally brief reference to a cherub in the Jerusalem temple was the catalyst for a later interpretation of the חַיּוֹת of chapter 1 as cherubim. This, in turn, led to the cherubim acquiring the characteristics of the חַיּוֹת. This would mean that the description in the Song of David, a more ancient text, may witness to an earlier conception of the cherubim as quadrupedal. Similarly, the idea that the cherubim possess a plurality of faces and four wings is something which is unique to Ezekiel and conflicts with the description of the

---

216 Although supernatural beings, they are not deities. There is no evidence that they were worshipped. The biblical evidence suggests that they were tutelary beings, who designated and guarded the presence of the deity.

cherubim in 1 Kings and Exodus, where they appear to have one face and one set of wings each. Our exegesis of the biblical passages suggests that the descriptions of the cherubim in Ezekiel are less likely to be representative of how the cherubim were originally conceived than those in the books of Kings and Exodus. Nevertheless, the notion of hybridity that is an overt characteristic of the cherubim in Ezekiel is only implicit in the rest of the cherubim texts. Thus the hybrid characteristics of the cherubim in Ezekiel are something that we will still need to consider as possible qualities of cherubim, even if these are only made explicit in a later and convoluted text.

As concerns the cultic contexts in which the cherubim appear, our exegetical work on the biblical passages highlighted several characteristic features of the cherubim. The tutelary function of the cherubim with regard to the divine locale is paramount. They are found within the Holy of Holies itself and they appear on the doors and walls of the temple, the veil of the tabernacle and on the bronze cult stands. Ezek 28:11–19 may also suggest that a cherub could be an appropriate image with which to decorate a seal, again indicative of an apotropaic function. The sacred trees and open flowers with which cherubim often occur (see Gen 3:24; 1Kgs 6:29–35; Ezek 28:14, 16; 41:18–20) also appear at the threshold of divine space. Cherubim often occur in pairs (Ex 25:18; 1 Kgs 6:23; 2 Chr 3:10), as sentinels, and can also appear with lions and oxen (1 Kgs 7:29). A cherub is able to transport the deity from the divine into the human sphere in Ps 18:11 = 2 Sam 22:11.[217] Thus our typological profile can be constructed. We are looking for supernatural, winged beings that often occur in pairs on cultic appurtenances, temple walls and doors and with sacred vegetation, lions and oxen. Possible other physical characteristics may include an element of hybridity (combining features of one or more animal, particularly human, leonine, bovine and aquiline[218]), one or more heads, one or two sets of wings, and the occurrence of hands and wings together. Cherubim are more likely to be quadrupedal but the possibility that they could be bipedal will also be considered. Other potential characteristics of

---

217 This is also implicit in Ezekiel's visions in chapters 1 and 10 and also in 1 Chr 28:18.

218 In the following discussion, we will use the terms "aquiline" and "eagle" to refer to any characteristics of a bird of prey. In Ezekiel 1 and 10, the Hebrew term נשׁר is used, which may refer to an eagle, vulture or falcon.

cherubim include their use as a design on signets (connected with their apotropaic function) and their ability to transport the deity.

§ 3.2 Delimiting the Evidence 2: Temporal and Spatial Parameters

As stated above, any demarcation of geographical and temporal boundaries within which we can reasonably expect to find comparative material for the biblical cherubim is essentially an artificial one. However, such demarcation is essential if we are to narrow down the vast amount of possible comparative material that we have available to us (see Freedman and O'Connor 1995: 316–318).[219] If we use the biblical texts as our guide, we can fix the temporal parameters according to the dates of our cherubim passages. Yet dating the biblical texts is far from an easy task. Those that speak of early events (e.g. 1 Samuel 4 and 2 Samuel 6) may in fact have been written at a much later date. An approximate guess, based on our exegetical discussion, would place the poem of Psalm 18 = 2 Samuel 22 as one of the earliest of our cherubim passages. Although it is impossible to date the text with any certainty, the earliest plausible time of its composition must be around the late tenth to the early ninth Century B.C.E. (see Smith 2004: xiii).[220] Among the latest of our texts, according to our exegesis, are 1 and 2 Chronicles, which were probably composed in the Persian period, in the 4th Century B.C.E. This dating of our texts, although approximate, would restrict our use of comparative archaeological material to those finds which date to a similar period (late 10th–4th centuries B.C.E.).

---

219 The need to set temporal and spatial parameters is mostly due to the space constraints of the current study. We do not wish to suggest that evidence lying beyond our parameters cannot illuminate the biblical cherubim. Rather, establishing parameters condenses the otherwise overwhelming body of evidence and helps to reduce the possibility of making inappropriate comparisons.

220 This dating is based on the assumption that the song presupposes the existence of the Solomonic temple. This seems likely considering the reference to the הֵיכָל in verse 7 (see § 1.3.3). The psalm displays many pre-exilic features and can be ascribed to this period quite confidently. For pre-exilic features of the psalms, see Day 2004: 225–250.

Delimiting the archaeological evidence on geographical grounds poses a greater problem. Foreign influence on the cults of Israel and Judah is recorded in the Hebrew Bible (e.g. 1 Kgs 16:31–34; 2 Kgs 21:2). The Phoenician contribution to the design and construction of the temple, recorded in 1 Kings 5; 7:13–45, may indicate that the Jerusalem cult had many features in common with that of Tyre.[221] The Babylonian invasion resulted in the end of the Solomonic temple cult (2 Kgs 24:13; 25:13–21), and the deportation of the people (2 Kgs 24:14–16; 2 Kgs 25:11) may have effected new Babylonian influence on the religion of the exiles. Thus it may be entirely fitting to look for comparative material to the biblical cherubim in Phoenician and Babylonian iconography. Yet, by far the safest geographical boundaries within which we can look for comparative material for the biblical cherubim are those of ancient Israel and Judah, so as not to make any inappropriate comparisons (see Keel et al. 1984: 239–241).[222] However, one of the most important collections of objects depicting "cherub-like" figures from the 10th–4th centuries in Israel is the hoard of ivories from Samaria. This group of carvings cannot be discussed responsibly without reference to other contemporary and remarkably similar collections of ivories found

---

221 It is striking that a text such as 1 Kings, which is so often said to be characterized by a polemic against religious syncretism and an emphasis on the centralization of the Jerusalem cult, should record foreign contribution at the heart of the temple cult design. The references in 1 Kings, going as they do against the grain of the ideology of the book as a whole, should not only be seen as confirmation of the importance of using skilled craftsmen (whatever their nationality) in the design of important institutional buildings, but also as strong evidence for the historicity of this information.

222 It may even seem strange to include material from the Northern Kingdom, given that nearly all of our cherubim texts can be linked to the Jerusalem temple in some way (according to our exegesis). If we discount evidence from Israel, we are left with seals as our primary source of iconographic evidence. The absence of 'cherub-like' images depicted on cultic objects from 10th-4th century Judah is unfortunate but probably not that significant. Indeed, very few cultic objects from Judah have been found at all. Seal images depicting 'cherub-like' figures witness to the fact that similar creatures were portrayed during this period in Judah, just as the biblical evidence suggests. The fact that we have more images from the Northern Kingdom is probably due to the fact that Israel was a more affluent and cosmopolitan state in the Iron II period than Judah. Nevertheless, whether or not the history written in 1 Kings is accurate, the Hebrew Bible links the manufacture of the temple decoration and furnishings to a time when the Southern and Northern Kingdoms were supposedly united. Hence it seems appropriate to include finds from the Northern Kingdom.

at Nimrud, Arslan-Tash and Khorsabad (see Beach 1993). It has even been argued that the same or a similar guild of craftsmen could have been responsible for ivories in more than one of the collections (see Crowfoot and Crowfoot 1938: 5 and Winter 1981). So, at times, we will have to travel outside the realms of Israel and Judah in order to deal with the archaeological evidence in a conscientious manner.

§ 3.3 The Megiddo Ivories

In the previous sections, we noted that the best possible comparative material for our purposes is that which depicts winged, supernatural beings found in Israel and Judah and dating from the late 10th–4th centuries B.C.E. Those figures occurring in pairs and depicted in similar cultic contexts to the biblical cherubim will be given special consideration. It is items that conform to these specifications which will constitute our primary source of comparative material for the biblical cherubim.

Having identified the specifications for our primary evidence, it is necessary to survey briefly some evidence that does not accord with our chronological constraints. The Megiddo ivories, excavated within the boundaries of ancient Israel and Judah and depicting "cherub-like" figures, date to a period much earlier than we suppose our earliest cherubim texts to have been written. Nevertheless, as discussed in § 1.1, many scholars (e.g. Mettinger 1982a and Haran 1978: 247–249) have argued that the Megiddo ivories depict cherubim. It is therefore important to include discussion on these ivories in order that we can dialogue with these scholars. Although our treatment of the Megiddo artifacts will precede the survey of our primary evidence (10th–4th Century material), this does not mean that it takes precedence. We merely include the Megiddo material first for chronological reasons. We can use the earlier Megiddo material to provide us with a useful springboard from which we can launch our more targeted survey. We may be able to detect early features in the Megiddo iconography which can be compared to the style of the later artwork, which constitutes our primary evidence.

The Megiddo ivories, although not primary comparative evidence, can be considered to represent cultic and iconographic convention which may have prefigured biblical traditions concerning the cherubim decoration.[223] Excavations of stratum VIIA of the site of ancient Megiddo yielded a cache of ivories including plaques, a model and an ivory box on all of which appear similarly depicted winged supernatural beings. They were discovered in what is thought to have been the palace treasury and date to the period from c. 1250 to 1150 B.C.E (see Barnett 1982: 26). The supernatural beings depicted display many features that accord with our typological profile of the biblical cherubim.

Our first piece in the Megiddo group is an ivory box (see Picture 1 and Loud 1939, pls. 1–3). Each of its four sides is decorated with winged, hybrid quadrupeds and lions. The winged quadrupeds appear in pairs with their leonine bodies facing away from each other, but human faces turned outwards. The faces are badly damaged but two plaits remain hanging down, indicating the position of the face. The hairstyles may be female in fashion (see Barnett 1982: 26). Barnett argues that the figures are Syrian in style and reminiscent of the large gateway statues of the Hittite capital of Hattuša.

Of the ivory plaques, one depicts a prince seated upon a throne flanked by two winged and hybrid quadrupeds with leonine bodies and anthropoid, crowned heads (see Picture 1 and Loud 1939 pl. 4: 2a and 2b). The prince is surrounded by tribute-bearers and musicians, and captives are paraded before him. Although only one quadruped is pictured, this is because the scene is represented from a side view (as is typical of Egyptian art). We can be fairly sure that another such quadruped was envisioned flanking the other side of the royal throne because we can compare it to the model of a similarly flanked throne which was also dug up with this Megiddo cache (see Picture 2 and Loud 1939 pl. 4: 3). The model throne is flanked by the same type of hybrid quadrupeds with winged leonine bodies, crowned anthropoid heads and eagles' wings. The figure seated on the throne is partially missing.

---

223 It used to be the case that scholars (e.g. Barnett 1982: 43) saw the period of transition from the Late Bronze to the Early Iron periods as something of a Dark Age in Syria-Palestine, which ended with the emergence of the Phoenicians, with their new and distinct language and cultural traditions, in the 10th Century. This theory, however, has since been discredited by the archaeological evidence. Markoe (2000: 11), for example, argues for a "continuity in tradition that characterized Phoenician history over a period of more than 1200 years, from the beginning of the Late Bronze Age (c. 1550 BC)... to the start of the Hellenistic period around 300 BC."

Similar creatures to these are also depicted on fragments of two other ivory plaques from the Megiddo hoard (Loud 1939 pl. 5: 4 and 5). They too have human heads, leonine bodies and aquiline wings. On these plaques, however, they are portrayed as predatory creatures, pouncing on caprids. Physically, they resemble the quadrupeds on the previous plaque and model very closely, especially in the detail of their wings and bodies. However, unlike the previous examples, they are bearded (although the head is only preserved on no. 5). The two fragmentary plaques are mirror images of each other (see Loud 1939: 13), suggesting that they once formed a pair of symmetrical panels, which would have been inserted into wooden furniture or used to decorate walls.

Another group of plaques depicting a similar image are a set of three delicately carved openwork ivories featuring a seated winged being with a leonine body and anthropoid head (see Loud 1939 pl. 7: 21, 22a, 22b, 23). On numbers 22 and 23, the image is the reverse of 21, again suggesting that there were once four such plaques, which were used to form two sets of symmetrical panels to be inserted into furniture. Unlike the quadrupeds depicted on the other ivories, these extend human hands, which hold a votive cup. This design of a seated and winged leonine/human quadruped with outstretched hands is found elsewhere on the base of a throne on which is seated Queen Mutnodjme, wife of Pharaoh Horemheb, 1321–1293 BCE (see Jordan 1998: 202). This throne thus dates to around one hundred years prior to our Megiddo examples.[224] In both, the quadrupeds display several female characteristics. The face is beardless and possesses elongated, effeminate features. Its crown is similar to that worn by the famous Egyptian queen, Nefertiti, with lotus blossoms protruding from the top. The leonine body has distinct teats on its underside, thus representing a lioness. On the Queen Mutnodjme example, the quadruped wears a rosette around its neck, which is thought to be symbolic of the goddess Astarte (see Jordan 1998: 203), another feminine feature.[225]

---

224 Similar designs occur a few times in Egypt and the style is reminiscent of that of the Armana period. This has caused some scholars to date these Megiddo openwork ivories to the 14th Century (see Frankfort 1954: 158).

225 Following the treaty between Rameses II and the Hittites, Egyptian trade with Phoenicia flourished. The existence of shrines to Baal and Astarte, dating to the

Similar quadrupeds occur on a small panel of Anatolian design also discovered in the Megiddo cache (see Loud 1939 pl. 11). The panel depicts registers of Hittite figures in relief, with two kings at the top supported by the Hittite pantheon (see Barnett 1982: 28). How this panel came to be at Megiddo is something of a mystery. It may have been imported (Loud 1939: 10) or it may have been carved locally as a record of a treaty between the two kings featured at the top (Barnett 1982: 28) or as a legitimation of succession. Barnett (1982: 28) conjectures that its presence at Megiddo may be due in some way to the peace treaty of Rameses II and the Hittite king Hattušiliš (1284 B.C.E.). The costume of the kings, and the double-headed monsters, with which they are depicted, are certainly features of Anatolian design. However, some of the smaller figures supporting the king are not (see Loud 1939: 10). This suggests that the panel was carved locally but that Hittite motifs were intentionally incorporated. For our purposes, it is the quadrupeds that flank the second and third registers that are of interest. At both ends of the third register are seated winged quadrupeds with leonine bodies, crowned anthropoid heads and eagles' wings. Physically, therefore, they are very similar to the creatures featured on the ivory box, model and plaques described previously. Like the previous examples, their wings extend upwards and outwards. They face outwards, guarding the assembly. Rosettes and sacred plants feature as space fillers surrounding all the creatures. A second set of quadrupeds are positioned underneath this first set on the second register. Their bodies face the same direction as the pair above them, but their faces are turned forwards. Physically, they differ from the pair above them. They have longer headdresses, hanging down, and their tails loop under their bodies rather than extending upwards. It is difficult to tell whether these creatures are winged or not. If they are, then their wings are short, extending from the chest rather than the back, and form a teardrop shape over their body. However, this shape may equally denote the mane or fur of the creature and may not be a wing at all. The panel is in such poor condition that it is difficult to ascertain.

---

period of Rameses II in Memphis, shows that a Phoenician community existed at this time in Egypt (Markoe 2000: 20). Hence the blend of Phoenician and Egyptian motifs during this period is unsurprising.

Our final examples from the Megiddo cache consist of four further plaques, depicting a different kind of winged quadruped (see Loud 1939 pl. 9, 32–35). Again, there is a set of two identical but reversed pairs (although the two with heads facing to the left are fragmentary). The ends are dovetailed for insertion, perhaps into corners or legs of furniture (see Loud 1939: 14). Unlike the previous examples, these quadrupeds possess leonine and aquiline features only (the anthropoid head being replaced by that of an eagle). Like some of the earlier examples (Loud 1939: pl. 7), they are featured in a seated position with their wings splayed out above them.

Several scholars (e.g. Albright 1938 and Mettinger 1982a) have made much of these Megiddo objects, arguing that some of the figures depicted must be cherubim. Although this is purely speculative, the similarities between the typical features of some of these figures and the typical features of the cherubim are striking. We shall proceed to compare these figures to the typological profile we have constructed for the cherubim. However, we must bear in mind that these artifacts date to a time much earlier than our cherubim texts.[226]

Physically, the Megiddo figures are all winged and hybrid quadrupeds, mostly combining human, leonine and aquiline features (though our last example combined only the latter two). They are depicted as sitting and standing and mostly with wings outstretched above them (compare e.g. 1 Kgs 6:27). Most interesting, for our purposes, is the fact that there appear to be both female and male types of the same creature. Those flanking the thrones, pouncing on caprids and guarding the Hittite assembly seem to be male, whereas the openwork examples and those surrounding the ivory box seem to be female. By comparison with similar winged quadrupeds (such as that depicted under the Queen Mutnodjme throne, those featured on the cult stand from Taanach and those featured on the walls of the ʿAin Dara temple), we can argue that these female "cherub-like" beings were often associated with a goddess. The Queen Mutnodjme example wears the rosette of the goddess Astarte around its neck (see Jordan 1998: 202). Those on the Taanach stand have long headdresses and guard the shrine to Astarte (see Keel and

---

226 Albright and Mettinger do not pay enough attention to the early date of these ivories.

Uehlinger 1998: 157–158 and description below). The ʿAin Dara examples possess female characteristics and hairstyles and protect the sanctuary which is dedicated to the goddess Ishtar (see Abu Assaf 1990: pls. 20–21). The gender of the noun כְּרוּב is evidence enough that the biblical כְּרֻבִים are masculine creatures. Yet the archaeological evidence may suggest that this fact is inextricably linked to the gender of the deity with whose cult they are associated.

The inclusion of hands rather than paws in the openwork examples is interesting. We have discussed the problems created by the inclusion of hands in Ezekiel's description of the cherubim (see §§ 1.3.4.3.1–2 and the discussion of Ezek 1:8; 10:7, 21). Our conclusion was that the attribution of hands to cherubim was somewhat strange and was perhaps indicative of editorial activity, which merged the description of the חַיּוֹת with the cherubim. The חַיּוֹת, being biped, could have hands, feet and wings. Cherubim, being quadruped, could only have feet and wings. What the Megiddo openwork examples show is that human characteristics could continue from the head down into the upper body of the winged quadruped. Hands are necessary in order for the creature to hold the votive cup. Thus human hands replace leonine paws. The hands, together with the female characteristics and association with a goddess, distance these quadrupeds from the biblical cherubim. Nevertheless, these examples do show that "cherub-like" images could be transmogrified in order to express more exactly what was in the mind of the craftsman. Likewise, in the biblical texts, the cherubim can be transmogrified to suit the purposes of the author (see, in particular, our discussion of Ezekiel 10).

The majority of the objects in the Megiddo cache depict the quadrupeds in pairs. This is one of the typical features of the cherubim, which are often described as occurring in pairs (Ex 25:18; 1 Kgs 6:23; 2 Chr 3:10 and Ezek 41:18). On the ivory box and the Anatolian panel, in particular, we can see pairs of winged quadrupeds performing the function of sentinels, protecting the valuable content of the box and the sacred Hittite assembly. On the ivory box, the quadrupeds occur with protective lions (a combination used in the design of the cult stands described in 1 Kgs 7:29). As we have seen in our exegetical sections, this apotropaic function is a key characteristic of the cherubim. The quadrupeds pouncing on caprids are testimony to the ferocity of the

Megiddo creatures, which may be linked to their function as guardians. The cherubim in Gen 3:24 and the Song of David appear to possess this same menacing quality.

Many of the Megiddo plaques seem to have been used as inlay on furniture (esp. Loud 1939 pls. 5, 7 and 9), inserted into chair backs, armrests, legs or footrests (see Barnett 1982: 27). Other inlays found in the same cache depict sacred trees, lotus blossom, palms and rosettes (see e.g. Loud 1939 pls. 5, 6, 8). The combination of "cherub-like" beings with sacred vegetation is reminiscent of the decoration on the walls, doors and other features of the Solomonic temple (described in e.g. 1 Kgs 6:29–32). The well-known reference to the rich elite reclining on beds inlaid with ivory in Amos 6:4 witnesses to the use of ivory inlay in Jerusalem and Samaria.[227] Yet the use of ivory inlay in the Jerusalem temple is not recorded in the Hebrew Bible. Nevertheless, similar decorative patterns may have been used on wood, gold and bronze. Hence the Megiddo inlays may represent designs similar to those used in the decoration of the Solomonic temple (albeit dating to 200–300 years earlier).

A final feature of the winged quadrupeds of the Megiddo collection is their function as guardians of the prince's throne. As has been discussed in §§ 1.1.1–3, scholars[228] who use the two Megiddo throne examples to argue that the cherubim formula refers to Yahweh "enthroned upon the cherubim" are asking too much of the archaeological evidence. The meaning of the formula must be sought, first, in Hebrew linguistic convention and, second, by appeal to the literary contexts in which the cherubim appear. In §§ 1.1.1–3 we argued that, on the basis of both Hebrew linguistic and literary conventions, the cherubim formula is less likely to mean "enthroned upon the cherubim" than it is to mean "ruler" or "dweller of the cherubim". It would thus refer to Yahweh's residence in the temple. The Megiddo plaque and model constitute the only real

---

227 In this particular oracle, the audience addressed is the elite of Samaria *and* Zion (Amos 6:1). 1 Kgs 10:22 describes Solomon's naval expeditions with King Hiram's fleet. They would return with, among other luxuries, ivory. 1 Kgs 22:39 notes that Ahab built a house of ivory and Amos 3:15 warns that the houses of ivory will be torn down. The annals of Assyrian kings record booty in the form of ivory taken from both Israel and Judah during this period. Samaria is listed as supplying ivory to Tiglath-pileser III (744–727) and Judah to Esarhaddon (see Winter 1981: 101).

228 E.g. Mettinger 1982a, Albright 1938 and Hendel 1988: 376

evidence for interpreting the cherubim formula as a reference to Yahweh's enthronement. Similarly flanked thrones occur on numerous Phoenician scarabs (especially from the Achaemenid Persian Period, see Boardman 2003: 62–66 and pls. 16–17) as well as Ahiram's sarcophagus (dating to the first half of the 12th Century or later)[229] and thus we may argue that this is a relatively common Phoenician motif which had considerable longevity. Nevertheless, examples of this motif do not occur in Israel or Judah apart from among the Megiddo ivories.[230] The throne on the plaque occurs in an elaborate but earthly court scene and witnesses to the importance of the king and royal ideology. We know from 1 Kgs 10:18–19 that Solomon's throne was guarded by lions, not cherubim. The figure on the model throne from Megiddo has worn away and we are unable to tell whether it was a deity or a king. The Phoenician scarabs do appear to depict a god, as well as kings, on similar thrones. Nevertheless, evidence from Israel and Judah and dating from the late 10th–4th centuries has not yet been discovered that depicts a god or king seated on such "cherub thrones". Although the Megiddo evidence testifies to the probable connection between "cherub-like" figures and thrones, and thus parallels the connection of the cherubim with Yahweh's throne in Ezekiel, it is not compelling enough to dictate our rendering of the cherubim formula or our interpretation of the cherubim statues in the Holy of Holies (1 Kgs 6:23–28) and on the כַּפֹּרֶת of the Exodus tabernacle. Neither the cherubim in Ezekiel nor the temple and tabernacle statues are said to form the throne of Yahweh. The reason for their appearance in the Holy of Holies is the same as the reason for the appearance of "cherub-like" beings flanking the thrones on the Megiddo ivories: they safeguard and

---

229 See Markoe 2000 pl. V and discussion on p. 144.

230 There is one other example of a Late Bronze Age model throne from Beth-Shean which has eagle-headed and winged leonine quadrupeds depicted on the sides (see Rowe 1940: 9, pls. 19 and 48). Keel and Uehlinger (1998: 168) refer to terracotta fragments of similar thrones from Iron Age Megiddo (see May 1935: pls. 25 and 28). They argue that these remnants "provide the only evidence that can support the idea that there was a continuity, right within the country, for cherub thrones, one that stretched from the Late Bronze to Iron Age IIA." However, these fragments may not have constituted a model throne. Indeed, they could have formed parts of pottery shrines (like others found in the same stratum, see May 1935: pl. 13) and thus may have more in common with the Taanach cult stand than the model throne from Late Bronze Megiddo. They certainly cannot be used as evidence of a continuity of these model thrones into the Iron Age periods.

demarcate the presence of the king/deity. It does not follow, however, that the cherubim statues in 1 Kings 6 physically comprise the throne of Yahweh.

§ 3.4 Archaeological Survey: Israel and Judah (Late 10th–4th Century B.C.E.)

We will proceed to survey evidence that conforms to our specifications outlined in §§ 3.1–2. The 10th–4th Century B.C.E. spans from the Iron II to the Persian period. The political situation in Israel and Judah shifted frequently during this time and the iconography reflects these changing circumstances. The artwork of the Iron I period in Israel and Judah is characterized, in part, by a decline in anthropomorphic representations (particularly of the goddess) compared to the Bronze Age (see Keel and Uehlinger 1998: 109–131). This continues in the iconography of the Iron IIA[231], where few anthropomorphic representations of deities are found (the Taanach cult stand being one notable exception, preserving a more ancient style). Instead, gods and goddesses are represented by their attribute animals or symbols. In the Iron IIB period, Israel and Judah existed as independent states and the iconography echoes this. Nevertheless, winged beings (some of them deities) come to the fore in the artwork of both states through the influence of Egyptian royal and solar symbolism. However, where in Judah the iconography retains conservative features, in Israel the inherited Egyptian elements are taken in new directions. Following the occupation of the Northern Kingdom by Assyria, this Egyptian symbolism diminishes in importance in the Iron IIC period and is replaced by Assyrian and Aramaean astral elements. In a similar way, pressure from the Babylonian and Persian empires leaves its imprint on the iconography of the Iron III and Persian periods respectively.

   A major source of evidence for the iconography of Israel and Judah from the 10th–4th Century comes from images on stamp and cylinder seals. Aside from these, various items (particularly from the Northern Kingdom) are also significant. These include the Taanach cult stand

---

231 For the separation of the Iron II period into these three phases see Keel and Uehlinger 1998: 13–16, 410.

(from the Iron IIA period), the Samarian ivories (from around the 8th Century) and certain objects from Hazor (from the 9th–8th centuries) as well as a rock drawing from Jerusalem. We will begin our survey by looking at the larger objects on which "cherub-like" beings are depicted. Following this review, we will proceed to examine the seal images. Both surveys will catalogue the objects chronologically.

§ 3.4.1 Larger objects, Ivories and a Cave Drawing

The Taanach cult stand (see Picture 3) is conspicuous among the material remains of Iron IIA Israel and Judah both because of its anthropomorphic representation of a goddess ("the mistress of the lions")[232] and for its inclusion of winged beings.[233] The stand consists of four registers, on which the second from the bottom depicts two winged quadrupeds with human heads and leonine bodies. They stand either side of an empty space. The cultic function of the stand and the symbolism of its iconography has been much discussed (e.g. by Hadley 2000: 169–176 and Beck 1990: 417–439). The best analysis is that given by Keel and Uehlinger (1998: 157–158), who view the stand as a model of a shrine to the goddess Astarte. According to their analysis, the lowest register (depicting the "Mistress of the Lions") is symbolic of desert regions (profane space). The second register symbolizes the entrance to the shrine with the winged quadrupeds guarding the open space that gives access to the holy place. The third register depicts caprids feeding from a sacred tree (representative of the *asherah*, bestowing blessings), which is guarded by lions. Finally, the topmost register depicts a quadruped animal (symbolic of the goddess) below a

---

232 Although the "mistress of the lions" is depicted anthropomorphically, the goddess to which the stand is devoted is represented by her attribute animal (a quadruped at the top of the stand). Scholars are divided as to the genus of the quadruped (see Keel and Uehlinger 1998: 157-158). It is most likely to be a horse, the attribute animal of Astarte.

233 A second stand, similar and roughly contemporary to this one, was also found in excavations at Taanach. Keel and Uehlinger (1998) describe the stand as being decorated with winged sphinxes (cherubim) alternating with lions. Unfortunately, the stand is in such fragmentary condition that an analysis of its symbolic value is difficult. For a description and a drawing of the reconstructed stand, see Keel and Uehlinger 1998: 155 and fig. 182a.

winged solar disk, which represents the heavens. The stand itself is made of terracotta and thus preserves more ancient iconography than that of contemporary objects made from other media (see Keel and Uehlinger 2000: 154). Such terracotta pieces were used in private "house cults" rather than larger, more official institutions. This means that they were rather conservative in style.

Like the examples from Megiddo, the winged quadrupeds depicted on the stand display several features which correspond to our typological profile of the biblical cherubim. Physically, they possess similar hybrid characteristics to the Megiddo examples. They occur as a pair, probably guarding the entrance way to the shrine (see Keel and Uehlinger 1998: 157–158) and thus possessing the apotropaic qualities of sentinels, like the cherubim. They occur both with lions (featured on the bottom and third registers) and sacred vegetation (on the third register). Finally, their appearance on a cult stand can be compared to the occurrence of the cherubim on the ten bronze stands described in 1 Kgs 7:27–39. Although the Taanach stand is a less sophisticated cult object than the stands described in 1 Kings 7, the pattern of symbolic elements and their arrangement in registers are similar. No complete wheeled bronze cult stands have been found in ancient Israel.[234] Yet remnants of one example have been found at Ekron, Philistia. This stand, dating to the 11th Century B.C.E., was wheeled and decorated with sacred vegetation, like those described in 1 Kings 7. It seems to have been of similar construction to a Phoenician wheeled stand from Enkomi in Cyprus, which dates to the 12th Century (see Catling 1964: 207–210). The Enkomi example depicts a winged quadruped on one of its sides. This quadruped (like those on the Taanach stand) possesses a human head, leonine body and aquiline wings and occurs with sacred vegetation. The stands in 1 Kings 7 are said to be much larger than any of the cult stands found in excavations of ancient Near Eastern sites. This may be due, partly, to exaggeration on the part of the biblical authors. Bloch-Smith (1997: 85) suggests that the dimensions of the lavers may reflect the superhuman size of the deity (see § 1.2.2.3 of this study). Whatever the reason for the difference in size, the function of

---

234 A fine example of a non-wheeled bronze stand has been found in the Iron I context of ancient Megiddo (see May 1935: pl. 18).

the Bronze and Terracotta stands seems to be similar: they were used as supports for bowls onto which offerings could be laid or into which libations could be poured (see Keel and Uehlinger 1998: 155). The cherubim on the wheeled lavers, like the winged quadrupeds on the Taanach stand, set apart the holy space on which the offering would have been made.

The winged quadrupeds on the cult stands from Taanach and Enkomi possess many similarities that accord with our typological profile of the cherubim. Nevertheless, the Taanach figures are undoubtedly connected with the cult of a goddess (most likely Astarte, see Keel and Uehlinger 1998: 160). The symbolic constellation of lions, sacred vegetation and these "cherub-like" beings seems to have been connected with the worship of a goddess here and elsewhere.[235] Nevertheless, the same constellation appears on the cult stands described in 1 Kings 7, albeit this time with the inclusion of oxen. Thus the symbols used for the demarcation of sacred space found on the cult stand dedicated to Astarte from Taanach (10th Century) persist in the description of the cult stands of Yahweh in 1 Kings 7.[236] This is testimony to the universality and potency of such symbol patterns, which could be adapted to suit different cultic contexts and ideologies.

A cave drawing (see Pictures 4 and 5 and de Vaux 1967: figs. 2a and b) depicting a winged quadruped with a leonine body and crowned human head, similar to some of those depicted on the Megiddo ivories, has also been dated to the Iron IIA period (see de Vaux 1967: 117). The cave is situated in quarries to the north-west of Jerusalem (see Metzger 1985: 332). Clermont-Ganneau (1896: 242–245) originally dated the drawing to the 8th–6th centuries on the basis of its similarity to

---

235 See the decoration of the temple at ʿAin Dara, dedicated to Ishtar. It is decorated all around with lions, winged sphinxes and palm trees (see Abu Assaf 1990: 25–31). These sphinxes have long headdresses and feminine characteristics because of their association with the goddess. The cherub-like beings on the Taanach cult stand also seem to have long headdresses, rather than the crowns of their Megiddo male counterparts (see above). See Keel and Uehlinger 1998: 186–187.

236 Zwickel (1987) suggests that the iconography of the stands described in 1 Kings 7 indicates that they were connected with the goddess Astarte in the Jerusalem temple. This argument is unnecessary. Lions became associated with male deities in the Iron I period (see Keel and Uehlinger 1998: 169). The addition of cattle to the symbol pattern of the stands described in 1 Kings 7 also brings the iconography closer to that used to symbolise the male weather god.

Mesopotamian hybrids. According to de Vaux, the cave in which this drawing was found was one of several that may have provided the stone for the buildings constructed in the Solomonic era, of which the Jerusalem temple was one. He argues (1967: 117), "le graffito peut avoir été inspire par la vue des chérubins du Temple." Thus, for de Vaux, this drawing "paraît être l'image la plus authentique d'un chérubin biblique." Although this is an overstatement, the drawing is particularly important because, with the exception of the glyptic, it is the only image from Judah that accords with our cherubim typology.

In the Iron IIB period, the states of Israel and Judah coexisted side by side. Owing to its favourable geographical position, Israel enjoyed close political and economic relations with the neighbouring city states of Tyre, Sidon and Damascus. Judah, on the other hand, did not benefit from such commercial and political allies, situated as it was far from the major trade routes. The iconography reflects this. Judah continued to preserve many of its older indigenous symbols, as well as Egyptian royal elements. By contrast, Israel's iconography exhibits greater autonomy and innovation in how inherited Egyptian symbols were used. It thus shows more in common with the iconography of its Phoenician and Syrian neighbours than it does with Judah.

Northern cities flourished during Iron IIB and it is from the sites of these ancient capitals that some of our most interesting comparative material from this period has been excavated. During this time, winged beings became more popular in the iconography of Israel. One recurring motif is that of a four-winged boy. On a bone carving (see Picture 6) discovered at Hazor and dating to the end of the 9th or beginning of the 8th Century, a four-winged youth is depicted, holding a branch of a small tree in each hand (Yadin 1958: pl. 151). According to Keel and Uehlinger (1998: 195), this boy is a solar deity or mediating being (which may have been identified with Baal). Similar figures have been found on bone handles and scarabs from Gezer, Dan and elsewhere in the Northern Kingdom.

The figure on the Hazor example displays several elements that correspond to our visual profile of the cherubim. It occurs with sacred vegetation (as do the cherubim in e.g. Gen 3.24; 1 Kgs 6.29–35; Ezek 28.14, 16 and 41.18–20). Its four wings are consistent with the description of the cherubim in Ezek 10:21, though in Ezekiel the cherubim also have four heads. Keel and Uehlinger (1998: 195) argue that the four wings are a sign of the deity's celestial and omnipresent nature.[237] Like Ezekiel's חַיּוֹת, this winged youth is biped, but it does not display the hybrid characteristics of these beasts. Its features (apart from the wings) are all fully human. Scarabs and seals from elsewhere in the Northern Kingdom (see Keel and Uehlinger 1998: pl. 211 a–c) show this figure on its own and sometimes flanked by two worshippers. These representations distance this four-winged boy from the cherubim. The symbolism suggests that this is a god, not a subsidiary guardian being.[238]

The style of the design on this bone handle has been classed as South Syrian (see Winter 1981: 115, n. 108 and Keel and Uehlinger 1998: 195). Since the discovery of several large ivory collections from Nimrud, Arslan-Tash, Samaria, Khorsabad and Salamis, scholars have posited the existence of two major schools of ivory carving during the first millennium: Phoenician and North Syrian. This differentiation is made on the grounds of stylistic differences and distribution (see Poulsen 1912: 38–53, Barnett 1939: 4–19 and Winter 1976). However, the ivory groupings have been further refined to include the prospect of a southern Syrian school which incorporated aspects from both the Phoenician and North Syrian disciplines but which had as its centre the Aramaean capital of Damascus (see Winter 1981). The squat proportions of human figures are said to be characteristic of this South Syrian style and the four-winged boy on the Hazor bone handle has a notably stocky physique.

A similar style is found on another object from Hazor, an ivory pyxis[239] (see Picture 7), which dates to the second half of the eighth century (Yadin 1958: pl. 155). The design on the pyxis consists of a kneeling male worshipper before plants. On the other side of the plant,

---

237 This further illuminates the cherubim-חַיּוֹת, celestial figures that symbolise the omnipresence of Yahweh.

238 Similar figures occur on the Samarian ivories, but this time with two wings and holding lotus blossoms. Originally, these probably occurred in pairs, flanking a central image. For an interpretation of these figures, see below.

239 The pyxis displays some similarities to the ivory box from Megiddo described above, yet the Hazor exampleis cylindrical. Boxes of a similar design have been found in the NW. Palace at Nimrud.

a winged leonine quadruped is featured, facing toward the plant and the man. Unfortunately the pyxis is fragmentary and the head of the quadruped is missing (for a discussion of the proposed restoration of the pyxis, see Yadin 1958: 41–43). This quadruped displays similar physical characteristics to those represented on the Megiddo ivories and Taanach cult stand. The stocky physique of the human figure links the style of this piece to that of the bone handle. The pose of the man is certainly one of veneration and thus the tree must be either emblematic of a deity or divine blessing in general. The winged quadruped looks on as sentinel to ensure this human encounter with the divine remains respectful. Just such an encounter between humanity and divinity, although this time inappropriate, is described in Genesis 2–3 (see § 1.3.1). The cherubim in Gen 3:24 are positioned to prevent humanity from infringing upon divine order (again symbolised by a tree). Hence the winged quadrupeds on the Hazor pyxis accord both with our physical and with our contextual profile of the biblical cherubim.

The southern Syrian style can also be found on several of the ivories from the Samarian group. The Samarian ivory collection is one of the largest and most important finds from pre-exilic Israel. The date of the ivories is uncertain. They were discovered in the ruins of a building which dates back to the time of King Omri or his son Ahab in the 9th Century B.C.E. (see Crowfoot and Crowfoot 1938: 2). However, the site was an important one into and even after the Hellenistic period, and the majority of the ivory fragments were found in a disturbed context, commingled with Rhodian and Hellenistic sherds (see Picture 8 and Crowfoot and Crowfoot 1938: 2). Thus, as Winter (1981: 124) argues, "at best, all that we have for the ivories is a *terminus ante quem* of the conquest of Samaria by Shalmaneser V in 722, completed in 720 by Sargon II."

In the main, the style of the ivory collection has been linked to the Phoenician school, which was characterized by an inclusion of Egyptian elements and a tendency towards realism and aestheticism. This is in contrast to the North Syrian School, with its heavily stylized designs (see Barnett 1982: 43–48). However, a few of the Samarian pieces have been classified as Syrian and may well have been linked to a southern Syrian guild centred at Damascus (Winter 1981: 127). As is typical of the iconography of the Iron IIB period, the ivories depict several types of winged beings. Generally speaking, these beings are Egyptian in origin, though the designs are by no means typical of Egyptian art. Thus it is likely that the ivories were either carved locally, or imported from Tyre, Sidon or Damascus (see Winter 1981: 127). One pair of winged figures, that are certainly Egyptian in origin, occurs on a scene which is spread over two plaques (see Picture 8 and Crowfoot and Crowfoot 1938: pl. 3). The figures are human in form and wear necklaces that hang down over the shoulder, as is typical in Egyptian art. They squat facing each other with a lotus blossom in each hand and the *djed* symbol of Osiris between them. The presence of this *djed* pillar allows us to identify these figures as the goddesses Isis and Nephthys, the sisters of Osiris (see Crowfoot and Crowfoot 1938: 16). Although these are winged figures occurring in pairs, and thus conform to some extent to our typological profile of the cherubim, the iconography is deeply rooted in Egyptian tradition and it is thus unlikely that these figures could have been identified as, or with, the cherubim.

More human winged figures occur on several fragments from the Samarian collection (for example, Picture 9 and Crowfoot and Crowfoot 1938: pls. 4, 14.2 and 15.7). The figures are standing and probably occurred in pairs, holding lotus flowers and facing a central object, possibly a sacred tree (see Crowfoot and Crowfoot 1938: 17). Very similar figures are depicted in the other large ivory hoards from Arslan Tash and Nimrud. At these sites, the figures are sometimes female and similar figures occur in later Phoenician art with the emblems of Isis and Nephthys. Thus it may be that these Samarian figures should also be identified as these Egyptian goddesses. Yet, on one of the fragments (Crowfoot and Crowfoot 1938: pl. 3), the garment worn by the figure appears to be male (see Crowfoot and Crowfoot 1938: 18). This would distance the Samarian figures from the goddesses. If male, these figures have more in common with the biblical cherubim. Indeed, Crowfoot and Crowfoot (1938: 18) argue that "the cherubim on the two ends of the mercy seat in the ark were undoubtedly of the same type" as these winged figures. Given the fragmentary state of these pieces, this statement seems a little forced. [240] The tutelary function of the figures is

---

240 Keel and Uehlinger (1998: 197) link these figures to winged youths of the type found on the Hazor bone handle, which depict Baal or a subsidiary genius.

suggested by their arrangement in pairs around a central figure. On one occurrence, this figure is a sacred tree (pl. 14.2) and, on another, it is a papyrus flower (pl. 15.8). The apotropaic function of the figures, as well as their connection with sacred vegetation, accords with our typological profile of the cherubim. Yet the fragmentary condition of these figures, together with the possible connection between them and Egyptian tutelary goddesses, means that any identification of them as or with the biblical cherubim remains extremely questionable.

In addition to winged human figures, the Samarian ivories also depict a variety of winged quadrupeds, some of which bear close similarities to those that we encountered on the Megiddo ivories, Taanach stand and Hazor pyxis. In the main, these quadrupeds are hybrids with leonine bodies, crowned human heads and aquiline wings. They are quite consistently depicted except for slight differences of style and dress.[241] However, on some fragments (pls. 8.1; 14.3, 4) a similar creature has an aquiline head (as was the case with one of our examples from Megiddo). Unfortunately, the examples of this eagle-headed kind are extremely fragmentary. There is one further type that we have not encountered previously, which depicts a ram-headed winged quadruped (pl. 6. 2). Tiny fragments of a pair of these figures were found together and have been matched to a design found at Arslan-Tash.[242] The Arslan-Tash figures show two leonine, ram-headed winged quadrupeds facing each other, with a sacred tree featured between them. As concerns their context, they agree with our typological profile of the cherubim. They occur in a pair and have a strong connection with a sacred tree. The ram's head is a physical feature we have not met before and is not something that is ever highlighted as a potential characteristic of the cherubim (either explicitly or implicitly).

As for the human-headed types (Crowfoot and Crowfoot 1938: pls. 5; 6.1; 7; 8; 10.3, 4, 5), these are depicted in a very similar manner to our examples from Megiddo, Taanach and the Hazor pyxis. However, generally, they are dressed in male regal garments and some of them are

---

241 Crowfoot and Crowfoot (1938: 23) observe that, although many of this type of quadruped are only preserved on small fragments, "the range of variation is narrow."

242 Crowfoot and Crowfoot show the fragments lying on top of a drawing of the Arslan-Tash design (pl. 6.2).

bearded. They have a closer connection with vegetation than the Megiddo and Taanach examples, depicted stalking through lotus thicket, in front of lilies or past palm trees. The most complete example of this type is depicted in a style more characteristic of the Syrian school (see Picture 10 and Crowfoot and Crowfoot 1938: pl. 5. 1, 2). It has full facial features, a stocky build and its Egyptian double crown is not accurately rendered. This is in contrast to other examples of such creatures in the collection (Picture 11 and Crowfoot and Crowfoot 1938: e.g. pl. 5.3; 7.6, 7), which are rendered in the Phoenician style. The Egyptian crown is correctly interpreted, and the physical features are realistic and stately. On several fragments (pls. 7; 8; 10), the quadrupeds seem to be battling with other animals, mostly with lions. On pl. 7.5, the creature rears up (in a similar manner to the winged quadrupeds pouncing on caprids in the Megiddo collection), perhaps in order to snatch its prey. Thus, again, the threatening qualities of this type of creature are highlighted, which may be connected to an apotropaic function.

As we have seen in our treatment of the Megiddo ivories, Taanach cult stand and Hazor pyxis, these human/leonine winged quadrupeds conform to our typological profile of the cherubim both physically and contextually. A detail which helps strengthen a link between these creatures and the cherubim is the various types of vegetation with which they are depicted. The vegetation tends to be in the form of palm trees (as in pl. 5.3), lotus flowers or lily blossoms (pl. 5.1, 2). This corresponds to the palm trees and 'open flowers' with which the cherubim are depicted in 1 Kgs 6:29, 32 and 1 Kgs 7:36.

The Samarian ivories, like those from Megiddo, derive from a palace complex rather than a temple or sanctuary. Some scholars have argued that Samaria was a secular city (established in order to improve trade links with Phoenicia and Syria) with its cult centre remaining at Bethel (see Winter 1981: 125). However, since the discovery of inscriptions from *Kuntillet ʿAjrud*, which speak of "Yahweh of Samaria", the existence of a shrine to Yahweh in Israel's capital seems more than likely (see Keel and Uehlinger 1998: 228). A close link between palace and temple is described in 1 Kings 6–7 and what was true of the Jerusalem palace/ temple complex may also have been true of Samaria. Thus, decoration of the royal residence may have been very similar to that of the divine residence. Beach (1993) has even argued that the ivory collections from

Khorsabad, Nimrud, Arslan-Tash and Samaria may have been integral to the *Marzeaḥ* ritual, in which the king was an active participant.[243] Thus the Samarian ivories may well feature designs similar to those envisaged by the writers of 1 Kings 6–7.

§ 3.4.2 The Glyptic

Figures that conform to our cherubim typology feature on Judahite and Israelite glyptic as early as the Late Bronze Age[244] and as late as the Persian period. Cylinder seals, common in the Late Bronze Age, were replaced with stamp seals from Iron I and, from the 8th Century B.C.E. onwards, became the principal method of sealing (see Collon 1987: 75). Concomitantly, literacy became more widespread in the 8th Century. These two trends meant that the use of iconography on seals decreases from this period. By their very nature, stamp seals could not accommodate the elaborate scenes depicted on cylinder seals. An increasingly literate society meant that it was no longer necessary to designate ownership by means of pictorial representations. Moreover, literacy was a mark of the elite and thus anepigraphic seals became associated with a lower status. These trends meant that, from the end of the 8th Century on, seals became increasingly aniconic (see Naveh 1982: 71).[245]

Despite this trend towards aniconism, iconic seals dating from the 8th Century onwards have still been found in Israel and Judah, albeit in smaller quantities. The principal function of a seal was to designate

---

243   Some of the finer details of Beach's argument have been called into question, rightly, by Albenda (1994: 60). Nevertheless, the possibility that the ivories collections were used as part of a religious or royal festival must be considered.

244   For example, on cylinder seals from Hazor (Yadin 1961: pl. 319.2) and Megiddo (Winter 1983: illus. 143) there appear creatures very similar to the winged quadrupeds depicted on the Megiddo ivories and Hazor pyxis.

245   It does appear that aniconism was more prevalent on seals from Judah in the 7th and 6th centuries than on contemporary seals from elsewhere in the ancient Near East. Although an aniconic trend can be traced in the glyptic from Ammon, Moab and elsewhere, it is not as distinct as it is in that from Judah. The prevalence of aniconism in Judahite glyptic has been linked to the biblical prohibition on idols (see Ex 20:23; 34:17; Lev 19:4; 26:1; Deut 4:16, 23, 25; 27:15). For discussion of this, see Uehlinger (1993: 278–288).

ownership or authority. Nevertheless, a supplementary function was a seal's capacity to act as an amulet. This amuletic value is stressed by Uehlinger (1993: 273–274), who argues that the term "seal-amulet" should be used to describe the majority of Northwest Semitic seals. As we noted in our discussion of Ezek 28:11–19, the choice of material and design used in the making of a seal was probably not arbitrary but rather was intimately connected with a seal's apotropaic powers. Precious stones are associated with magical properties in Mesopotamian texts and Ex 39:10–14 also suggests that jewels were not chosen purely for aesthetic purposes. In a similar way, the design on a signet may also have been connected with its prophylactic qualities. A cherub, as a tutelary being, may well have been an ideal image with which to decorate a seal.

Determining the origin of a seal is a notoriously difficult task. Seals could travel long distances, could have considerable longevity and could be easily reused (see Collon 1987: 120–122). As previously noted, there is a general correlation between age and epigraphy, anepigraphic seals being more common in earlier periods. The principal method of establishing the date and provenance of a seal is by means of palaeography and thus the origin of anepigraphic seals is more difficult to determine. The onomastics, the orthography and the style of writing are all important factors and these can be supplemented by studying the iconography (where applicable) and the findspot of the seal, if known (see Sass 1993: 195–197 for a discussion of these problems and method). Most of the seals we will discuss will be linked to Israel or Judah by means of the inscription. Anepigraphic seals can be linked to Israel or Judah only by means of their findspot. Only seals dating approximately from the late 10th–4th Century will be included.

One type of being that we encounter on Israelite seals from the Iron II period is a winged male figure. This figure can have four wings (like the winged boy on the Hazor bone handle) but can also be pictured with two (like some of the figures on the Samarian ivories). According to Sass (1993: 235), when some of these bipterous figures are depicted in profile, they should really be considered four-winged, with only one pair of wings being visible. One four-winged example occurs on a seal from Gezer (Keel and Uehlinger 1998: illus. 211a), at which site were also found bone handles (like the Hazor piece) depicting similar winged beings. The figure is quite crudely rendered and the seal is anepigraphic. Both these features may point to an early date and local provenance. As noted in our discussion of the Hazor bone handle, the four-winged male figure is a recurring motif in Northern iconography from the 8th Century and normally holds lotus blossom in each hand. Although its possession of four wings agrees with the description of the cherubim in Ezek 10:21, other representations of the same figure (e.g. Keel and Uehlinger 1998: illus. 211b–c) suggest that this winged being is a god, possibly to be identified with Baal (see Keel and Uehlinger 1998: 195–198). On one seal from Tell el-Farʿah (south), a similar four-winged male is depicted with the head of a falcon and a sun disk above its head (Keel and Uehlinger 1998: illus. 213). Keel and Uehlinger argue that the use of these Egyptian solar elements serve to identify the four-winged Baal with the sun god. An identical figure to this one (although this time in profile, with two visible wings) is found on a seal of unknown provenance (classified as Hebrew by Sass 1993: 235, illus. 141). This figure again has an aquiline head and holds lotus blossom in each hand. It seems, therefore, that this winged male is a god that became associated with the Egyptian solar deity. It is unlikely, therefore, that this winged male would have been recognized as a cherub. It may be that the bipterous standing figures holding lotus blossom that we encountered on the Samarian ivories (Crowfoot and Crowfoot 1938: pls. 4, 14.2 and 15.7) should be identified with this god.

Winged quadrupeds, with leonine bodies but aquiline heads (sometimes crowned), are popular on iconic seals from both Israel and Judah in the Iron II period (see Lemaire 1990: 98–99 for a full list). We encountered this type of creature in the Megiddo ivory collection (Loud 1939 pl. 9, 32–35) and on fragments from the Samarian cache (Crowfoot and Crowfoot 1938: pls. 8.1; 14.3, 4). The Megiddo example is depicted seated on its own, with its wings splayed out above it. The Samarian pieces are extremely fragmentary and difficult to reconstruct with certainty. On two eighth century anepigraphic seals from Megiddo (Keel and Uehlinger 1998: illus. 231a–231b), two such quadrupeds are depicted in the middle register facing a central stylised tree. Their appearance on a seal and in a pair, and their close connection to a tree, are all factors which accord with our cherubim typology. On one of these seals, the upper register shows a vulture attacking a rabbit and the lower register depicts a lion attacking a caprid. According to Keel and Uehlinger (1998: 233–234), these scenes "contrast strongly with the carefully guarded tree in the middle." Thus the iconography of the seal denotes a vigilantly protected divine or central order surrounded by peripheral peril and disorder. The symbolism may well have been thought to enhance the prophylatic power of the seal.

A pair of these creatures also occurs on two scarabs from Tell en-Naṣbeh and Tel Dan respectively (see McCown 1947, pl. 52.12 and Keel and Uehlinger 1998: illus. 248), but this time they flank a *uraeus*.[246] Like the stylised tree (see Keel and Uehlinger 1998: 233–236), the *uraeus* could be a general symbol of divine power. On the Tel Dan example, the register depicting the winged quadrupeds is framed above and below by rows of good luck symbols. Again, the iconography emphasises the apotropaic power of the seal. The position of the winged quadrupeds, facing towards the *uraeus*, is identical to that of those that flank the stylised tree. Thus, again, the guardian function of these winged quadrupeds is evident.

On several other Hebrew seals dated to the 8th Century, the same type of eagle-headed winged quadruped occurs on its own (see Keel and Uehlinger 1998: illus. 250a–254b, 258c and 259a; Sass 1993: fig. 120–122). When featured on its own, this creature nearly always wears a crown, be it the double crown of Egypt, or a sun disk (see Picture 12). This is in contrast to the pairs depicted on the seals described above, which never have crowns. The only example of this type of creature occurring on its own but without a crown occurs on a scaraboid of Phoenician design but owned by a Judahite (Sass 1993: fig. 122).[247] The inscription was probably added to an originally anepigraphic seal. The quadruped is depicted with its foot on a stylised lotus blossom, its head

---

246 The *uraeus* is the cobra symbol of Lower Egypt and was associated with divinity and royalty. As an Egyptian solar symbol it became popular from the 8th century onwards in Israel and particularly Judah. Winged varieties were especially popular, in accordance with solar trends, and on our scarab from Tell en-Nasbeh, the *uraeus* is winged. Four-winged *uraei* were particularly popular in Judah in the 7th-6th Century (see Sass 1993: 196, 212–213).

247 The inscription displays Judahite orthography but the design has been linked to Phoenician artisans by Gubel (1993: 107), who compares it with similar designs of Phoenician origin. Particularly close is the design on several ivories from Nimrud (see Mallowan 1966: figs. 455, 456, 485, 558, 559).

turning backwards and a man thrusting a spear into its beak. Sass (1993: 228) argues that there is no struggle between the two because the quadruped shows no sign of resistance. However, by comparison with very similar designs on ivories from Nimrud (Mallowan 1966: figs. 455–456, 485, 558–559), this is not the case. On two examples (figs. 456 and 559), the creature's legs kick back and upwards into the air, a sure sign of struggle. Indeed, the creature's turned head suggests that it has been caught unawares.[248] On our scaraboid, the quadruped has its paw on a lotus blossom (as it does on several of the Nimrud ivories). Although speculative, the lotus blossom (or what it represents) may be the cause of the fight.[249] In this way, the symbolism on this scaraboid may be compared to that on the Hazor pyxis described earlier. It represents an encounter between humanity and divinity (perhaps represented by sacred vegetation).

Other seals depicting winged quadrupeds with aquiline heads and leonine bodies show it crowned and facing an *ankh* (sometimes in a cartouche) or similar protective symbol (see Picture 12 and Keel and Uehlinger 1998: 252–256, illus. 250a–254b and Sass 1993:226, figs. 120–121). On these seals, the creatures have a stately air and are normally featured in a standing position, although sometimes they are portrayed crouching or reclining. This type of image is particularly popular on name seals. According to Keel and Uehlinger (1998: 256), the *ankh* symbol replaces the sacred tree that is featured on the two anepigraphic seals from Megiddo. Thus, the earlier scene of a pair of these hybrids guarding a tree has been supplanted by a more simplistic motif of one such hybrid guarding an *ankh* symbol. This shift in imagery concurs with the general trend towards aniconism on seals. The earlier anepigraphic seals display more complex and realistic scenes compared to the later epigraphic seals with their more stylised and simplistic

---

248   On several of the ivories from Nimrud (e.g. Mallowan 1966: figs. 507, 517, 526–527), identical creatures are depicted eating from vegetation. The creature on our scaraboid has its foot on a lotus blossom and one of the Nimrud ivories depicts an identical creature in a similar position (fig. 506). Thus, it is not inconceivable that the creature on our scaraboid is envisaged as having been attacked while feeding.

249   On one of the examples from Nimrud (Mallowan 1966: fig. 456), the struggle takes place on a mountain rather than among lotus blossom. It is tempting to see an equation between sacred vegetation and sacred mountain in these designs (as is drawn in Ezek 28:13–14).

motifs. Despite this shift, the overall symbolism of the images remains the same.

Interestingly, there is one seal (see Picture 13 and Sass 1993: 123) that depicts a human-headed winged lion (of a kind very similar to those depicted on the Megiddo and Samarian ivories and Taanach stand) standing in front of an *ankh* symbol. The posture of this hybrid in relation to the *ankh* is identical to that of the eagle-headed types that occur more frequently. This fact may point to some kind of identification of the eagle-headed winged lions with their human-headed counterparts.[250] Another human-headed example occurs on an eighth century[251] seal from Megiddo (Lamon and Shipton 1939: pl. 67.34), this time featured reclining and with winged *uraei* in the upper register. Although both the human and eagle-headed types are usually depicted with a crown or sun disk, Keel and Uehlinger (1998: 256) argue that they are not to be regarded as incarnations of a deity or king. Instead, the headdress connects the creature with Egyptian royal and solar aspects, which came to the fore in both Israel and Judah in the 8th Century. They are thus to be regarded as guardian beings who served the deity, conceived of in solar terms. The protection which they afforded the deity was conveyed, by extension, upon the seal owner.

In our survey of "cherub-like" beings depicted on the ivories and other objects, we saw that human-headed winged lions were the most prevalent type. On the seals, however, eagle-headed winged lions predominate. According to Sass (1993: 226), the preference for aquiline rather than human features was the result of a desire to avoid anthropomorphic images. Although it is true that there is a decline in anthropomorphic images (particularly of deities) from the Iron I period onwards, human figures were still represented in Israel and Judah in all periods. It is not necessarily the case, therefore, that human features were considered more taboo than those of animals. Indeed, Sass (1993: 198, 243–246) links this supposed evasion of anthropomorphic images to the prohibition of idols mentioned in the Hebrew Bible (Ex 20:4, 23; 34:17; Lev 19:4; 26:1; Deut 4:16, 23, 25; 27:15). Yet Deut 4:16–17 suggests

---

250 We have already seen how depictions of the four-winged boy on Israelite glyptic occasionally substituted the human head for that of an eagle.

251 The seal was found in a sixth century context but should be dated to the eighth century on palaeographical grounds.

that all idols, human and animal alike, were considered taboo. Moreover, the biblical prohibition is generally thought to have arisen only after the collapse of the Northern Kingdom and possibly not until even later (see Dohmen 1985). Thus it would be odd for the imagery of eighth century seals to have been affected by this ideology.[252] If Sass's explanation for the preference of aquiline heads is erroneous, we will need to look for a reason for this predilection elsewhere. We have already seen that the human head of the four-winged boy popular in the iconography of eighth century Israel could be substituted for an aquiline head. It may be considered, therefore, that the eagle-headed and human-headed winged lions were essentially the same type of creature.[253] The aquiline head (an Egyptian solar symbol) would serve to connect this creature with the solar aspects of the deity. Lemaire (1990: 97–101) argues that the popularity of these aquiline/leonine hybrids on seals from Israel (determined either by the inclusion of a – *yw* name or by the findspot) suggests that they derive from a northern seal workshop, possibly centred in Samaria.

Keel and Uehlinger (1998: 177–181) view this Egyptian solar symbolism as a characteristic of Israelite and Judahite iconography in the Iron IIB period (9th–8th Century). After the occupation of Israel (722–720 B.C.E.), influence from Assyria meant that these Egyptian elements were suppressed, although they were not lost altogether (see Sass 1993: 199). Assyria's conquest of Israel meant that the North became deurbanized. In reaction, Judah operated policies of centralization in order to unify the country and cope with refugees from Israel. At first, Judah, being situated as it was off the major trade routes, was not targeted by Assyria. However, when Sennacherib began his Western Campaign in 701 (the aim of which was to advance into Egypt), Judah too succumbed to Assyrian pressure. According to the biblical account (2 Kings 17–21), Hezekiah managed to prevent the capture of Jerusalem but lost many of Judah's western and southern settlements. He and his son Manasseh were forced to pay sizable tributes to Assyria, and Judah was eventually subjected to vassalage.

---

252 Furthermore, how far the population of Israel and Judah would have regarded depictions on seals as "idols" is uncertain. Although they were considered to have prophylactic powers, these images were not designed to be worshipped.

253 This issue will be discussed further in the following section.

Cylinder seals, which had been replaced by stamp seals in Israel and Judah in the Iron I-Iron IIB periods, have been found in Israel in archaeological contexts dating from the last third of the eighth century. The appearance of these seals is evidence of the Assyrian occupation of Israel during this period. One Iron IIC cylinder seal, discovered in Samaria and dated to the 7th Century, includes a cuneiform inscription (see Keel and Uehlinger 1998: 288). They were most likely brought to Israel by Assyrian officials who were stationed in Israelite settlements after the conquest of the Northern Kingdom. This is confirmed by the iconography, which is markedly different from the Phoenician and Egyptian inspired designs we have encountered on eighth century stamp seals.

As these cylinder seals were mostly imported into Israel, any "cherub-like" figures must be regarded as images that were indigenous to Assyrian culture. However, such figures could have been identified as or with the cherubim by local Israelites.[254] Indeed, the Assyrians had been influenced by Aramean culture since the 9th Century (see Keel and Uehlinger 286–287) and, given the political and cultural[255] ties between Syria and Israel, some degree of consonance between the Assyrian and Israelite symbol systems should perhaps be expected. It is thus not too surprising that we find leonine/aquiline hybrids, similar to those we encountered on the 8th Century stamp seals, on seals from Iron IIC Israel. However, although the physical form of the creatures remains similar, the iconographic contexts in which they appear are different from those in which they occurred previously. For example, on one Assyrian cylinder seal from Megiddo (see Picture 14 and Lamon and Shipton 1939: pl. 66.11), two such hybrids appear battling with a warrior (perhaps a deity or a king). Although a similar hybrid is attacked by a human figure on the Phoenician style scaraboid (Sass 1993: fig. 122) described earlier, the Assyrian seal depicts a more complex scene. The figures are surrounded by astral symbols, an eight-pointed Venus star and the Pleiades. These astral elements are characteristic of Assyrian icono-

---

254 In Judah, locally produced glyptic was mostly aniconic in this period (see Sass 1993: 198–200 and Avigad 1986).

255 The South Syrian school of ivory carving posited by Winter (1981) had its centre at Damascus. Many of the designs found on artefacts from Israelite cities can be linked to this school.

graphy and contrast with the solar symbols that Israel and Judah inherited from Egypt. The battle scene depicted on this seal is one of several in the Assyrian cylinder collection from Israel. Given Assyria's political ambitions during this period, conflict is not a surprising theme to find on these seals. However, all of these combat scenes take place in the heavenly sphere (represented by the astral elements) and thus symbolise the triumph of cosmos over chaos. If this is a correct interpretation, the hybrid creature represents the chaotic realm. The cherubim are never depicted in such a negative light in the Hebrew Bible.[256] Although menacing creatures (Gen 3:24; Ps 18:11 = 2 Sam 22:11), they work in harmony with divine order and do not threaten it.

On another Assyrian cylinder seal from Iron IIC Palestine (see Picture 15 and Parker 1949: no. 172), a stylised version of a similar leonine/aquiline hybrid occurs as the target of an archer.[257] Similar scenes but depicting a variety of different beasts as the target occur on many cylinder seals from the Assyrian empire (see Keel and Uehlinger 1998: 291). On one example from Gezer, the target is a horned snake. Keel and Uehlinger (1998: 291) view these scenes as depictions of mythological battles between gods and various chaos monsters. They argue that the leonine/aquiline hybrid on the cylinder seal is a representation of the Anzu dragon. In Mesopotamian mythology, this dragon was killed by the god *Ninurta*, after stealing the tablet of destinies. Although sometimes described as having a lion's head, in certain texts it is described as having a "beak like a saw", which suggests features of a bird of prey (see Green and Black 1992: 107). In which case, the aquiline/leonine hybrid on this seal (as well as those on the Assyrian cylinder seal from Megiddo) may depict this (or a similar) chaos monster, as Keel and Uehlinger suggest. What is interesting, therefore, is that the leonine/aquiline hybrid depicted on Assyrian glyptic can have completely different connotations to that depicted on the Hebrew name seals we examined earlier. The Assyrian creature is a symbol of chaos, which must be overcome by the king or deity. By contrast, the Hebrew

---

256 Ezek 28:11-19 (MT) does depict a cherub in a pejorative light. Yet the poem is intentionally subversive.

257 Parker (1949: 38) argues that the rough drill-hole cutting is characteristic of seals from the 9th Century. However, the iconography is certainly Assyrian and its appearance in Palestine is probably the result of the Assyrian domination in Iron IIC.

examples are prophylactic images designed to protect the owner of the seal.

Nevertheless, aquiline/leonine hybrids do still appear in the Iron IIC period with similar positive overtones to those depicted in the Iron IIB period. For example, the constellation of an aquiline/leonine hybrid facing a stylised tree or other object, which is familiar on the eighth century Hebrew name seals, appears again on an Iron IIC seal from Samaria (Keel and Uehlinger 1998: illus. 292). The hybrid is portrayed facing a branch or stylised tree under a crescent moon. The Egyptian solar elements are no longer prominent and the lunar disc (the emblem of the moon god Sin) appears instead. On one conoid seal from Gezer (Keel and Uehlinger 1998: illus. 293a), the same hybrid is featured again below a lunar disk but faces a worshipper.[258]

According to Keel and Uehlinger (1998: 298–316), lunar and astral elements were incorporated into the iconography associated with the god El, and possibly also Yahweh, as a result of Assyrian influence. On a cylinder seal from Beth-Shean these lunar and astral elements are depicted together with an enthroned deity and winged leonine/aquiline hybrids (similar to those we have encountered previously). The stratum in which the seal was discovered is uncertain and thus dating the seal has proved difficult (see Parker 1949: 28 and James 1966: 104). Keel and Uehlinger (1998: 312) argue that the style and iconography suggest that the seal was carved locally and should be dated to the end of the 8th or beginning of the 7th Century. This would mean that the Assyrian astral and lunar aspects have been adopted by local craftsmen and integrated with more traditional motifs. The hybrid on the lower register is depicted sitting opposite a stylised tree (a motif familiar to us from the Hebrew stamp seals). Above it, however, is a rhombus (a symbol prevalent in Assyrian art) which represents the heavenly sphere above the hybrid (Keel and Uehlinger 1998: 314). It would seem, therefore, that the familiar design of a hybrid guarding a tree has been integrated into a more complex scene depicting the god El conceived of as a lunar deity. A similar aquiline/leonine hybrid also occurs on the upper register. This time it is portrayed in a recumbent position in front of an archer who is

---

258   This piece was discovered in a fifth century tomb but is linked to the Iron IIC by means of its iconography.

aiming at a leaping caprid above the hybrid. The scene on the upper register is somewhat disjointed, which has caused Keel and Uehlinger (1998: 313) to argue that it depicts paratactically arranged motifs that are symbolic, in a general way, of the heavenly realm.[259]

Also depicted on the upper register of the Beth-Shean cylinder seal is a winged human figure holding two caprids by the feet. A non-winged figure in the same stance is common in the iconography of Judah and Israel in the Iron I-IIB periods (see Keel and Uehlinger 1998: 116, 140, 182–184). The animals held by the human figure vary from crocodiles and scorpions to ostriches and caprids. This type of figure is known as "Lord of the Animals" or "Mistress of the Animals", depending on its gender (see Keel and Uehlinger 1998: 182–184, 313). It represents the mastery of the deity over nature.[260] On the Beth-Shean seal, the gender of the figure is uncertain. Unlike the figures from the Iron I-IIB periods, the Beth-Shean example has grown wings. According to Keel and Uehlinger (1998: 313), this may well be the result of influence from Assyrian iconography, in which winged "Lords of the Animals" are frequently portrayed. Thus, although a winged being, it is unlikely that this figure would have been identified with, or as, a cherub.[261]

Winged human figures that should probably also be identified as deities are represented on two unique name seals from the Iron IIC period. One (Sass 1993: illus. 142) dates to the end of the 8th or beginning of the 7th Century and is of unknown provenance. It has been classified as

---

259 They also suggest that the different elements may be representative of certain star signs (the caprid and the archer being obvious astral symbols).

260 The "Mistress of the Lions" that we encountered on the Taanach cult stand is a female version of the same figure.

261 The same can be said of the winged bulls being held by a "Lord of the Animals" on an Assyrian style cylinder seal from Dor (Keel and Uehlinger 1998: illus. 284). Although this time it is the animals, and not the deity, that are winged, the addition of wings merely helps to bring the familiar scene into the heavenly realm. Keel and Uehlinger (1998: 290) argue: "Even though this seal may not have come from the 'imperial' production in the centre of Assyria, but rather from a provincial workshop, it still ought to be considered an import. We find neither the 'Lord of the Animals' nor winged bulls in any works attributable to local stamp seal production." Moreover, as has been stated previously, the biblical cherubim are never described as at odds with the divine sphere. On the contrary, they serve and protect the deity.

Hebrew on palaeographical grounds.[262] The figure is a nude four-winged woman depicted *en face* and holding a floral staff in each hand. A horned headdress signals that the figure is a deity and, based on iconographic traditions at this time, has been identified as the 'Queen of Heaven', who was either the goddess Astarte or Asherah (see Keel and Uehlinger 1998: 338–340). The same goddess may also feature on another unique Hebrew name seal (see Picture 16 and Sass 1993: illus. 143). This time the goddess appears above a stylized palmetto tree. Owing to the female and divine characteristics of these figures, they are not to be viewed as appropriate comparative material for the cherubim.

On the same seal just mentioned (Sass 1993: illus. 143), there appear two further winged beings. One is a bipterous[263] male figure, its horned headdress signifying that he is to be identified as a god. The other is more illuminating for our purposes. Under the male deity, a winged quadruped is featured with a human head wearing an elaborate crown. Its body faces the palmetto tree under the goddess but its head is turned to face outwards. There are several intriguing features about this design and the iconography is so unique among Northwest Semitic seals that scholars have sometimes doubted the seal's authenticity (see Sass 1993: 237). The scene is elaborate and would thus be more ideally suited to a cylinder seal, where a greater surface area could allow for more detail. The seal incorporates aspects of Urartian and Assyrian art but no notably Egyptian elements.

The winged quadruped displays several characteristics that comply with our typological profile of the cherubim. Indeed, it is somewhat similar to those that we encountered on the Megiddo and Samarian ivories, the Taanach stand and the Hazor pyxis. Yet, physically, it displays one important unique feature: its body is bovine. Ezekiel's vision of the hybrid characteristics of the חַיּוֹת incorporates bovine elements (Ezek 1:7, 10). However, these are notably missing from the

---

262 The haphazard spacing of the inscription suggests that it was added later. In which case, the iconography (which characterizes this seal as unique among Hebrew seals) may suggest that the seal originated from further a field. This depiction of a four-winged goddess *en face* was particularly popular on Assyrian seals dating to eighth and seventh centuries (see Keel and Uehlinger 1998: 338).

263 Again, this figure is depicted in profile and was probably conceived as having four wings with only two being visible.

second vision, where the חַיּוֹת are identified as cherubim. The quadruped on our seal is the only example of a human-headed winged bovine in the extant iconography of Israel and Judah. In every other instance, human-headed winged quadrupeds have leonine bodies. Winged bulls with human heads are a distinctive feature of Mesopotamian art, the most famous examples being the gateway guardians of Assyrian palaces (see *ANEP* figs. 646–647). The foreign elements of the design and its uniqueness among Northwest Semitic glyptic mean that this seal probably travelled to Israel from elsewhere. Indeed, the placing of the inscription suggests that this was originally an anepigraphic seal to which the Hebrew name was added later (see Keel and Uehlinger 1998: 340).

A second interesting characteristic of this quadruped, for our purposes, concerns its position below the male deity. It is possible that the scene on this seal should be divided into two registers (see Sass 1993: 236). If this is the case, the quadruped would be depicted facing the palmetto tree (in a similar position to the quadruped on the Hazor pyxis) and would have no relation to the god featured above it. However, Sass (1993: 236) argues that the design should be viewed as a single scene for compositional reasons. If this is the case, the god appears above the quadruped, whereas the goddess appears above the tree. This arrange-ment begs for a comparison with the biblical texts that allude to the manifestation and transportation of Yahweh on or above a cherub/cherubim, particularly 2 Sam 22:11=Ps 18:11. In ancient Near Eastern art, gods are often pictured as standing on quadrupeds of one kind or another. As Keel and Uehlinger (1998: 340) argue: "A local *interpretatio judaica* by a Judahite owner could have connected this constellation of images with Yahweh (above a 'cherub'; see Ps 18:11) and Asherah as 'Queen of Heaven' (above a stylized tree)". Thus, although the iconography is not indigenously Hebrew, a Judahite owner could have identified this quadruped as a cherub.

In the Iron III period, which lasted from the capture of Jerusalem by the Babylonians in 587 until the establishment of the province of Yehud in around 450[264], cylinder seals again became outmoded.[265] Instead,

---

264 For this periodization, see Keel and Uehlinger 1998: 410.
265 Only one Neo-Babylonian style cylinder seal has been found in Palestine (see Parker 1949: no. 7). On this seal, from Tell Jemmeh, a bird-man with lion's paws and a

conoid stamp seals (both iconic and aniconic) were popular in this period. Winged beings are not common on Babylonian style seals from Palestine but occur frequently on Persian style glyptic. Typically, these winged beings tend to be in the form of winged bulls or caprids, similar to those found on the Assyrian style cylinder seal from Dor (described above, n. 50). On several of these Persian style seals (Keel and Uehlinger 1998: illus. 361a–c), the winged beings are held up by a crowned human figure (probably the king), in a stance reminiscent of the "Lord of the Animals". The winged sun disc hovers above the king, thus bringing the scene into the heavenly realm. The design is probably symbolic of the cosmic dominance of the king. Similar scenes (although this time only featuring one winged creature, leonine or bovine) occur on a bulla from Samaria and a scaraboid from Tell Keisan (see Keel and Uehlinger 1998: illus. 360 a–b). These winged beasts can be identified with those depicted with the "Lord" or "Mistress of the Animals" on seals and scarabs from Judah and Israel from the Iron I-Iron IIB periods. Although the motif is indigenous to the area, the addition of wings to the animal and human figures that occurs in the Iron IIC-Persian periods may be the result of Mesopotamian influence. The wings serve to push the scene into the celestial sphere. This, in turn, underscores the cosmic powers of the king. It is unlikely, therefore, that these creatures would ever have been identified as or with the biblical cherubim. Indeed, as we noted earlier, the cherubim work with, and not against, the cosmic order.

Similar designs to those described above occur on several of the Wadi Daliyeh seal impressions (Leith 1997: pls. 17 and 18). Some feature the "Master of the Animals" with wingless lions (pl. 17) but one worn impression seems to depict a "Master of the Animals" holding winged creatures (pl. 18, WD 3B). Two (pl. 18, WD 4 and 8) depict the Persian king smiting a lone winged animal. The Wadi Daliyeh bullae are a collection of sealings found in caves near Samaria. Originally, they sealed official documents written on papyri, remnants of which were also found at the same site. The documents were composed and

---

scorpion's tail stands on a platform, facing the goat-fish of Ea on an altar. The goat-fish has the ram staff of Ea on its back. These figures are typical of Neo-Babylonian iconography. Although the scorpion hybrid accords physically, to some extent, with our typological profile of the cherubim, contextually it does not. The iconography is deeply-rooted in Babylonian religion and does not display features that are present on local stamp seal glyptic (see Keel and Uehlinger 1998: 374).

sealed in Samaria in the 4th Century B.C.E. and the bullae constitute important evidence for the iconography of the Persian period. From 539–332, Samaria (as well as the rest of former Israel and Judah) was part of the fifth satrapy of the Achaemenid Persian Empire. The documents are written in Aramaic, the *lingua franca* of the Persian Empire. The iconography reflects the cosmopolitan culture of this period, incorporating Hellenistic, Phoenician, Babylonian and Persian elements (see Leith 1997: 20–24). The similarity of some of the motifs to designs on Judaean and Samarian coinage of this period may suggest that the seal rings or stamps were carved locally. Alternatively, they may have been produced by Syro-Phoenician craftsmen for the wealthy Samarian officials. Although the Hellenistic designs perhaps witness to the non-conformist attitude of the seal owners, some of the more Near-Eastern designs reflect the Court Style of the Achaemenid Empire. This is particularly the case with those that depict winged figures.

Aside from those occurring on the bullae depicting the "Master of the Animals", "cherub-like" figures appear relatively frequently in the Wadi Daliyeh collection, some in similar forms and contexts to those encountered in earlier Judahite and Israelite iconography. The main problem, however, in comparing these figures to the biblical cherubim concerns how far we can regard these images as reflecting the religious beliefs of the Samarians to whom they belonged. Many of the seal owners bear Yahwistic names and thus probably worshipped Yahweh. However, according to Leith (1997:24), although the owner may have believed his or her seal to have amuletic properties, "there may have been no overwhelming impulse in Persian-period Samaria to associate seal imagery with personal religious orientation." Thus, rather than reflecting private religious beliefs, the motifs may have functioned more generically as prestigious emblems. It is also true that, by this time, religious traditions concerning the cherubim could have shifted considerably. Following the exile and probably largely due to the Ezekiel traditions, the cherubim took on a somewhat more mystical status. This can be seen clearly in later texts such as *The Songs of the Sabbath Sacrifice* and the Enochic texts. In our exegesis of Ezekiel and Chronicles, we detected the first signs of this conceptual shift concerning the cherubim.

Winged quadrupeds (like those we have encountered on the objects and eighth century seals discussed earlier) with leonine bodies and human heads are a very common design in the Wadi Daliyeh impressions (see Picture 17). Normally, they are depicted with the head of the Persian king or hero (see Leith 1997: pl. 15, WD 53 and WD31; pl. 19, WD3A and WD 24; pl. 21, WD 48 and WD 15A). However, they are also depicted wearing the Egyptian double crown (pl. 20: WD 13 and WD 41), a feature of some of those appearing in the Samaria ivory collections. According to Leith (1997: 29), the designs with quadrupeds wearing double crowns may be variations on a Court Style motif, probably produced in Phoenicia (hence the Egyptian rather than Persian headdress). Similarly, WD 15A, which depicts a pair of winged quadrupeds flanking a central lotus blossom or palmette, may also be of eastern manufacture.[266] In general, these quadrupeds occur in pairs (for example, Picture 17 and Leith 1997: pl. 19, WD 3A, WD 24; pl. 20, WD 13, WD 41; pl. 21, WD 48, WD 15A) but occasionally appear on their own (pl.15, WD 53, WD 31).

One interesting design depicts two of these human-headed winged lions flanking a human figure (probably the king) in a smiting position (WD 3A, WD 10A, WD 11B, WD12, WD 24). The motif is typical of the Achaemenid Court Style but is quite crudely rendered, which causes Leith (1997: 221–223) to argue that the seal ring responsible for these impressions must have been manufactured locally. What is interesting about this design is that, unlike the other impressions depicting these hybrids, this one portrays them in a pejorative light. According to Leith (1997: 223), the Persians adopted the Mesopotamian traditions concerning these creatures. As we discussed earlier, Assyrian and Babylonian iconography represent such hybrids as ambivalent creatures, capable of being both sentinels of divine and royal order and also menacing opponents of a deity or king. Such quadrupeds are never associated with these negative connotations on objects or glyptic from Judah or Israel prior to the Assyrian invasion. The biblical cherubim are never described as opponents to the natural or cosmic order, although

---

266 The flower has two tendrils which may be volutes, a characteristic of Phoenician flowers (see Winter 1976: 6).

their ability to protect or safeguard does necessarily suggest menacing characteristics (Gen 3:24; Ps 18:11 = 2 Sam 22:11).

Another motif of Mesopotamian origin is the pair of scorpion men depicted on WD 25. Again, this is a standard design of the Achaemenid Empire's Court Style (Leith 1997: 235). The two figures, which have scorpion tails, stick legs and the head of the Persian Hero, are depicted facing each other. Significantly, the only other hybrid with scorpion characteristics that we have encountered in our survey is that depicted on the only Neo-Babylonian cylinder seal to be found in Palestine (Parker 1949: no. 7, see above n. 56).[267] Although, physically, this creature is somewhat different, scorpion features are found frequently on Mesopotamian hybrids (see Green and Black 1992: 161). According to Leith (1997: 235), "artists in the Achaemenid Empire produced a new variation on the Mesopotamian scorpion-man by giving him the head of the Persian Hero, a guise in which the Persian king also appears." Although a Perso-Babylonian motif, a Samarian coin (probably minted in Samaria in the 4th Century) depicts an identical Persian Hero scorpion-man. According to Leith (1997: 235), this may indicate that the design had some importance to Samarians in this period. Thus although the design derives from eastern iconography, the seal that produced this image may have been manufactured locally.

The variety of "cherub-like" figures on the Wadi Daliyeh seal impressions is likely due to Mesopotamian influences on Persian iconography. Winged and non-winged hybrids of countless types occur in Assyrian and Babylonian artwork (see Green and Black 1992: 64–65). It seems that some of these were incorporated into the official iconography of the Persian Empire. The craftsmen responsible for cutting the seals and minting coins for use in small provinces of the empire, such as Samaria, would have adopted some of these designs.

Whether or not some, or all, of these figures were identified by the Samarian officials with the biblical cherubim is difficult to say. As noted earlier, the Ezekiel traditions change the status of the cherubim significantly. Instead of statues and designs that are intimately linked to the Jerusalem temple, they become more mystical creatures

---

267 There also exists an unprovenanced cylinder seal with a scorpion man and an Aramaic inscription (see Leith 1997: 236, n.8).

connected with the universal presence of Yahweh. The physical
description of the cherubim in Ezekiel is so convoluted that it becomes
almost impossible to define their exact corporeal nature. Thus, it may
be that the Samarian seal owners would not have made a connection
between the hybrid creatures depicted on the Wadi Daliyeh bullae and
the biblical cherubim.

§ 3.5 Evaluation

Following our survey of "cherub-like" images in the iconography of
Israel and Judah from the late 10th–4th Century B.C.E., it is necessary
to evaluate what we have gleaned in more detail. There are several
different types of creature that could potentially qualify as cherubim.
However, some of these conform more closely to our typological
profile than others. In general, winged human figures tend to depict
deities rather than subsidiary tutelary beings. This concurs with the
results of our exegetical work. The possibility that the cherubim were
envisaged as bipedal creatures is only suggested by Ezek 1:5–7 and,
therefore, is dependent on the equation of the cherubim with the חַיּוֹת
in Ezek 10:15, 20 and 22. As our exegesis has shown, this equation is
the result of later editorial activity and was not original to the text. It
is, therefore, more likely that the cherubim were conceived of as
quadrupeds (in accordance with 2 Sam 22:11 = Ps 18:11) at least until
the exilic period.

Turning to representations of winged quadrupeds in the extant
iconography of Israel and Judah, there are four different per-
mutations.[268] The first is the ram-headed winged lion that occurs on
tiny fragments discovered in the Samarian ivory cache. Although they
occur in a pair and face a sacred tree (a configuration which can only

---

268 We are discounting here the winged beasts depicted on seals from the Iron IIC and
     Persian periods that are held upside down by the "Lord" or "Mistress of the
     Animals" and occur on their own on the Wadi Daliyeh bullae. As we noted in our
     survey, these animals are merely winged in order to bring an earlier common motif
     into the celestial sphere. They do not conform closely to our typological profile of the
     biblical cherubim. We will also discount the scorpion-men (of which we only have
     three examples). These were indigenous to Mesopotamian iconography and only
     absorbed into Samarian glyptic in the 4th Century B.C.E.

be determined by comparison with a similar design found at Arslan-Tash), ovine features are never attributed to the cherubim. Moreover, ram-headed hybrids are prominent in Egyptian art, often representing avatars of the god Amun.[269] The fact that we only have one extant example of this type of winged quadruped is perhaps an indication that this was not a prominent figure in Israelite or Judahite iconography.

The second type of winged quadruped also only occurs once in the existing artwork of ancient Israel and Judah. This is the human-headed winged bull that we encountered on the unique Hebrew name seal (Sass 1993: fig. 143). This type of winged quadruped is common in Assyrian iconography and, given the date of this seal, it may be that the seal came into the possession of its Judahite owner from elsewhere in the Assyrian empire. Although the owner of the seal may well have associated this creature with a cherub, this type of image is not likely to have inspired the iconography of Israel and Judah prior to the Assyrian invasion

The type of winged quadruped that conforms most closely to our typological profile of the biblical cherubim is the human-headed winged lion. It occurs in pairs in the Samarian ivory collections as well as on the Taanach cult stand. In the Samarian ivories, it is always depicted in male garments and has a very close connection to sacred vegetation. It is used as decoration on wall panels, the Taanach cult stand and on seals. Although the wall panels were used in the decoration of palaces, some consonance is to be expected between the ornamentation of state and cultic buildings. This type of creature is especially associated with an apotropaic function and is often depicted as a menacing creature. On the cult stand, one is positioned on each side of the entrance to the model shrine and demarcates the sacred space. This human-headed winged lion thus matches our typological profile of the biblical cherubim very well.

A fourth type of winged quadruped in the artwork from Israel and Judah that accords with our cherubim typology is an aquiline

---

269 The god Amun was worshipped in Canaan in the Late Bronze and Iron I periods, when the country was under Egyptian control. It may be that this design is a vestige of this time and continued to be incorporated into Israelite and Phoenician artwork during the Iron II.

headed winged lion. Although only occurring on fragments from the Samarian hoard, it is a common image on seals from the Iron II-Iron III periods. On the Hebrew name seals of the 8th Century, it occurs in exactly the same positive iconographic contexts as human-headed types. Assyrian versions of a similar creature are portrayed in a pejorative light on cylinder seals found in Israel. These examples are likely to be creatures indigenous to Assyrian iconography and do not conform closely to our contextual profile of the cherubim.

The results of our survey show that there are two types of winged being in the extant iconography of Israel and Judah from the 10th–4th Century B.C.E. that conform most closely to our profile of the biblical cherubim. These are the human and eagle-headed winged lions. Although it is not possible to identify one or other (or both) as a cherub with certainty, it does seem most likely that it is a being such as these that was envisaged by the authors of our cherubim texts. What has also become apparent from our analysis of the archae-ological evidence is that the eagle-headed winged lions may be essentially the same type of creature as the human-headed types. Indeed, Egyptian solar symbolism allowed eagle and human heads to be interchanged on deities. It may be that this substitution could also occur on subsidiary beings.

Freedman and O'Connor (1995: 314), in their analysis of the texts and iconography pertaining to the biblical cherubim, maintain that the word כְּרוּב "does not denote a single type of creature like that represented on certain monuments but refers rather to a variety of winged creatures associated with a sacred landscape." They continue by arguing that כְּרֻבִים "denotes beings that resemble birds, bipeds, and quadrupeds" (Freedman and O'Connor 1995: 218). Our analysis of the textual and archaeological material has shown that such a remark is actually rather short sighted. Our survey of the archae-ological evidence discourages the identification of the cherubim with bipeds or birds. Instead, it is winged quadrupeds (probably with leonine bodies and with either aquiline or human heads) that are most likely envisaged by the biblical writers. Although the archae-ological record preserves winged lions with both human and aquiline heads, this does not mean that they are two different types of creature. Egyptian symbolism (which inspired the iconography of

Judah, Israel and Phoenicia) allowed deities to change in appearance and yet retain their individual identities. By analogy with the substitution of human for aquiline heads on deities depicted in the iconography of Israel, it may be that the same thing could happen to a subsidiary guardian being. Thus the human and aquiline winged quadrupeds may be the same type of creature. It is this creature that conforms most closely to the biblical cherubim.

§ 3.6 Summary

Although any comparison between textual and material artefacts should be tentative, our survey of "cherub-like" figures in the iconography of Israel and Judah does illuminate the biblical cherubim. Not only does it help us to imagine the kind of creature that the biblical writers were envisaging but it also supports the conclusions that we made purely on the basis of our exegesis. No figures with the physical characteristics described in the Ezekiel cherubim texts have been found in the extant iconography. Multi-faced creatures are entirely absent and four-winged creatures are usually to be identified as deities. Likewise, winged bipeds have human features and tend to be deities rather than subsidiary beings. Thus our view that cherubim were probably envisaged as quadrupedal (in accordance with 2 Sam 22:11 = Ps 18:11) is substantiated. The human and aquiline-headed winged lions conform most closely to our typological profile of the cherubim. If we are to attribute a degree of historicity to the account of the temple building in 1 Kings 6–7, then the archaeology corresponds to the biblical account. The human–headed winged lions are especially associated with Phoenician designs and occur in the iconography of the state buildings in Samaria (8th Century). The possibility that the designs had some religious impetus cannot be discounted (see Beach 1993). Thus, chronologically and contextually, these designs correspond to those described in 1 Kings 6–7.

In Part I, we argued that there is not enough evidence to support Mettinger's theory of a biblical "cherubim throne" concept. The archaeological evidence has shown that, although "cherub-like" figures flanked thrones in the Megiddo ivories, there are no "cherubim thrones" after the Late Bronze period. This corroborates our argument that there is no reason to import a "cherubim throne" concept into the biblical material. Historically, there may have been a cherubim throne in Israel, but there is no evidence of this in the biblical texts. We will need further archaeological to come to light in the future in order to claim the existence of such a throne in the cults of ancient Samaria and Jerusalem.

Just as the cherubim in the biblical passages, there is evidence to suggest that "cherub-like" figures depicted in Israelite and Judahite iconography could be transmogrified. An ability to metamorphose is not evidence that the word כְּרוּב refers to a variety, rather than a single type, of winged beings (as Freedman and O'Connor 1995 argue). Indeed, the iconography seems to indicate that the craftsmen were aware that divine beings were not constrained by a fixed corporeal reality. In a similar way, the final form of Ezekiel allows the cherubim to transcend their manufactured reality (as described in 1 Kings 6–7). They are transformed into creatures whose physical form is difficult for the author to describe and almost impossible for readers to envisage.

Conclusion

Our synthetic study of the biblical כְּרֻבִים has allowed us to engage with types of evidence other than that provided by the texts: archaeological and etymological data. This has enabled us to dialogue with scholars, such as Dhorme (1926) and Mettinger (1982a), who view these other types of evidence as integral to understanding the biblical כְּרֻבִים and whose conclusions have shaped cherubim scholarship to date. However, unlike the works of these scholars, this study has given precedence to the biblical texts because the כְּרֻבִים exist, first and foremost, as a biblical phenomenon.

In Part I, our analysis of the biblical literature highlighted the development of ideas concerning the cherubim (for a summary of our findings arising from biblical exegesis, see §1.4). In texts such as The Song of David and 1 Kings 6–8, the cherubim are conceived as apotropaic beings that function as guardians of the divine locale. They are understood as quadrupeds with one face and one set of wings. In exilic and post-exilic texts (Ezekiel and 1–2 Chronicles), the first signs of a shift concerning cherubim traditions can be detected. In Ezekiel, the cherubim acquire the physical characteristics of the חַיּוֹת and a connection between the cherubim and seraphim can be perceived for the first time (Ezek 1:11; 3:12). This connection is developed in post-biblical literature, for example *The Songs of the Sabbath Sacrifice* and the Enochic texts, where the cherubim become agents of praise and form part of a divine hierarchy. Thus, over time, the apotropaic role of the cherubim was supplanted by one of obeisance. Likewise, the use of the term מֶרְכָּבָה in 1 Chr 28:18 can be viewed as a precursor to the more developed *merkābāh* theology of later Judaism, which was based on the visions of Ezekiel 1 and 10.[270]

---

270 In *The Songs of the Sabbath Sacrifice*, the cherubim and the wheels (familiar from Ezekiel 10) are explicitly stated to form chariots. Both כרובים and אופנים are linked to

In Part II, an examination of the etymological evidence pertaining to the biblical כְּרֻבִים showed that there is no proof concerning the derivation of the lexeme. We argued, against Dhorme, that a possible link with the Akkadian word *kurību* is not evidence of the intercessory role of the cherubim. Indeed, the Akkadian lexeme, if cognate, would actually underscore the apotropaic qualities of the כְּרֻבִים. This would strengthen our argument (based on the biblical texts) that the primary function of the cherubim was to guard the divine locale.

Evaluation of the archaeological evidence, in Part III, corroborated our conclusions made on the basis of biblical exegesis. We found no "cherubim thrones" in our targeted survey. The only thrones flanked by "cherub-like" beings occur among the Late Bronze Megiddo ivories and there are only two examples. It is thus unwarranted to import a "cherubim throne" concept into the biblical material based on these two early pieces. Likewise, there are no extant images in the archaeological record of ancient Israel and Judah that conform to the physical description of the cherubim in Ezekiel 8–11. The most common winged figures, occurring in contexts similar to those in which the biblical כְּרֻבִים feature, are aquiline and human-headed winged lions. These occur in pairs and have a close link to sacred vegetation, suggestive of an apotropaic function. It is likely that it was creatures such as these that were envisaged by the authors of 1 Kings 6–8 and the Song of David when they mention the כְּרֻבִים.

Further Trajectories

Our discussion of the biblical כְּרֻבִים has drawn attention to several topics that would merit further discussion. First, the cherubim throne as a biblical concept has been taken for granted in recent academic literature. Following this study, it is hoped that scholars will reassess the evidence for the existence of such a throne, not only in the biblical literature but also in the historical cults of ancient Israel and Judah. The biblical texts give us no information about a cherubim throne. The archaeological record does not provide us with "cherub" flanked

---

the *markabot* (chariots) in 4Q403 1 ii 15, where both appear with 3mp suffixes referring back to *markabot* at the beginning of the line (see Newsom 1985:237).

thrones from Israel and Judah in the 10th–4th centuries. Thus we need more substantial evidence to sustain claims that such a throne existed in the cults of ancient Israel and Judah. If such evidence comes to light in the future, we will then need to ask why the cherubim throne is absent in the biblical literature.

Second, the possible historical connection between the cherubim and Phoenicia may be an area worthy of future investigation. The biblical tradition of Phoenician input into the temple design and the connection between a cherub and the King of Tyre in Ezekiel 28 may point to a link between the cherubim and Phoenician culture. The archaeological evidence also points in this direction, with "cherub-like" figures occurring most frequently in Phoenician artwork.

Finally, biblical scholarship could benefit from a study focussing on the link between the seraphim and cherubim. A connection between these two types of heavenly creature is only made explicit in post-biblical literature but is implicit in the book of Ezekiel (Ezek 1:11; 3:12). Moreover, the development of ideas in the Qumran texts concerning the position of the cherubim would be an interesting and profitable area of future study, as would the conception of the cherubim elsewhere in early Jewish and Christian art and literature. It is hoped that the present study may provide a useful starting point for future research.

Bibliography

Abu Assaf, Ali.
1990 *Der Tempel von 'Ain Dara.* Damaszener Forschungen 3; Mainz: Philip von Zabern

Ackroyd, Peter.
1972 "The Temple Vessels: A Continuity Theme." in *Studies in the Religion of Ancient Israel.* Edited by Helmer Ringgren. (SVT 23. Leiden: Brill), 166–181

Ahlström, Gosta.
1975 "The Travels of the Ark: A Religio-Political Composition." *JTS* 26, 141–149

Albenda, Pauline.
1994 "Some Remarks on the Samaria Ivories and other Iconographic Resources." *BA* 57, 60.

Albright, William F.
1938 "What were the Cherubim?" *BA* 1, 1–3.
1939 *From the Stone Age to Christianity.* (Baltimore: John Hopkins Press)
1949 *The Archaeology of Palestine.* Middlesex: Penguin Books
1969 Archaeology and the Religion of Israel. (Garden City, NY: Doubleday, 5th ed)

Alexandre, Monique
1986 "L'Epée de Flamme (Gen. 3:24): Textes Chrétiens et Juives." in *Hellenica et Judaica.* Edited by André Caquot, Mireille Hadas-Lebel and Jean Riaud. (Leuven: Peeters), 403–441

Allen, L. C.
1990 *Ezekiel 20–48* (WBC 29; Dallas, TX: Word Books)
1994 *Ezekiel 1–19* (WBC 28; Dallas, TX: Word Books)

Assmann, J. (ed.)
1982 *Funktionen und Leistungen des Mythos: drei altorientalische Beispiele.* Orbis biblicus et orientalis 48; Freiburg, Schweiz: Universitäts-verlag; Göttingen: Vandenhoeck & Ruprecht

Auld, A. G.
1994 *Kings without Privilege* (Edinburgh: T & T Clark)
2004 Samuel at the Threshold: Selected Works of Graeme Auld. (Aldershot: Ashgate)

Avigad, N.
    1986   *Hebrew Bullae from the Time of Jeremiah: Remnants of a Burnt Archive.* (translated by R. Grafman; Jerusalem: Israel Exploration Society)

Baumgartner, W. and L. Kohler
    1995   The Hebrew and Aramaic Lexicon of the Old Testament: Volume 2 Tet-Ayin. (Leiden: Brill)
Barnett, R. D.
    1939   "Phoenician and Syrian Ivory Carving." *PEQ* 71, 4–19
    1969   "Ezekiel and Tyre," *Eretz Israel* 9, 6–13
    1982   Ancient Ivories in the Middle East and Adjacent Countries. (Qedem 14; Jerusalem: Hebrew University)
Barr, J.
    1961   *The Semantics of Biblical Language.* (Oxford: Oxford University Press)
    1992a   "'Thou Art the Cherub': Ezekiel 28:14 and the Post-Ezekiel Understanding of Genesis 2–3." in *Priests, Prophets and Scribes: Essays on the Formation of Second Temple Judaism in Honour of Joseph Blenkinsopp.* Edited by E. Ulrich *et al.*, (JSOTSup. 149; Sheffield: JSOT Press), 213–223
    1992b   The Garden of Eden and the Hope of Immortality. (SCM Press: London)
    2000   History and Ideology in the Old Testament: Biblical Studies at the End of a Millennium. (Oxford: Oxford University Press)
Barrick, W. B.
    1982   "The Straight-Legged Cherubim of Ezekiel's Inaugural Vision (Ezekiel 1:7a)." *CBQ* 44, 543–550
Barton, J.
    1996   *Reading the Old Testament: Method in Biblical Study.* (2nd Edition; London: Darton, Longman & Todd)
Batto, B. F.
    1991   "Paradise Reexamined." in *The Biblical Canon in Comparative Perspective.* Edited by K. L. Younger Jr., et. al. (Ancient Near Eastern Texts and Studies 11; Lewiston, NY: Edwin Mellen), 33–66
Beach, E. F.
    1993   "The Samaria Ivories, Marzeaḥ, and Biblical Text." *BA* 56/2 94–104
Beck, P.
    1990   "The Taanach Cult Stands: Iconographic Traditions in the Iron I Cult Vessels." in *From Nomadism to Monarchy: Archaeological and Historical Aspects of Early Israel.* Edited by N. Na'aman and I. Finkelstein. (Jerusalem: Yad Izhak Ben-Zvi), 417–446 (in hebrew)

Bevan, A. A.
1903   "The King of Tyre in Ezekiel XXVIII." *JTS* 4, 500–505

Black, J. and A. Green
1992   Gods, Demons and Symbols of Ancient Mesopotamia: An Illustrated Dictionary. (London: British Museum Press)

Black, J., A. George, N. Postgate (eds.)
2000   *A Concise Dictionary of Akkadian.* (2nd Corrected Printing; Wiesbaden: Harrassowitz Verlag)

Bloch-Smith, E.
1994   "'Who is the King of Glory?' Solomon's Temple and its Symbolism." in *Scripture and Other Artifacts: Essays on the Bible and Archaeology in Honor of Philip J. King.* Edited by M. D. Coogan et. al. (Louisville, KY: Westminster/John Knox), 18–31
2002   "Solomon's Temple: The Politics of Ritual Space." in *Sacred Time, Sacred Place.* Edited by B. M. Gittlen. (Winona Lake, Ind: Eisenbrauns), 83–94

Block, D. I.
1988   "Text and Emotion: A Study in the 'Corruptions' in Ezekiel's Inaugural Vision (Ezekiel 1:4–28)." *CBQ* 50, 418–442
1997   *The Book of Ezekiel: Chapters 1–24.* NICOT; (Grand Rapids, Michigan: Eerdmans)
1998   *The Book of Ezekiel: Chapters 25–48.* NICOT; (Grand Rapids, Michigan: Eerdmans)

Boardman, J.
2003   *Classical Phoenician Scarabs: A Catalogue and Study.* Studies in Gems and Jewellery 2; (Oxford: British Archaeological Reports)

Bogaert, P.-M.
1983   "Montagne sainte, jardin d'Eden et sanctuaire (hierosolymitain) dans un oracle d'Ézéchiel contre le prince de Tyr (Éz 28, 11–19)." in *Le mythe, son langage et son message. Actes du colloque de Liège et Louvain-la-Neuve 1981.* Edited by H. Limet and J. Ries. Homo Religiousus vol. 9; (Louvain-la-Neuve: Centre d'histoire des religions), 131–153

Borger, R.
1956   *Die Inschriften Asarhaddons Königs von Assyrien.* Archiv für Orientforschung 9; (Graz: E. Weidner)

Borowski, E.
1995   "Cherubim: God's Throne?" *BAR* 21, 36–41

Brovarski, E.
1977   "The Doors of Heaven." *Orientalia* 46, 107–115

Brown, J. P.
1968   "Literary Contexts of the Common Hebrew-Greek Vocabulary." *JSS* 13, 184–188

Busink, T. A.
1970   Der Tempel von Jerusalem von Salomo bis Herodes: 1. Der
            Tempel von Salomos. (Leiden: Brill)

Callender, D. E.
1998   "The Primal Man in Ezekiel and the Image of God." in *Society of
            Biblical Literature Seminar Papers*. (Atlanta, Georgia: Society of
            Biblical Literature), 606–625
Campbell, A. F.
1975   The Ark Narrative (1 Sam 4–6; 2 Sam 6): A Form-Critical and
            Traditio-Historical Study. SBL Dissertation Series 16; (Cambridge
            Mass: Scholars' Press,)
Carley, Keith W.
1974   *The Book of the Prophet Ezekiel*. The Cambridge Bible Commentary
            on the New English Bible; (Cambridge: Cambridge University)
Carlson, R. A.
1964   David, the Chosen King: A Tradition-Historical Approach to the
            Second Book of Samuel. (Almquist & Wiksells: Uppsala)
Cassuto, U.
1961   *A Commentary on the Book of Genesis, Part I*. Translated by
            I. Abrahams; (Jerusalem: Magnes Press)
1967   *A Commentary on the Book of Exodus*. Translated by I. Abrahams;
            (Jerusalem: Magnes Press)
Catling, H. W.
1964   Cypriot Bronzework in the Mycenaean World. (Oxford:
            Clarendon Press)
Childs, B.
1960   Myth and Reality in the Old Testament. SBT 27; (London: SCM
            Press)
Clements, R. E.
1965   *God and Temple*. (Oxford: Blackwell)
Cleveland, R. L.
1963   "Cherubs and the 'Tree of Life' in Ancient South Arabia." *BASOR*
            172, 55–61
Clifford, R. J.
1972   *The Cosmic Mountain in Canaan and the Old Testament*. HSM 4;
            (Cambridge, Mass: Harvard University Press)
1984   "The Temple and the Holy Mountain." in *Temple in Antiquity*.
            Edited by T. G. Madsen. (Salt Lake City, Utah: Bookcraft), 47–71
Clines, D. J. A.
1968   "The Image of God in Man." *TynBul* 19, 53–103
1987   "The Parallelism of Greater Precision: Notes from Isaiah 40 for a
            Theory of Hebrew Poetry." in *Directions in Biblical Hebrew Poetry*.
            Edited by E. R. Follis JSOTSup. 40; (Sheffield: Sheffield Academic
            Press), 77–100

Collins, J. J.
2005   The Bible after Babel: Historical Criticism in a Postmodern Age.
        (Grand Rapids, Michigan: Eerdmans)

Collon, D.
1993   First Impressions: Cylinder Seals in the Ancient Near East.
        (London: British Museum Press)

Cooke, G. A.
1936   A Critical and Exegetical Commentary on the Book of Ezekiel.
        (ICC; Edinburgh: T&T Clark)

Cornelius, I.
2004   The Many Faces of the Goddess: The Iconography of the Syro-
        Palestinian Goddesses Anat, Astarte, Qedeshet, and Asherah c.
        1500–1000 B.C.E. (OBO 204; Fribourg: Academic Press;
        Göttingen: Vandenhoeck & Ruprecht)

Cross, F. M.
1973   Canaanite Myth and Hebrew Epic: Essays in the History of the
        Religion of Israel. (Cambridge, Mass: Harvard University Press)

Cross, F. M. and D. N. Freedman
1953   "A Royal Song of Thanksgiving: II Samuel 22 = Psalm 18." *JBL* 72,
        15–34

Crowfoot, J. W. and G. M. Crowfoot
1938   *Early Ivories from Samaria.* Samaria-Sebaste Reports 2; (London:
        Palestine Exploration Fund)

Curtis, J. E.
1988   Bronze-Working Centres of Western Asia c.1000–539 B.C.
        (London: Kegan Paul)

Dahood, M.
1966   *Psalms I.* AB; (Garden City, N.Y.: Doubleday)

Davis, E.
1989   Swallowing the Scroll: Textuality and the Dynamics of Discourse
        in Ezekiel's Prophecy. JSOTSup. 78 (Sheffield: Almond Press)
1999   "'And Pharaoh Will Change his Mind…' (Ezekiel 32:31):
        Dismantling Mythical Discourse." in *Theological Exegesis: Essays
        in Honour of Brevard S. Childs.* Edited by C. Seitz and K. Greene-
        McCreight. (Grand Rapids, MI: Eerdmans), 224–239

Day, J.
2004   In Search of Pre-exilic Israel: Proceedings of the Oxford Old
        Testament Seminar. JSOTSup. 406; (London: T & T Clark)

Dessenne, A.
1957   *Le Sphinx, Etude Iconographique. I. Des origins à la fin du second
        millénnaire.* Bibliothèque des écoles françaises d'Athènes et de
        Rome, 186; (Paris: Boccard)

Dhorme, É.
1926   "Les Chérubins. I: Le Nom." *Revue Biblique* 35, 328–339

Dibelius, M.
1906   Die Lade Jahves: Eine religionsgeschichtliche Untersuchung.
            FRLANT 7; (Göttingen: Vandenhoeck & Ruprecht)
Dijk, H. J. Van
1968   *Ezekiel's Prophecy on Tyre (Ez. 26,1–28,19): A New Approach*. Biblica
            et Orientalia 20; (Rome: Pontifical Biblical Institute)
Dijkstra, M.
1986   "The Glosses in Ezekiel Reconsidered: Aspects of Textual
            Transmission in Ezekiel 10." in *Ezekiel and His Book: Textual and
            Literary Criticism and their Interrelation*. Edited by J. Lust. BETL 74;
            (Leuven: Leuven University Press), 55–77
Dohmen, C.
1985   Das Bilderverbot: seine Entstehung und seine Entwicklung im
            Alten Testament. Bonner biblische Beiträge 62; (Bonn: Hanstein)
Donner, H. and W. Röllig
2002   *Kanaanäische und aramäische Inschriften*. Band 1. 5th edition; (Har-
            rassowitz Verlag)
Douglas, M.
1966   *Purity and Danger*. (London: Routledge & Kegan Paul)
Durham, J. I.
1987   *Exodus*. WBC 3; (Waco, TX:Word Books)
Dürr, L.
1917   Ezekiels Vision von der Erscheinung Gottes (Ez. c. 1 und 10) im
            Lichte der vorderasiatischen Altertumskunde. (Würtzberg: Rich-
            ter)

Eichrodt, W.
1968   *Ezekiel* (translated by C. Quin; OTL; Philadelphia: Westminster)
Eissfeldt, O.
1966a   *Kleine Schriften* 3. (Tübingen: Mohr)
1966b   The Old Testament, an Introduction including the Apocrypha
            and Pseudepigrapha, and also the Works of Similar Type from
            Qumran: The History of the Formation of the Old Testament.
            Translated by P. R. Ackroyd from 3rd German edn. (Oxford: Basil
            Blackwell)
Engnell, I.
1955   "'Knowledge' and 'Life' in the Creation Story." in *Wisdom in
            Israel and the Ancient Near East: Essays presented to Professor H. H.
            Rowley*. Edited by M. Noth and D. Winton Thomas. SVT 3;
            (Leiden: Brill), 103–109
Eynikel, E.
2000   "The Relation between the Eli Narratives (1 Sam. 1–4) and the
            Ark Narrative (1 Sam. 1–6; 2 Sam. 6:1–19)." in *Past, Present,
            Future: The Deuteronomistic History and the Prophets*. Edited by J.
            C. de Moor and H. F. Rooy. OTS 44; (Leiden: Brill), 88–106

Fechter, F.
1992   Bewältigung der Katastrophe: Untersuchungen zu ausgewählten
        Fremdvölkersprüchen im Ezechielbuch. BZAW 208; (Berlin: W.
        de Gruyter)

Fincke, A.
2001   The Samuel Scroll from Qumran: 4QSamᵃ restored and compared
        to the Septuagint and 4QSamᶜ. Studies on the Texts of the Desert
        of Judah XLIII; (Leiden: Brill)

Fokkelman, J. P.
1993   Narrative Art and Poetry in the Books of Samuel; A Full
        Interpretation Based on Stylistic and Structural Analyses, vol. IV:
        Vow and Desire (I Sam 1–12). (Assen: Van Gorcum)

Fokkelman, J. P.
2003   Major Poems of the Hebrew Bible: at the Interface of Prosody and
        Structural Analysis. V 3, the remaining 65 psalms. Studia Semi-
        tica Neerlanica 43; (Assen: Van Gorcum)

Foote, T. C.
1903   "The Cherubim and the Ark." *JAOS* 25, 279–286

Frankfort, H.
1954   The Art and Architecture of the Ancient Orient. (Harmonds-
        worth: Penguin)

Freedman, D. N. and M. P. O'Connor
1995   "כרוב *kᵉrûb*." in *Theological Dictionary of the Old Testament*. Edited
        by G. J. Botterweck, H. Ringgren and H-J. Fabry. Translated by
        D. E. Green. Volume VII, (Grand Rapids, Michigan: Eerdmans),
        307–319

Frolov, S.
2004   The Turn of the Cycle: 1 Samuel 1–8 in Synchronic and Dia-
        chronic Perspectives. BZAW 342; (Berlin: W. de Gruyter)

Gadon, E.
1989   The Once and Future Goddess: A Symbol for Our Time. (San
        Francisco: Harper & Row)

Gaster, T. H.
1938   "Ezekiel and the Mysteries." *JBL* 60, 289–310
1950   Thespis: Ritual, Myth and Drama in the Ancient Near East. (New
        York: Schuman)
1969   Myth, Legend and Custom in the Old Testament. (New York:
        Harper & Row)

Gelb, I. J. (et al.)
1956–1961 The Assyrian Dictionary of the Oriental Institute of the Uni-
        versity of Chicago. (Chicago: The Oriental Institute)

Geller, S. A.
1979   *Parallelism in Early Biblical Poetry*. HSM 20; (Harvard: Scholars
        Press)

Geyer, J. B.
    1986   "Mythology and Culture in the Oracles against the Nations." *VT* 36, 129–145

Gibson, J. C. L.
    1982   Textbook of Syrian Semitic Inscriptions, Volume III. (Oxford: Clarendon Press)
    1994   Davidson's Introductory Hebrew Grammar ~ Syntax. Fourth Edition; (T&T Clark: Edinburgh)

Goff, B.
    1956   "The Role of Amulets in Mesopotamian Ritual Texts." *Journal of the Warburg and Courtauld Institutes* 19, 1–39

Goldberg, I.
    1989   "The Poetic Structure of the Dirge over the King of Tyre." In Hebrew. *Tarbiz* 58/2, 277–281

Görg, M.
    1977   "Keruben in Jerusalem." *BN* 4, 13–24
    1990   "יָשַׁב *yāšaḇ*." in *Theological Dictionary of the Old Testament*. Edited by G. J. Botterweck, H. Ringgren and H-J. Fabry. Translated by D. E. Green. Volume VI, (Grand Rapids, Michigan: Eerdmans), 420–438

Gowan, D. E.
    1975   *When Man Becomes God: Humanism and Hybris in the Old Testament* Pittsburgh Theological Monograph Series 6; (Pennsylvania: Pickwick Press)

Graham, W. C. and H. G. May.
    1936   Culture and Conscience: An Archaeological Study of the New Religious Past in Ancient Palestine. (Chicago: University of Chicago)

Gray, J.
    1970   *I & II Kings: A Commentary*. OTL; (London: SCM Press)

Greenberg, M.
    1983   *Ezekiel 1–20*. AB 22; (New York: Doubleday)
    1986   "What Are Valid Criteria for Determining Inauthentic Material in Ezekiel?" in *Ezekiel and his Book: Textual and Literary Criticism and their Interrelation*. Edited by J. Lust. (Leuven: Leuven University Press), 123–135
    1997   Ezekiel 21–37: A New Translation with Introduction and Commentary. AB 22A; (New York: Doubleday)

Grelot, P.
    1957   "Sur une pointe de flèche à inscription Phénicienne." *Orientalia* 26, 273–279

Grøndahl, F.
    1967   *Die Personennamen der Texte aus Ugarit*. (Rome: Typis Pontificiae Universitatis Gregoriae)

Gubel, E.
  1993   "The Iconography of Inscribed Phoenician Glyptic." in Studies in
          the Iconography of Northwest Semitic Inscribed Seals: Procee-
          dings of a Symposium held in Fribourg on April 17–20, 1991.
          Edited by B. Sass and C. Uehlinger. Orbis Biblicus et Orientalis
          125; (Fribourg/Göttingen: University Press/Vandenhoeck &
          Ruprecht), 101–129
Gunkel, H.
  1910   *Genesis, übersetzt und erklärt*. Third Revised Edition. First printed
          in 1901; HAT; Göttingen: Vandenhoeck & Ruprecht)

Hadley, J. M.
  2000   The Cult of Asherah in Ancient Israel and Judah: Evidence for a
          Hebrew Goddess. (Cambridge: Cambridge University Press)
Halperin, D.
  1988   *Faces of the Chariot: Early Jewish Responses to Ezekiel's Vision*, Texte
          und Studien zum Antiken Judentum; (Tübingen: J.C.B. Mohr)
Hals, R. M.
  1989   *Ezekiel*. The Forms of the Old Testament Literature 19; (Grand
          Rapids, MI: Eerdmans)
Haran, M.
  1959   "The Ark and the Cherubim." *IEJ* 9, 30–38, 89–94
  1978   Temples and Temple Service in Ancient Israel. (Oxford:
          Clarendon)
Hendel, R. S.
  1985   "'The Flame of the Whirling Sword': A Note on Genesis 3:24."
          JBL 104, 671–674
  1988   "The Social Origins of the Aniconic Tradition in Early Israel."
          CBQ 50, 365–382
Herdner, A.
  1963   Corpus des Tablettes en Cunéiformes Alphabétiques: Decou-
          vertes à Ras Shamra de 1929 À 1939. (Paris: Imprimerie Natio-
          nale, Geuthner)
Hillers, D.
  1968   "Ritual Procession of the Ark and Ps 132." *CBQ* 30, 48–55
Hirth, V.
  1989   "Die Keruben – Vorstellung und Wirklichkeit zur Zeit des Alten
          Testaments." *Theologische Versuche* 17, 15–22
Hoheisel, K.
  1984   "Kerube im Zweiten Tempel und die Anfänge der Kabbala" in
          Vivarium. Edited by E. Dassmann. (Münster: Aschendorff), 175–
          187
Hölscher, G.
  1924   *Hesekiel, der Dichter und das Buch*. BZAW 39; (Gießen: Töpelmann)

Houtman, C.
  2000   *Exodus*. Translated by S. Woudstra. Historical Commmentary on
              the Old Testament 3; (Leuven: Peeters)
Huehnergard, J.
  1987   *Ugaritic Vocabulary in Syllabic Transcription*. HSM 32; (Atlanta,
              Georgia: Scholars Press)
Humbert, P.
  1940   *Études Sur le Récit du Paradis et de la Chute dans Genèse*. Neuchâtel
              University Mémorial 14; (Neuchâtel: Secrétariat de l'Université)
Hurowitz, V. A.
  1992   I Have Built You an Exalted House: Temple Building in the Bible
              in Light of Mesopotamian and Northwest Semitic Writings.
              JSOTSup. (115; Sheffield: Sheffield Academic Press)
  2005   "Yhwh's Exalted House – Aspects of the Design and Symbolism
              of Solomon's Temple." in *Temple and Worship in Biblical Israel*.
              Edited by J. Day. Library of Hebrew Bible/Old Testament Studies
              422; (London: T&T Clark), 63–110
Hyatt, J. P.
  1971   *Exodus*. NCB; (London: Oliphants)

Irwin, W. A.
  1943   *The Problem of Ezekiel*. (Chicago: University of Chicago Press)

Janowski, B.
  1989   "Das Königtum Gottes in den Psalmen," *ZThK* 86, 389–454
  1992   "Keruben und Zion. Thesen zur Entstehung der Zionstradition."
              in *Ernten, was man sät: Festschrift für Klaus Koch zu seinem 65. Ge-*
              burtstag. Edited by D. R. Daniels, Uwe Glessmer and Martin
              Rösel. (Neukirchen-Vluyn: Neukirchener Verlag), 231–264
Japhet, S.
  1993   *I & II Chronicles: A Commentary*. (Louisville, Kentucky: West-
              minster/John Knox Press)
Jenni, E.
  1952   "Das Wort ʿolam im AT." *ZAW* 64, 197–248
Jensen, R. M.
  1995   "Of Cherubim and Gospel Symbols," *BAR* 21, 42
Jemielity, T.
  1992   *Satire and the Hebrew Prophets*. (Louisville, Kentucky: West-
              minster/John Knox Press)
Jeppesen, K.
  1991   "You are a Cherub, but no God!" *SJOT* 1, 83–94
Jeremias, J.
  1965   Theophanie: Die Geschichte einer alttestamentliche Gattung.
              WMANT 10; (Neukirchen-Vluyn: Neukirchener, 1965)

Johnstone, W.
1997   *1 & 2 Chronicles: Volume 1*. JSOTSup. 253; (Sheffield: Sheffield Academic Press)

Jordan, P.
1998   *Riddles of the Sphinx*. (Stroud: Sutton Publishing)

Joüon, P.
1993   *A Grammar of Biblical Hebrew*. Translated and revised by T. Muraoka. (Roma: Editrice Pontificio Istituto Biblico)

Joyce, P.
1989   Divine Initiative and Human Response in Ezekiel. JSOTSup. 51; (Sheffield: JSOT Press)

Kapelrud, A. S.
1950   "The Gates of Hell and the Guardian Angels of Paradise," *JAOS* 70, 151–156

Kaufmann, Y.
1961   The Religion of Israel from its Beginnings to the Babylonian Exile. Translated by M. Greenberg. (London: Allen & Unwin)

Keel, O.
1972   The Symbolism of the Biblical World: Ancient Near Eastern Iconography and the Book of the Psalms. Translated by T. J. Hallett. (London: SPCK)
1977   Jahwe-Visionen und Siegelkunst: Eine neue Deutung der Majestätsschilderungen in Jes 6, Ez 1 und 10 und Sach 4. SBS 84/85. (Stuttgart: Katholisches Bibelwerk)

Keel, O., M. Küchler and C. Uehlinger
1984   Orte und Landschaften der Bibel: Ein Handbuch und Studienreiseführer, Vol. 1: Geographisch-geschichtliche Landeskunde. (Köln: Benziger; Göttingen: Vandenhoeck und Ruprecht)

Keel, O. and C. Uehlinger
1991   *Göttinnen, Götter und Gottessymbole: Neue Erkentnisse zur Religionsgeschichte Kanaans und Israels aufgrund bislang unerschlossener ikonographischer Quellen*. Quaestiones Disputatae vol. 134; (Freiburg: Herder)

Keel, O. and C. Uehlinger.
1998   *Gods, Goddesses and Images of God in Ancient Israel*. Translated by T. H. Trapp; (Fortress Press: Minneapolis)

King, L.
1910   A History of Sumer and Akkad: An Account of the early Races of Babylonia, to the Foundation of the Babylonian Monarchy. History of Babylonia and Assyria 1; (London: Chatto & Windus)

Koehler, L. and W. Baumgartner
1995   *The Hebrew and Aramaic Lexicon of the Old Testament: Volume 2*. Revised by W. Baumgartner and J. Stamm. (Leiden: Brill)

Kugel, J. L.
1981   The Idea of Biblical Poetry: Parallelism and its History. (New Haven: Yale University Press)
Kuntz, J. K.
1983   "Psalm 18: A Rhetorical-Critical Analysis." *JSOT* 26, 3–31

Lambert, W. G.
2002   "The Background of the Neo-Assyrian Sacred Tree." in *Sex and Gender in the Ancient Near East*. Edited by S. Parpola and R. M. Whiting. Proceedings of the 47th Rencontre Assyriologique Internationale. (Helsinki: Eisenbrauns), 321–326
Lamon, R. S. and G. M. Shipton
1939   *Megiddo I: Seasons of 1925–34, Strata I–IV*. University of Chicago Oriental Institute Publications 62. (Chicago: Chicago University Press)
Landsberger, B.
1928   "Das 'Gute Wort'." Mitteilungen der Altorientalischen Gesellschaft, 294–321.
Landsberger, F.
1947   "The Origin of the Winged Angel in Jewish Art." *HUCA* 20, 227–254
Langdon, S.
1923   *The Babylonian Epic of Creation Restored from the Recently Recovered Tablets of Assur*. (Oxford: Clarendon press)
Launderville, D.
2003   "Ezekiel's Cherub: A Promising Symbol or a Dangerous Idol?" *CBQ* 65, 165–183
Leith, M. H. W.
1997   *Wadi Daliyeh I: The Wadi Daliyeh Seal Impressions*. DJD 24. (Oxford: Clarendon Press)
Lemaire, A.
1990   "Cinq Nouveaux Sceaux Inscrits Ouest-Sémitiques." *Studi Epigrafici e Linguistici sul Vicino Oriente Antico* 7, 97–109.
Lohfink, N.
1987   "Der Begriff des Gottesreichs vom Alten Testament her gesehen." in *Unterwegs zur Kirche: alttestamentliche Konzeptionen*. Edited by J. Schreiner. (Freiburg: Herder), 33–86
Loud, G.
1939   *The Megiddo Ivories*. The University of Chicago Oriental Institute Publications 52; (Chicago: Chicago University Press)
1948   *Megiddo II: Seasons of 1935–1939*. The University of Chicago Oriental Institute publications 62; (Chicago: University of Chicago Press)

Lust, E. J.
   1986   *Ezekiel and his Book: Textual and Literary Criticism and their Inter-relation*. (Leuven: Leuven University Press)
Lyons, J.
   1977   *Semantics I/II*. (Cambridge: Cambridge University Press)

Mackay, C. M.
   1934   "The King of Tyre," *Church Quarterly Review* 117, 239–258
Maimonides, M.
   1919   *The Guide for the Perplexed*. Translated by M. Friedländer. (London: Routledge)
Mallowan, M. E. L.
   1966   Nimrud and its Remains: Volume II. (London: Collins)
Mandelkern, S.
   1896   Veteris Testameni Concordantiae Hebraicae atque Chaldaicae. (Lipsiae: Veit)
Margulit, B.
   1989   *The Ugaritic Poem of Aqht*. BZAW 182; (Berlin: W. de Gruyter)
Markoe, G.
   2000   *Phoenicians*. Peoples of the Past. (London: British Museum Press)
May, H. G.
   1935   *Material Remains of the Megiddo Cult*. University of Chicago Orien-tal Institute Publications 26; (Chicago: Chicago University Press)
   1962   "The King in the Garden of Eden: A Study of Ezekiel 28:12–19." in *Israel's Prophetic Heritage: Essays in Honour of James Muilenburg*. Edited by B. W. Anderson and W. Harrelson. (New York: Harper & Brother), 166–176
McCown, C. C.
   1947   Tell en-Naʄbeh: Excavated under the Direction of the Late Wil-liam Frederic Badè. Vol. 1: Archaeological and Historical Results. (Berkeley: Palestine Institute)
McKenzie, J. L.
   1956   "Mythological Allusions in Ezek 28:12–18," *JBL* 75, 322–327
Mettinger, T. N. D.
   1976   King and Messiah: The Civil and Sacred Legitimation of the Israelite King. Coniectanea Biblica 8. (Lund: C. W. K.Gleerup)
   1982a   "Yhwh Sabaoth: The Heavenly King on the Cherubim Throne." in *Studies in the Period of David and Solomon and other Essays: International Symposium for Biblical Studies, Tokyo*. Edited by T. Ishida. (Winona Lake IN: Eisenbrauns), 109–138
   1982b   *The Dethronement of Sabaoth: Studies in the Shem and Kabod Theologies*. Translated by F. H. Cryer. Coniectanea biblica 18. (Lund: C. W. K. Gleerup)

1999   "Cherub," in *Dictionary of Deities and Demons in the Bible*. Edited
            by K. van der Toorn, B. Becking and P. W. van der Horst. 2nd
            Edition. (Leiden: Brill), 189–192

Metzger, M.
1985   Königsthron und Gottesthron: Thronformen und Thron-
            darstellungen in Ägypten und im Vorderen Orient (Alter Orient
            und Altes Testament 15; Neukirchener: Butzon & Bercker
            Kevelaer)
1993   "Keruben und Palmetten als Dekoration im Jerusalemer
            Heiligtum und Jahwe, 'der Nahrung gibt allem Fleisch.'" in *Zion:
            Ort der Begegnung*. Edited by Ferdinand Hahn. (Bodenheim:
            Athenäum), 503–529
1994   "Jahwe, der Kerubenthroner, die von Keruben flankierte
            Palmette und Sphingenthrone aus dem Libanon." in "Wer ist wie
            du, Herr, unter den Göttern?" Studien zur Theologie und
            Religionsgeschichte Israels für Otto Kaiser zum 70. Geburtstag.
            Edited by I. Kottsieper. (Göttingen: Vandenhoeck & Ruprecht),
            75–90

Meyers, C.
1976   The Tabernacle Menorah: A Synthetic Study of a Symbol from
            the Biblical Cult. ASOR Dissertation Series 2. (Montana: Scholars
            Press)
1992   "Cherubim." in *ABD* 1. Edited by D. N. Freedman. (New York:
            Doubleday), 899–900

Milik, J. T.
1956   "An Un-Published Arrow-Head with Phoenician Inscription of
            the 11th–10th Century B.C.," *BASOR* 143, 3–6
1961   "Flèches à inscriptions phéniciennes au Musée National Liba-
            nais," *Bulletin du Musée de Beyrouth* 16, 105–106

Millard, A. R.
1984   "The Etymology of Eden," *VT* 34, 103–106
1997   "King Solomon in his Ancient Context." in *The Age of Solomon:
            Scholarship at the Turn of the Millennium*. Edited by L. K. Handy.
            Studies in the History and Culture of the Ancient Near East XI.
            (Leiden: Brill), 30–53

Miller, J. M.
1991   "Is it Possible to Write a History of Israel without Relying on the
            Hebrew Bible?" in *The Fabric of History: Text, Artifact and Israel's
            Past*. Edited by D. V. Edelman. JSOTSup. 127; (Sheffield: Sheffield
            Academic Press), 93–102

Miller, P. D.
1965   "Fire in the Mythology of Canaan and Israel." *CBQ* 27, 256–261.

Miller, P. D. and J. J. M. Roberts
1977   Hand of the Lord: A Reassessment of the "Ark Narrative" of
            1 Samuel. (John Hopkins University Press: Baltimore)

Mitchell, C. W.
  1987   *The Meaning of BRK "To Bless" in the Old Testament.* SBL Disser-
             tation Series 95. (Atlanta Georgia: Scholars Press)
Montgomery, J. A. and H. S. Gehman
  1960   A Critical and Exegetical Commentary on the Book of Kings.
             ICC. (T & T Clark: Edinburgh)
de Moor, J. C. and K. Spronk
  1987   A Cuneiform Anthology of Religious Texts from Ugarit. SSS 6.
             Leiden: Brill)
Morgenstern, J.
  1938   "The Mythological Background of Psalm 82," *HUCA* 14, 29–126
  1942   "The Ark, the Ephod and the Tent of Meeting," *HUCA* 17, 153–
             266
  1960   "The King-God among the Western Semites and the meaning of
             Epiphanes." *VT* 10, 138–197
Mowinckel, S.
  1962   "Drive and/or Ride in O.T." *VT* 12, 278–299

Naveh, J.
  1982   *The Early History of the Alphabet: An Introduction to West Semitic
             Epigraphy and Palaeography.* (Leiden: Brill)
Neiman, D.
  1969   "Eden, the Garden of God." *Acta Antiqua Academiae Scientiarum
             Hungaricae* 17, 109–24
Newsom, C. A.
  1984   "Maker of Metaphors: Ezekiel's Oracles against Tyre."
             Interpretation 38, 151–64
  1985   *Songs of the Sabbath Sacrifice: A Critical Edition.* HSS 27. (Atlanta,
             Georgia: Scholars Press)
Noth, M.
  1960   *Exodus.* OTL. (Philadelphia: Westminster Press)
  1968   *Könige.* BKAT 9.1. (Neukirchen-Vluyn: Neukirchener Verlag)

Obbink, K. T.
  1929   "Jahwebilder." *ZAW* 47, 264–274
Olmo Lete, G. del and J. Sanmartín
  2003   A Dictionary of the Ugaritic Language in the Alphabetic
             Tradition: Part One ['a/i/u – k]. Translated by W. G. E. Watson.
             (Leiden: Brill)
Olyan, S.
  1993   A Thousand Thousands Served Him: Exegesis and the Naming
             of Angels in Ancient Judaism. Texte und Studien zum antiken
             Judentum 36. (Tübingen: J.C.B. Mohr)

Ornan, T.
1995   "Symbols of Royalty and Divinity." *BAR* 21, 38–39

Page, H. R.
1996   *The Myth of Cosmic Rebellion: A Study of its Reflexes in Ugaritic and Biblical Literature.* SVT 65. (Leiden: Brill)

Parker, B.
1949   "Cylinder Seals from Palestine." *Iraq* 11, 1–43

Parpola, S.
1993   "The Assyrian Tree of Life: Tracing the Origins of Jewish Monotheism and Greek Philosophy." *JNES* 52, 161–208

Petersen, D. L.
1997   "Creation in Ezekiel: Methodological and Theological Prospects." in *SBL Seminar Papers.* SBL Seminar Papers 36. (Atlanta, GA: Scholars Press), 490–500

Petersen, D. L. and K. H. Richards
1992   *Interpreting Hebrew Poetry.* (Minneapolis: Fortress Press)

Pfeiffer, R.
1997   "Cherubim." *JBL* 41, 249–250

Platt, E. E.
1992   "Jewellery, Ancient Israelite." in *ABD III.* Edited by D. N. Freedman. (New York: Doubleday), 823–834

Pope, M. H.
1955   *El in the Ugaritic Texts.* (Leiden: Brill)
1977   *Song of Songs: A New Translation with Introduction and Commentary.* AB. (New York: Doubleday)

Poulsen, F.
1912   Der Orient und die frühgriechische Kunst. (Leipzig: B. G. Teubner)

Powell, M. A.
1992   *The Bible and Modern Literary Criticism: a Critical Assessment and Annotated Bibliography.* Compiled by M. A. Powell with the assistance of C. G. Gray and M. C. Curtis. (New York: Greenwood Press)

Preuss, H. D.
1991   Theologie des Alten Testaments I: JHWHs erwählendes und verpflichtendes Handeln. (Stuttgart: Kohlhammer)

Pritchard, J. B.
1996a   *The Ancient Near East in Pictures Relating to the Old Testament.* 2nd Edition with Supplement; (Princeton: Princeton University Press)
1969b   *Ancient Near Eastern Texts Relating to the Old Testament.* 3rd Edition. (Princeton: Princeton University Press)

Rooke, D. W.
2000   Zadok's Heirs: The Rule and Development of the High Priest-hood in Ancient Israel. Oxford Theological Monographs. (Oxford: Oxford University Press)

Rossenvasser, A.
1971   "Kerub and Sphinx: More on the Phoenician Paradise," *Milla wa-Milla* 12, 28–38.

Rost, L.
1926   Die Überlieferung von der Thronnachfolge Davids. BWANT 6. (Stuttgart: W. Kohlhammer)

Rowe, A.
1940   *The Four Canaanite Temples of Beth-Shan: Part 1 The Temples and Cult Objects.* Publications of the Palestinian Section of the Museum of the University of Pennsylvania 2. (Philadelphia: University of Pennsylvania Press)

Sass, B.
1993   "The Pre-Exilic Hebrew Seals: Iconism vs. Aniconism." in *Studies in the Iconography of Northwest Semitic Inscribed Seals: Proceedings of a Symposium held in Fribourg on April 17–20, 1991.* Edited by B. Sass and C. Uehlinger. Orbis Biblicus et Orientalis 125. (Fribourg/Göttingen: University Press/Vandenhoeck & Ruprecht), 194–256

Sasson, J. M.
2000   "The Lord of Hosts Seated over the Cherubs." in *Rethinking the Foundations. Historiography in the Ancient World and in the Bible: Essays in Honour of John Van Seters.* Edited by A. L. McKenzie and T. Römer. BZAW 294. (Berlin: W. de Gruyter), 227–234

Sawyer, J. F. A.
1967   "Root-meanings in Hebrew." *JSS* 12, 37–50

Schley, D. G.
1989   *Shiloh: A Biblical City in Tradition and History.* JSOTSup. 63. (Sheffield: Sheffield Academic Press)

Schmitt, R.
1972   *Zelt und Lade als Thema Alttestamentlicher Wissenschaft.* (Gütersloh: Gütersloher Verlagshaus G. Mohn)

Sherlock, C.
1983   "Ezekiel 10: A Prophet Surprised." *Reformed Theological Review* 42, 42–44

Sjöberg, Å. W.
1994   "Eve and the Chameleon." in *In the Shelter of Elyon: Essays on Palestinian Life and Literature in Honour of G. A Ahlström.* Edited by W. B. Barrick, and J. R. Spencer. JSOTSup. vol. 31. (Sheffield: JSOT Press), 217–225

Skinner, J.
  1910   *A Commentary on the Book of Genesis.* ICC; (Edinburgh: T & T
              Clark)
Smelik, K.
  1989   "The Ark Narrative Reconsidered." in *New Avenues in the Study of
              the Old Testament.* Edited by A. S. Van der Woude. OTS 25.
              (Leiden: Brill), 128–144
  1992   *Converting the Past: Studies in Ancient Israelite and Moabite Historio-
              graphy.* OTS 28. (Leiden: Brill)
Smend, R.
  1880   *Der Prophet Ezechiel.* Kurzgefasstes exegetisches Handbuch zum
              Alten Testament. (Leipzig: S. Hirzel)
Smith, M.
  1996   *The Pilgrimage Pattern in Exodus.* JSOTSup. vol. 239. (Sheffield:
              JSOT Press)
  2004   *The Memoirs of God: History, Memory, and the Experience of the
              Divine in Ancient Israel.* (Minneapolis: Fortress Press)
Steck, O.
  1998   *Old Testament Exegesis: A Guide to the Methodology.* Translated by
              J. D. Nogalski. (Atlanta: Scholars Press)
Strange, J.
  1985   "The Idea of Afterlife in Ancient Israel: Some Remarks on the
              Iconography in Solomon's Temple." *PEQ* 117, 35–40
Strenski, I.
  1987   *Four Theories of Myth in Twentieth-Century History: Cassirer, Eliade,
              Levi-Strauss and Malinowski.* (Iowa: University of Iowa Press)
Stordalen, T.
  2000   *Echoes of Eden: Genesis 2–3 and Symbolism of the Eden Garden in
              Biblical Hebrew Literature.* Contributions to Biblical Exegesis and
              Theology 25. (Leuven: Peeters)
Stuart, D. K.
  1976   *Studies in Early Hebrew Meter.* HSM 13. (Missoula: Scholars Press)
Sukenik, E. L.
  1938   "Notes on Hebrew Letters on the Ivories." in *Early Ivories From
              Samaria.* Edited by J. W. Crowfoot and G. M. Crowfoot. Samaria-
              Sebaste 2. (London: Palestine Exploration Fund), 7–8
Sullivan, K. P.
  2004   Wrestling with Angels: a Study of the Relationship between
              Angels and Humans in Ancient Jewish Literature and the New
              Testament. Arbeiten zur Geschichte des antiken Judentums und
              des Urchristentums 55. (Leiden: Brill)

Tarragon, J. M.
1981   "La Kapporet est-elle une fiction ou un élément du culte tardif?"
        Revue Biblique 88, 5–12
Thureau-Dangin, F.
1975   *Rituels Accadiens.* (Osnabrück: O. Zeller)
Torrey, C. C.
1930   *Pseudo-Ezekiel and the Original Prophecy.* (New Haven: Yale
        University Press)
Tuell, S. S.
2004   "Contemporary Studies in Ezekiel: A New Tide Rising." in
        Ezekiel's Hierarchical World: Wrestling with a Tiered Reality. Edited
        by S. L. Cook and C. L. Patton. SBL Symposium Series 31.
        (Atlanta: SBL, 2004), 241–254

Uehlinger, C.
1993   "Northwest Semitic Inscribed Seals, Iconography and Syro-
        Palestinian Religions of Iron Age II: Some Afterthoughts and
        Conclusions." in *Studies in the Iconography of Northwest Semitic
        Inscribed Seals: Proceedings of a Symposium held in Fribourg on April
        17–20, 1991.* Edited by B. Sass and C. Uehlinger. Orbis Biblicus et
        Orientalis 125. (Fribourg/Göttingen: Universitätsverlag/Van-
        denhoeck & Ruprecht), 257–288

Van Seters, J.
1983   *In Search of History: Historiography in the Ancient World and the
        Origins of Biblical History.* (New Haven, CT: Yale University
        Press)
1989   "The Creation of Man and the Creation of the King." *ZAW* 101,
        333–342
1997a   "Solomon's Temple: Fact and Ideology in Biblical and Near
        Eastern Historiography." *CBQ* 59, 45–57
1997b   "The Chronicler's Account of Solomon's Temple-Building: A
        Continuity Theme." in *The Chronicler as Historian.* Edited by M. P.
        Graham, K. G. Hoglund and S. L. McKenzie. JSOTSup. 238.
        (Sheffield: Sheffield Academic Press), 283–300
Vaux, R. de.
1967   "Les Chérubins et l'Arche d'Alliance, les Sphinx Gardiens at les
        Trônes Divins dans l'Ancien Orient." in *Bible et Orient.* (Paris:
        Cerf), 231–259
Vincent, L. H.
1926   "Le Concept Plastique," *Revue Biblique* 35, 340–358, 481–495
Vincent, L. H. and A. M. Stève
1956   *Jérusalem de l'Ancien Testament.* (Paris: Gabalda)

Von Rad, G.
    1958   "Zelt und Lade." in *Gesammelte Studien zum Alten Testament.*
                (München: C. Kaiser), 109–129
    1962   *Old Testament Theology I.* Translated by D.M.G. Stalker. (Edin-
                burgh: Oliver and Boyd)
    1968   *Genesis: A Commentary.* OTL. (Philadelphia: Westminster)
Von Soden, W.
    1936   "Die Unterweltsvision eines assyrischen Kronprinzen." *ZA* 9, 1–
                31
    1965–1981 *Akkadisches Handwörterbuch.* 3 vols. (Wiesbaden: Harrasowitz)

Washburn, D. L.
    2002   *A Catalog of Biblical Passages in the Dead Sea Scrolls.* SBL Text-
                Critical Studies 2. (Atlanta: SBL)
Waterman, L.
    1915   "Bull-Worship in Israel." *AJSL* 31, 229–255
Watson, W. G. E.
    1995   "Ugaritic Onomastics (4)." *AuOr* 13, 217–229
    1996   "Ugaritic Onomastics (5)." *AuOr* 14, 93–106
Wellhausen, J.
    1883   *Prolegomena zur Geschichte Israels.* Zweite Ausgabe. (Berlin:
                Reimer)
Wenham, G. J.
    1987   *Genesis 1–15.* WBC 1. (Waco, TX: Word Books)
Westermann, C.
    1974   *Genesis 1–11.* BKAT vol. 1/1. (Neukirchen-Vluyn: Neukirchener
                Verlag)
Westermann, C.
    1981   *Genesis 12–36.* BKAT vol. 1/2. (Neukirchen-Vluyn: Neukirchener
                Verlag)
Wevers, J. W.
    1969   *Ezekiel.* (NCB; Nelson)
Widengren, G.
    1950   *The Ascension of the Apostle and the Heavenly Book: King and Saviour
                III.* Uppsala Universitets Årsskrift 7. (Uppsala: Lundequistska
                Bokhandeln)
    1951   *The King and the Tree of Life in Ancient Near Eastern Religion: King
                and Saviour IV.* Uppsala Universitets Årsskrift 4. (Uppsala/
                Wiesbaden: Lundequistska Bokhandeln/Harrassowitz)
    1958   "Early Hebrew Myths and their Interpretation." in *Myth, Ritual,
                and Kingship.* Edited by S. H. Hooke. (Oxford: Clarendon), 165–
                176

Williams, A. J.
1976   "The Mythological Background of Ezekiel 28:12–19." *Biblical Theological Bulletin* 6, 49–61
Wilson, R. R.
1984   "Prophecy in Crisis: The Call of Ezekiel." *Interpretation* 38, 117–130
1987   "The Death of the King of Tyre: The Editorial History of Ezekiel 28." in *Love & Death in the Ancient Near East: Essays in Honour of Marvin H. Pope.* Edited by J. H. Marks and R. M. Good. (Guilford, CT: Four Quarters), 211–218
Winter, I.
1976   "Phoenician and North Syrian Ivory Carving in Historical Context: Questions of Style and Distribution." *Iraq* 38, 1–22
1981   "Is there a South Syrian Style of Ivory Carving in the Early First Millennium B.C.?" *Iraq* 43, 101–130
Winter, U.
1983   Frau und Göttin: Exegetische und ikonographische Studien zum weiblichen Gottesbild im Alten Israel und in dessen Umwelt. Orbis Biblicus et Orientalis 53. (Fribourg/Göttingen: Universitäts-verlag/Vandenhoeck & Ruprecht)
Wood, A.
2006   "כְּרוּב" Semantics of Ancient Hebrew Database, http://www2.div.ed.ac.uk/research/sahd/krwb.pdf [Accessed 07/03/2007]
Wright, G. E.
1957   *Biblical Archaeology.* (London: Westminster Press)
Wyatt, N.
1986   "The Hollow Crown: Ambivalent Elements in West Semitic Royal Ideology." *UF* 18, 424–429
1996   Myths of Power: A Study of Royal Myth and Ideology in Ugaritic and Biblical Tradition. Ugaritisch-Biblische Literatur 13. (Münster: Ugarit-Verlag)
1998   Religious Texts from Ugarit: The Words of Ilimilku and his Colleagues. (Sheffield: Sheffield Academic Press)
2002a   "Ilimilku the Theologian: The Ideological Roles of Athtar and Baal in KTU 1.1 and 1.6." in *Ex Mesopotamia et Syria Lux: Festschrift für Manfried Dietrich.* Edited by O. Loretz, K. Metzler and H. Schaudig. Alter Orient und Altes Testament 281. (Münster: Ugarit-Verlag), 845–856
2002b   *Religious Texts from Ugarit.* 2nd Edition. The Biblical Seminar 53. (London: Continuum)

Yadin, Y.
1958   *Hazor I*. (Jerusalem: Magnes Press)
1991   *Hazor III–IV: Plates*. (Jerusalem: Magnes Press)
1975   *Hazor*. (London: Weidenfeld and Nicolson)
Yaron, K.
1964   "The Dirge over the King of Tyre." *ASTI* 3, 45–49
Yeivin, S.
1958   "Sur une pointe de flèche inscrite provenant de la Beqaa (Liban)." *Revue Biblique* 65, 585–589

Zimmerli, W.
1969a   *Ezechiel 1*. BKAT 13. Neukirchen/Vluyn: Neukirchener Verlag des Erziehungsvereins. English translation by R. Clements. (Hermeneia. Philadelphia: Fortress Press 1979)
Zimmerli, W.
1969b   *Ezekiel 2*. BKAT 13. Neukirchen/Vluyn: Neukirchener Verlag des Erziehungsvereins. English translation by J. D. Martin. (Hermeneia. Philadelphia: Fortress Press)
Zimmerli, W.
2003   *The Fiery Throne: The Prophets and Old Testament Theology*. Edited by K. C. Hanson. (Minneapolis: Fortress Press)
Zwickel, W.
1987   "Die Kesselwagen im salomonischen Tempel," *UF* 18, 459–461

Pictures

Picture 1 Ivory plaque, Megiddo (Keel and Uehlinger 1998: illus. 65)

Picture 2 Throne model, Megiddo (Keel and Uehlinger 1998: illus. 66b)

Picture 3 Cult stand, Taanach (Keel and Uehlinger 1998: illus. 184)

Picture 4 Cave drawing, Jerusalem (De Vaux 1967: fig. 2a)

Picture 5 Cave drawing, Jerusalem (De Vaux 1967: figs. 2b)

Picture 6 Bone handle, Hazor (Keel and Uehlinger 1998: illus. 210)

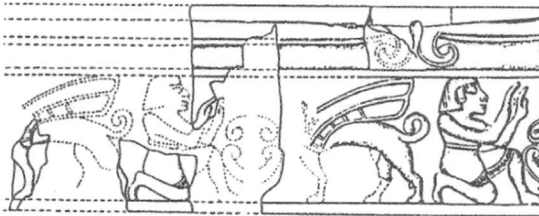

Picture 7 Ivory pyxis, Hazor (Keel and Uehlinger 1998: illus. 234a)

Picture 8 Ivory plaque, Samaria (Keel and Uehlinger 1998: illus. 243)

Picture 9 Ivory plaque, Samaria (Keel and Uehlinger 1998: illus. 212a)

Picture 10 Ivory plaque showing Syrian style winged quadruped, Samaria (Keel and Uehlinger 1998: illus. 232a)

Picture 11 Ivory plaque showing Phoenician style winged quadruped, Samaria (Keel and Uehlinger 1998: illus. 232b)

Picture 12 Stamp Seal, Megiddo (Keel and Uehlinger 1998: illus. 250b)

Picture 13 Stamp seal, Lachish (Keel and Uehlinger 1998: illus. 249)

Picture 14 Assyrian style cylinder seal, Megiddo (Keel and Uehlinger 1998: illus. 282c)

Picture 15 Assyrian style cylinder seal (Keel and Uehlinger 1998: illus. 284a)

Picture 16 Unique Iron IIC stamp seal (Keel and Uehlinger 1998: illus. 331b)

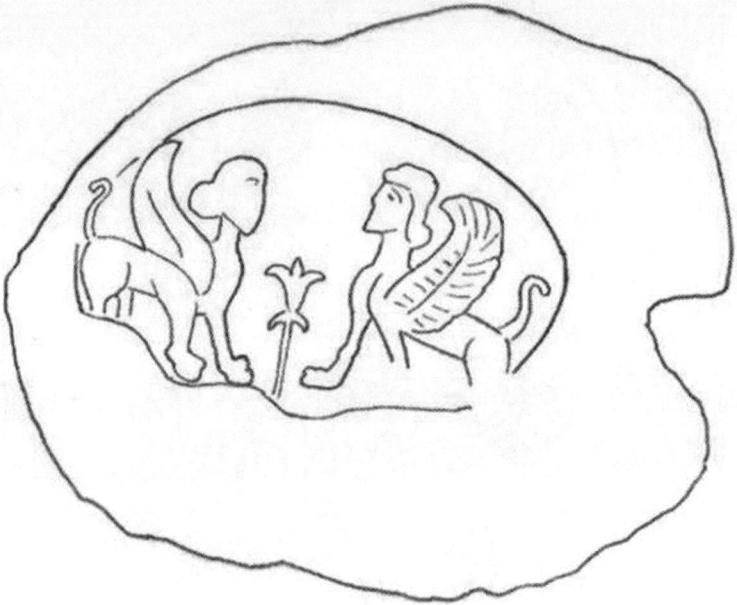

Picture 17 Seal impression, Wadi Daliyeh (Leith 1997: pl. 21, WD 15A)

Index of Biblical References

Hebrew Bible

Genesis

1	70, 110
1–11	51, 60
1:2	56
1:26	51, 70
2–3	49, 57, 59, 80
2:4b–3:24	51, 63, 66, 68
2:7	59
2:8	52, 66
2:8–9	65
2:10	40
2:11–12	65
2:12	79
2:16–17	59
3	6
3:5	58, 66
3:8	60, 80
3:21	60
3:22	57–59, 63, 66
3:24	6, 8, 14, 33, 37, 51–52, 54–56, 60–61, 69, 83, 87, 91, 94, 110, 126, 133, 139, 148, 151, 155, 171, 179, 191, 199
4:20	13
5:22	60
5:24	60, 80
6:1–4	51, 68
6:9	60, 80
11:7	51
17:1	80
19:21	55
19:25	55
19:29	55
41:43	44

Exodus

3:1	67
3:6	27
14:25	44
15:14	10
16:3	28
16:10	88
18:5	67
20:4	3, 189
20:23	3, 183, 189
24:13	67
25	80
25–26	6, 23
25–31	7, 77
25:17	24
25:18	7, 33, 37, 45, 95, 170
25:18–22	2, 98, 107, 136
25:20	25–27, 29–31, 33, 36, 44, 70
25:22	9, 11, 25–26, 29–31, 45
26:1	23, 32, 151
26:7	23, 32
26:26	32
26:31	23, 48
26:33	32, 43
28:15–20	78–80
29:13	80
30:17–21	38
31:3	80
31:5	80

34:15	13	29:22	55
34:17	3, 183, 189	32:40	58
35–40	7, 77	33:2	51
36–37	6, 23		
36:14	23, 32	*Joshua*	
37:7–9	2, 10, 23, 29		
40:3	26–27, 33	18:1	15, 52
40:34–38	88	22:28	79
		24:18	13
Leviticus			
		Judges	
4:3	39		
4:14	39	1:9 13	
15:9	88	3:22	53
16	114	5	39
16:4	110	5:20	51
16:12	110	7:13	54
16:12–13	110–111, 124,	11:21	13
	129		
19:4	3, 184, 189	*1 Samuel*	
22:23	39		
26:1	3, 184, 189	1–3	17, 19
		1–4	15
Numbers		1–7	19
		1–8	21, 103
7:89	8–9, 11–12, 26,	1:11	15
	29–31, 45	2:12–16	38
10:34–36	20	3	16
11:15	62	4–6	21–22
14:25	13	4:4	8–9, 12, 16–22
17:7	88	5:4	95
21:1	12–13	5:4–5	108
21:27–30	57	6:19–21	19
34:40	13	7:2	19
		8:11	45
Deuteronomy			
		2 Samuel	
4:16	3, 184, 189		
4:16–18	79, 189	5:6	10
4:23	3, 184, 189	6	15, 19, 21–22,
4:25	3, 184, 189		163
5:24	62	6:2	8–9, 14, 16–22
10:1–5	20, 30	22	84–85, 93, 163
12:11	52	22:5–7	84
17:1	39	22:11	2, 8, 14, 18, 51,
27:15	3, 184, 189		57, 84–87, 90–

	91, 94, 97, 123, 133, 137, 139, 140, 152, 161, 191, 195, 199–200, 203
22:12	89–91
22:12–13	110

1 Kings

1:31	58
4:7	19
5	159, 164
6–8	6–7, 34, 43, 106, 138, 205–206
6:18	37
6:22	111
6:23–28	2, 20, 22, 28, 34, 36, 47, 107, 172
6:27	169
6:29	33, 37, 53, 171, 182
6:31–32	48
6:32	33–34
6:32–35	34
6:34–35	107
6:36	40
7	38, 175–176
7:13–45	159, 164
7:14	77, 70
7:22	115
7:27–39	38, 107, 113, 139, 175
7:29	34, 162, 171
7:36	53, 184
8	20, 28
8:6–7	19–22, 28–31, 34, 45, 47, 49, 91, 94
8:8	107
8:12–13	10, 14
8:43	20
8:64	106
10:18–19	172
10:22	171
16:10	79

22	104
22:19–22	51, 56
22:35	44
22:39	171

2 Kings

13:6	88
17–21	189
19:15	8, 15–16
21:2	164
21:13	55
23:11	44
24:13	164
24:14–16	164
25:11	164
25:13–21	164

1 Chronicles

13:6	8–9, 14, 16
13:7	88
28	43, 45
28:2	45
28:11	43, 45
28:18	26, 42, 44, 46–47, 106, 162, 205

2 Chronicles

3	36, 49
3–5	37, 106
3:6	79
3:7	8, 37
3:10	22, 35, 170
3:10–13	34, 43, 45, 47, 50, 136
3:14	43, 48
4:1	106
4:6	38
4:14	38, 113
5:7–8	45, 47, 49
7:7	106
34:31	44
35:24	88

Ezra

2:59	2, 8

Nehemiah

2:3	58
7:61	2, 8

Job

37:12	55
38	67
39:23	53

Psalms

7:2	39
17:8	26
18	84–85, 93, 163
18:11	2, 8, 14, 18, 44, 51, 57, 84–87, 89–91, 94 97, 115, 123, 133, 137, 139–140, 152, 161–162, 191, 195, 199–200, 203
18:12	89–91
18:12–13	110
19:2	110
45:4	88
48:3	67
50:4	107
77:19	109–110
80	14
80:1	8–9
82	64, 68
83:14	109
91:4	26–27
99:1	8, 15
104:3	86
104:4	51, 53, 56, 126
106:18	53
140:8	26–27
148:2	51
148:8	53

Proverbs

12:7	55
14:4	39

Isaiah

5:24	54
5:28	109, 113
6	51, 93, 104, 126, 133, 142, 152
6:2	27, 134, 137
6:6	131
6:6–7	152
11:6–9	40
13:19	55
14:11	66
14:12–14	64, 66
17:13	109
28:28	109
31:3	82
37:16	8–9, 14–16
42:25	53

Jeremiah

7:3	52
20:16	55
47:3	109, 113
49:18	55
50:40	55

Ezekiel

1	45, 92–94, 98, 100, 104, 115, 117, 120–121, 124–128, 133–138, 140, 162, 205
1–11	50, 106, 114
1:4–5	116
1:5 2,	125
1:5–7	136, 200

1:6	47		111, 113, 126, 127, 129
1:7	2, 47, 161, 195		
1:8	170	10:3	111–112, 130
1:10	25, 125, 195	10:4	8, 95, 108, 111–
1:11	134, 137, 205, 207		112, 117–119, 122, 127, 130
1:13	126–127	10:6	112–113, 122, 127, 131
1:13–1:14	126–127, 134, 137	10:7	8, 115, 123, 125–128, 131, 137, 161, 170
1:16	115		
1:17	115	10:8	8, 97, 114–115, 122–123, 125, 128
1:18	115		
1:22	96		
1:22–26	109	10:9–17	125
1:23	133–134, 137	10:10	96, 115
1:24	130	10:11	115
1:26–27	106	10:12	96, 115, 123, 125–126, 137
1:28	106		
3:12	137, 140, 205, 207	10:14	116, 149, 170, 205
8:1	98	10:14–16	98
8:1–11:25	95, 97, 99, 105, 120–123, 128, 135, 138	10:15	45, 92, 96–97, 99, 102, 121– 123, 200
8:2–3	106	10:18	100, 131–132, 172
8:4	106, 108		
8:7	108	10:19	118–119, 130, 132
8:14	108		
8:16	108	10:20	45, 102, 104, 122
9:2	98		
9:3	8, 95, 100, 101, 107–108, 110, 111, 127, 132	10:21	25, 125, 170, 178, 185
9–11	6, 51, 100–102, 105, 134–136	11	118
		11:1	108, 119
10	2, 12, 18, 31 , 44, 98, 102, 104, 120–121, 125– 126, 128–129, 133–135, 140, 159, 170, 205	11:22–23	118
		11:23	114, 130
		17	74
		23:24	109, 113
		26:10	109, 113
		27:3–4	78
10:1	8, 18, 31, 108, 110–112, 117, 121, 129, 131	27:11	78
		28	37, 61, 64–66, 73, 207
10:2	70, 96, 98, 100– 101, 108, 110–	28:2	66
		28:5	77

28:7	78	*Hosea*	
28:11–19	49, 63–65, 66, 68–71, 73–76, 82, 86, 140, 162, 184, 191	4:19	86, 91
		Amos	
28:12	83		
28:12–13	76	1–2	57
28:13	52, 65–66, 79, 81	*Jonah*	
28:13–14	37, 60, 66, 70, 187	3:4	55
28:14	8, 65, 67, 69, 72–73, 80–84, 148	*Nahum*	
28:16	72, 74, 82	2:6	26–27
29:3	74	3:3	53
31:2b–9	74		
41:27	36, 148	*Zephaniah*	
41:18–25	2, 37, 49–50, 53, 106, 139, 148, 170	1:9–10	95, 108
43:10	77	*Haggai*	
46:2	108		
47:1	108	22:2	55
Daniel		*Zecharaiah*	
7	134–135	5:9	86, 91
12:7	58	9:5–6	11

Index of Names and Subjects

Aaron 110–111, 114, 126, 130
ᶜAin Dara 35, 157, 169–170, 176
Akkadian 34–35, 54–55, 57, 77–78, 81, 142–152, 154–155, 206
Assyrian 41, 150, 153–154, 171, 173, 190–196, 198–199, 201–202
altar 38–39, 43, 56, 98, 106, 110–111, 129, 131, 196
amulet 83, 159, 184, 197
angel 1, 104, 134, 138, 145
apotopaic 26, 29–33, 49, 60, 83, 94, 136, 138–140, 153–155, 162–163, 171, 175, 181–182, 184, 186, 201, 205–206
aquiline 117, 137, 162, 167, 169, 175, 181, 185, 187–193, 202
aniconism 183, 188, 190, 196
ankh 187–188
anthropomorphic 87, 154, 173–174, 188–189
archaeology 3, 19, 211
ark 9, 14, 18–23, 26, 28–29, 31, 33–34, 44–47, 69–70, 88, 98, 107, 129, 139, 180
artifact 3, 158
Arslan-Tash 165, 178, 181, 183, 201
Asherah 159, 175, 194–195
Astarte 159, 168, 170, 174, 176, 194

Baal 16, 19, 65, 147, 168, 177, 181, 185
Babylonian 142, 150, 152, 164 , 173, 196–199
battle 18–19, 26, 31, 94, 191
bovine 47, 96, 116–117, 137, 149, 162, 194–196
bull 97, 117, 149, 152, 193, 195–196, 201

Canaanite 15, 61–63, 65, 67
caprid 186, 193
cattle 39–40, 176
chariot 44–47, 49, 87–88, 91–92, 109, 149
cherubim formula 9–22, 26, 139, 171–172
cloud 14, 88–91, 94, 110–112
Cupid/Eros 1
curtains 23, 32–33, 37, 139

divine being 3, 54–55, 60, 63–64, 66–67, 73, 152–153, 204
divine council 51, 67, 104, 112, 134, 152
divine presence 10–11, 24, 26–27, 37, 80, 95, 107, 137–139

eagle 97, 116–117, 148–149, 162, 167–169, 172, 181, 186, 188–189, 202
Egyptian 11, 26, 34, 75, 166–168, 173, 177, 180–182, 185–186, 188–190, 192, 194, 198, 201–203
El 15–18, 22, 54, 62, 65–66, 81, 112, 192–193
etymology 3, 141–143, 145–146, 149, 151
eyes 115–116, 138

face 2, 25, 27, 33, 36, 43, 46–47, 49, 96–98, 116–120, 125, 133, 140, 148–149, 161–162, 166–167, 168, 205
feet 36, 43, 46–47, 49, 125, 154, 161, 170, 193
fire 53–55, 57, 65, 68, 75, 81, 91, 109–110–114, 124–131
flame 51–56, 60, 91
flowers 33, 148, 162, 180, 182, 198

Garden of Eden 37, 40, 52, 60–61,
    68–70, 75, 78, 80, 82, 136, 140,
    148, 151
glyptic 177, 183, 188, 190, 192, 195,
    196, 198, 200
Greek 12, 51, 63–64, 72, 86, 90, 121,
    127, 135, 146

hand 16, 54–55, 59, 95, 97–98, 109–
    111, 114–116, 118, 123, 125–128,
    131–133, 153–154, 161–162, 167,
    170, 177, 180, 185, 194
Hazor 174, 177–179, 181–185, 187,
    194–195
heaven 64, 84–85, 89, 133–134, 140,
    152, 194–195
Hiram 43, 77, 80
Holy of Holies 29, 32, 34, 35, 39, 43,
    45, 47–48, 50, 98, 100–101, 107,
    110–111, 139, 150–151, 153, 162,
    172–173
host 1, 14, 16, 31, 57, 87, 94
human 1–2, 38, 49–50, 53, 58, 63, 66,
    70, 81–82, 87, 97, 106–107, 117–
    118, 125, 137, 153–154, 162, 166–
    167, 169–170, 174–176, 178–182,
    188–189, 191, 193–196, 198, 200–
    203, 206
hybrid 25, 31, 45, 99, 157, 162, 166,
    169, 175, 178, 188, 191–193, 195–
    196, 199–200

iconography 11, 26, 39, 50, 55, 57, 82,
    92, 100, 106, 109, 112, 116, 122,
    133, 136, 138, 148, 157, 159–160,
    164–165, 173–177, 180, 183–186,
    189–204
image 3, 8, 54–55, 57, 62, 68, 71, 75–
    76, 79–84, 87, 93, 95, 157–158,
    160, 162, 167, 177–178, 184, 187,
    199, 201–202
intecessory 3, 143, 149–152, 154–155,
    206
Ishtar 35, 39, 157, 170, 176
Isis 180,

ivories 160, 164–167, 169, 172–174,
    176, 178–185, 187–188, 194, 201,
    204, 206

Jerusalem 6, 11, 15, 20–21, 23, 25, 27,
    29–30, 36, 99, 106, 110–111, 114,
    122, 134 , 139, 161, 164, 171, 174,
    176–177, 183, 190, 195, 200, 204
jewel 65, 68, 78–80, 184
Josephus 1, 41, 136

kāribu 3–4, 142–143, 149–152, 154
kurību 4, 152–155, 206
Khorsabad 165, 178, 183

lamassu 149–150, 152–154
leonine 50, 117, 137, 162, 166–170,
    172, 174–179, 181–182, 185, 187,
    189, 190–193, 195–196, 198, 202
lion 2, 39–40, 97, 116–117, 148, 153,
    157, 162, 166–167, 171–172, 174–
    176, 182, 186, 188–189, 191, 193,
    196, 198, 200–203, 206
locomotive 45–46, 49, 134, 136–137,
    140
lotos blossom 171, 180, 185, 187, 198

Marzeaḥ 183
Megiddo 11, 138, 165–173, 175, 179,
    181–185, 188, 190–191, 194, 204,
    206
merkabah 12, 45–46, 139, 205
messenger 54, 91
Mesopotamian 38, 57, 61, 67, 75, 78,
    151, 177, 184, 191, 195–196, 198–
    200
monster 54, 153–154, 168, 191
Moses 25, 27, 28, 30, 48
mountain 13, 40, 60, 62, 66–67, 75,
    80, 82, 119, 130, 132, 140, 187

Nephthys 180
Nimrud 165, 178–180, 183, 187

palm trees 33, 37, 40, 50, 148, 176, 182
Persian 163, 172–173, 183, 196–200
Phoenician 2, 11, 18, 42, 56, 64, 76–80, 84, 143–144, 146–147, 164, 166, 168, 172, 175, 177–180, 182, 186–187, 190–191, 197–198, 203, 207
plants 33, 148, 168, 179
platform 18, 94, 108–112, 121, 134, 140, 196
prayer 147, 152, 154
Punic 16, 146
Putto 1

quadruped 2, 115, 123, 136, 140, 166–167, 169–170, 174–176, 179, 181, 186, 187, 194–195, 201–202
Qumran 1, 7, 127, 136, 207

Samaria 164, 171, 178–179, 182–183, 190, 192, 196–199, 203–204
seal 57, 75–78, 83–84, 159–160, 162, 164, 174, 178, 183–202
šedu 149–150, 152–154
semantics 3, 12, 21–22, 138, 141–142
Seraphim 27, 93 –94, 133–134, 137, 140, 142, 152, 159, 205, 207
Shiloh 6, 15–22, 139
sphinx 11, 16, 18, 174, 176
statue 47, 49–50, 98, 100–101, 104, 107, 111–112, 129, 136, 139, 142, 151–154, 158, 166, 172–173, 199
sword 53–57, 78
Syrian 166, 177–180, 182, 190

Taanach 159, 169–170, 172–176, 179, 181–182, 188, 193–194, 201
tabernacle 3, 6–8, 10–11, 14, 19–20, 22–24, 26, 28–35, 37–38, 43, 45, 47–49, 51–53, 61, 77, 83, 91, 94, 107, 139, 158–159, 162, 172–173
temple 3, 6–8, 14–17, 19–22, 24, 26, 28–29, 31, 33–35, 37, 39–51, 53, 61, 77–80, 83, 91–92, 94–96, 98–99, 101–104, 106, 108–109, 111–113, 116, 118–119, 121–124, 128–130, 132–139, 148–150, 153, 157, 161–164, 169, 171–173, 176–177, 182–183, 200, 203, 207
tent 15, 23, 28, 32, 90
theophany 84–85, 89, 91–94, 110–111, 133–134, 137
threshold 33, 40, 52, 95, 107, 130, 139, 162
throne 2, 10–20, 22, 26–27, 29–31, 33–34, 49, 65, 82, 87–88, 92–94, 99, 101, 108–109, 117–118, 122, 129, 131, 133–135, 137–140, 152, 160, 166–167, 169, 171–173, 203–204, 206–207
Tree of Life 33, 37, 52–53, 57–60, 69–70, 148, 151
trees 25, 57–58, 162, 171

Ugaritic 15–17, 35, 54, 56, 65, 81, 143–146, 148, 155

vehicle 84, 115–119, 121–124, 126, 128–129, 131–134, 137–138
veil 23, 26–27, 32–33, 43, 48, 162

Wadi Daliyeh 196–200
weapon 53–57, 60, 94, 139
wheel 46, 49, 92, 96–97, 109, 113–126, 129, 133–134, 137–139, 205
wheeled lavers 34, 38, 49, 139, 176
wind 53, 56, 87–89, 91, 94, 96, 116–117, 134
wings 2, 10–11, 19–20, 25–31, 33, 36, 45–47, 85–89, 91, 93–94, 97, 112, 115–116, 118–119, 125, 133–134, 137–138, 140, 161–162, 167–170, 175, 178, 181, 184–185, 193, 196, 205

Zion 21, 28, 171